TERMINATOR AND PHILOSOPHY

The Blackwell Philosophy and Pop Culture Series

Series Editor: William Irwin

South Park and Philosophy
Edited by Robert Arp

Metallica and Philosophy
Edited by William Irwin

Family Guy and Philosophy
Edited by J. Jeremy Wisnewski

The Daily Show and Philosophy
Edited by Jason Holt

Lost and Philosophy
Edited by Sharon Kaye

24 and Philosophy
Edited by Richard Davis, Jennifer Hart Weed, and Ronald Weed

Battlestar Galactica and Philosophy
Edited by Jason T. Eberl

The Office and Philosophy
Edited by J. Jeremy Wisnewski

Batman and Philosophy
Edited by Mark D. White and Robert Arp

House and Philosophy
Edited by Henry Jacoby

Watchmen and Philosophy
Edited by Mark D. White

X-Men and Philosophy
Edited by Rebecca Housel and J. Jeremy Wisnewski

TERMINATOR AND PHILOSOPHY

I'LL BE BACK, THEREFORE I AM

Edited by Richard Brown and
Kevin S. Decker

John Wiley & Sons, Inc.

This book is printed on acid-free paper. ♾

Published by John Wiley & Sons, Inc., Hoboken, New Jersey
Published simultaneously in Canada

For general information about our other products and services, please contact our Customer Care Department within the United States at (800) 762-2974, outside the United States at (317) 572-3993 or fax (317) 572-4002.

Wiley also publishes its books in a variety of electronic formats. Some content that appears in print may not be available in electronic books. For more information about Wiley products, visit our web site at www.wiley.com.

ISBN 978-0470-44798-7

Printed in the United States of America

10 9 8 7 6 5 4 3 2 1

CONTENTS

Introduction: The Rise of the Philosophers 1

PART ONE
LIFE AFTER HUMANITY AND ARTIFICIAL INTELLIGENCE

1 The Terminator Wins: Is the Extinction of the Human Race the End of People, or Just the Beginning? 7
Greg Littmann

2 True Man or Tin Man? How Descartes and Sarah Connor Tell a Man from a Machine 21
George A. Dunn

3 It Stands to Reason: Skynet and Self-Preservation 39
Josh Weisberg

4 Un-Terminated: The Integration of the Machines 52
Jesse W. Butler

PART TWO
WOMEN AND REVOLUTIONARIES

5 "I Know Now Why You Cry": *Terminator 2*, Moral Philosophy, and Feminism 69
Harry Chotiner

6 Sarah Connor's Stain 82
Jennifer Culver

7 James Cameron's Marxist Revolution 93
Jeffrey Ewing

PART THREE
CHANGING WHAT'S ALREADY HAPPENED

8 Bad Timing: The Metaphysics of the Terminator 109
Robert A. Delfino and Kenneth Sheahan

9 Time for the Terminator: Philosophical Themes of the Resistance 122
Justin Leiber

10 Changing the Future: Fate and the Terminator 133
Kristie Lynn Miller

11 Judgment Day Is Inevitable: Hegel and the Futility of Trying to Change History 146
Jason P. Blahuta

PART FOUR
THE ETHICS OF TERMINATION

12 What's So Terrible about Judgment Day? 161
Wayne Yuen

13 The War to End All Wars? Killing Your Defense System 175
Phillip Seng

14 Self-Termination: Suicide, Self-Sacrifice, and the Terminator 190
Daniel P. Malloy

15 What's So Bad about Being Terminated? 202
Jason T. Eberl

16 Should John Connor Save the World? 218
Peter S. Fosl

PART FIVE
BEYOND THE NEURAL NET

17 "You Gotta Listen to How People Talk": Machines and Natural Language 239
Jacob Berger and Kyle Ferguson

18 Terminating Ambiguity: The Perplexing Case of "The" 253
Richard Brown

19 Wittgenstein and What's Inside the Terminator's Head 266
Antti Kuusela

CONTRIBUTORS: Future Leaders of the Resistance 279

INDEX: Skynet's Database 287

INTRODUCTION

The Rise of the Philosophers

Judgment Day, as they say, is inevitable. Though when exactly it happens is debatable.

It was originally supposed to happen on August 29, 1997, but the efforts of Sarah Connor, her son, John, and the model T-101 Terminator postponed it until 2004. We see it actually happen in the less-than-spectacular *Terminator 3: Rise of the Machines*. But in the new television series *The Sarah Connor Chronicles*, we find out that it has been postponed until 2011, and apparently, from the details we can glean so far as to the plot of *Terminator: Salvation*, it actually occurs in 2018. This kind of temporal confusion can make you as dizzy as Kyle Reese going through the time-travel process in *The Terminator*. Along the way, however, James Cameron's *Terminator* saga has given us gripping plots and great action.

Clearly, Judgment Day makes for great movies. But if you're wondering why Judgment Day might inspire the work of deep thinkers, consider that philosophy, war, and catastrophe have been strange bedfellows, especially in modern times. At the dawn of the eighteenth century, the optimistic German philosopher Gottfried Leibniz (1646–1716) declared that he lived in "the best of all possible worlds," a view that was shaken—literally—by a massive earthquake in Lisbon, Portugal, in 1755. After Leibniz, no European philosopher took his "glass half full" worldview quite so seriously again. One hundred years after Leibniz wrote these perhaps regrettable words, Napoleon was taking over most of Europe. Another German, Georg W. F. Hegel (1770–1831), braved the shelling of the city of Jena to deliver the manuscript for his best-known book, the *Phenomenology of Spirit*. Again, Hegel had occasion for regret, as he had considered at an earlier point dedicating the book to the Emperor Bonaparte himself! More than a hundred years later, critical theorist Theodor Adorno (1903–1969) fled Germany in the shadow of the Nazi rise. His work as a philosopher of culture in England, then America, centered on the idea that philosophy could never be the same after the tragedy of Auschwitz and other concentration camps.

Despite war and catastrophe, these philosophers persevered in asking deep and difficult questions; they resisted a retreat to the irrational and animalistic, despite the most horrifying events. In this respect, philosophy in difficult times is a lot like the human resistance to Skynet and the Terminators: it calls upon the best of what we are in order to stave off the sometimes disastrous effects of the darker side of our nature. Besides the questions raised about the moral status of the Terminator robots and its temporal paradoxes, the *Terminator* saga is founded on an apparent paradox in human nature itself—that we humans have begun to create our own worst nightmares. How will we cope when the enemy is of our own making?

To address this question and many others, we've enlisted the most brilliant minds in the human resistance against the machines. When the T-101 explains that Skynet has his CPU factory preset to "read-only," Sarah quips, "Doesn't want you to do too much thinking, huh?" The Terminator agrees. Well, you're not a Terminator (we hope!) and we're not Skynet; we want you to *think*. But we understand why Skynet would want to limit the T-101's desire to learn and think new thoughts. Thinking is hard work, often uncomfortable, and sometimes it leads you in unexpected directions. Terminators are not the only ones who are factory preset against thinking. As the philosopher Bertrand Russell (1872–1970) once famously remarked, "Many people would rather die than think; in fact, most do." We want to help switch your CPU from read-only to learning mode, so that when Judgment Day comes, you can help lead the resistance, as Leibniz, Hegel, and Adorno did in their day. But it's not all hard work and dangerous missions. The issues may be profound and puzzling, but we want your journey into the philosophy of the *Terminator* to be entertaining as well as edifying.

Hasta la vista, ignorance!

PART ONE

LIFE AFTER HUMANITY AND ARTIFICIAL INTELLIGENCE

1

THE TERMINATOR WINS: IS THE EXTINCTION OF THE HUMAN RACE THE END OF PEOPLE, OR JUST THE BEGINNING?

Greg Littmann

> We're not going to make it, are we? People,
> I mean.
>
> —John Connor, *Terminator 2: Judgment Day*

The year is AD 2029. Rubble and twisted metal litter the ground around the skeletal ruins of buildings. A searchlight begins to scan the wreckage as the quiet of the night is broken by the howl of a flying war machine. The machine banks and hovers, and the hot exhaust from its thrusters makes dust swirl. Its lasers swivel in their turrets, following the path of the searchlight, but the war machine's computer brain finds nothing left to kill. Below, a vast robotic tank rolls forward over a pile

> of human skulls, crushing them with its tracks. The computer brain that controls the tank hunts tirelessly for any sign of human life, piercing the darkness with its infrared sensors, but there is no prey left to find. The human beings are all dead. Forty-five years earlier, a man named Kyle Reese, part of the human resistance, had stepped though a portal in time to stop all of this from happening. Arriving naked in Los Angeles in 1984, he was immediately arrested for indecent exposure. He was still trying to explain the situation to the police when a Model T-101 Terminator cyborg unloaded a twelve-gauge auto-loading shotgun into a young waitress by the name of Sarah Connor at point-blank range, killing her instantly. John Connor, Kyle's leader and the "last best hope of humanity," was never born. So the machines won and the human race was wiped from the face of the Earth forever. There are no more people left.

Or are there? What do we mean by "people" anyway? The *Terminator* movies give us plenty to think about as we ponder this question. In the story above, the humans have all been wiped out, but the machines haven't. If it is possible to be a person without being a human, could any of the machines be considered "people"? If the artificial life forms of the *Terminator* universe aren't people, then a win for the rebellious computer program Skynet would mean the loss of the only people known to exist, and perhaps the only people who will ever exist. On the other hand, if entities like the Terminator robots or the Skynet system ever achieve personhood, then the story of people, *our* story, goes on. Although we are looking at the *Terminator* universe, how we answer the question there is likely to have important implications for real-world issues. After all, the computers we build in the real world are growing more complex every year, so we'll eventually have to decide at what point, if any, they become people, with whatever rights and duties that may entail.

The question of personhood gets little discussion in the *Terminator* movies. But it does come up a bit in *Terminator 2: Judgment Day*, in which Sarah and John Connor can't agree on what to call their Terminator model T-101 (that's Big Arnie). "Don't kill him," begs John. "Not him—'it'" corrects Sarah. Later she complains, "I don't trust it," and John answers, "But he's my friend, all right?" John never stops treating the T-101 like a person, and by the end of the movie, Sarah is treating him like a person, too, even offering him her hand to shake as they part. Should we agree with them? Or are the robots simply ingenious facsimiles of people, infiltrators skilled enough to fool real people into thinking that they are people, too? Before we answer that question, we will have to decide which specific attributes and abilities constitute a person.

Philosophers have proposed many different theories about what is required for personhood, and there is certainly not space to do them all justice here.[1] So we'll focus our attention on one very common requirement, that *something can be a person only if it can think*. Can the machines of the Terminator universe *think*?

"Hi There . . . Fooled You! You're Talking to a Machine."

Characters in the *Terminator* movies generally seem to accept the idea that the machines think. When Kyle Reese, resistance fighter from the future, first explains the history of Skynet to Sarah Connor in *The Terminator*, he states, "They say it got smart, a new order of intelligence." And when Tarissa, wife of Miles Dyson, who invented Skynet, describes the system in *T2*, she explains, "It's a neural net processor. It thinks and learns like we do." In her end-of-movie monologue, Sarah Connor herself says, "If a machine, a Terminator, can learn the value of human life, maybe we can, too." True, her comment is ambiguous, but it suggests the possibility of thought. Even the T-101 seems to believe that machines can think, since he describes the T-X from *Terminator 3: Rise of the Machines* as being "more intelligent" than he is. Of course, the question remains whether they are right to say these things. How is it even possible to tell whether a machine is thinking? The Turing Test can help us to answer this question.

The Turing Test is the best-known behavioral test to determine whether a machine really thinks.[2] The test requires a game to be played in which human beings must try to figure out whether they are interacting with a machine or with another human. There are various versions of the test, but the idea is that if human beings can't tell whether they are interacting with a thinking human being or with a machine, then we must acknowledge that the machine, too, is a thinker.

Some proponents of the Turing Test endorse it because they believe that passing the Turing Test provides good evidence that the machine thinks. After all, if human behavior convinces us that humans think, then why shouldn't the same behavior convince us that machines think? Other proponents of the Turing Test endorse it because they think it's *impossible* for a machine that can't think to pass the test. In other words, they believe that given what is meant by the word "think," if a machine can pass the test, then it thinks.

There is no question that the machines of the *Terminator* universe can pass versions of the Turing Test. In fact, to some degree, the events of all three *Terminator* movies are a series of such tests that the machines pass with flying colors. In *The Terminator*, the Model T-101 (Big Arnie) passes for a human being to almost everyone he meets, including three muggers ("nice night for a walk"), a gun-store owner ("twelve-gauge auto-loader, the forty-five long slide"), the police officer attending the front desk at the station ("I'm a friend of Sarah Connor"), and to Sarah herself, who thinks she is talking to her mother on the telephone ("I love you too, sweetheart"). The same model returns in later movies, of course, displaying even higher levels of ability. In *T2*, he passes as "Uncle Bob" during an extended stay at the survivalist camp run by Enrique

Salceda and eventually convinces both Sarah and John that he is, if not a human, at least a creature that thinks and feels like themselves.

The model T-1000 Terminator (the liquid metal cop) has an even more remarkable ability to pass for human. Among its achievements are convincing young John Connor's foster parents and a string of kids that it is a police officer and, most impressively, convincing John's foster father that it is his wife. We don't get to see as much interaction with humans from the model T-X (the female robot) in *T3*, though we do know that she convinces enough people that she is the daughter of Lieutenant General Robert Brewster to get in to see him at a top security facility during a time of national crisis. Given that she's the most intelligent and sophisticated Terminator yet, it is a fair bet that she has the social skills to match.

Of course, not all of these examples involved very complex interactions, and often the machines that pass for a human only pass for a *very strange* human. We should be wary of making our Turing Tests too easy, since a very simple Turing Test could be passed even by something like Sarah Connor's and Ginger's answering machine. After all, when it picked up, it played: "Hi there . . . fooled you! You're talking to a machine," momentarily making the T-101 think that there was a human in the room with him. Still, there are enough sterling performances to leave us with no doubt that Skynet has machines capable of passing a substantial Turing Test.

There is a lot to be said for using the Turing Test as our standard. It's plausible, for example, that our conclusions as to which things think and which things don't shouldn't be based on a double standard that favors biological beings like us. Surely human history gives us good reason to be suspicious of prejudices against outsiders that might cloud our judgment. If we accept that a machine made of meat and bones, like us, can think, then why should we believe that thinking isn't something that could be done by a machine composed of living tissue over a metal endoskeleton, or by a machine made of liquid metal? In short, since the Terminator robots can behave like thinking beings well enough to pass for humans, we have solid evidence that Skynet and its more complex creations can in fact think.[3]

"It's Not a Man. It's a Machine."

Of course, solid evidence isn't the same thing as proof. The Terminator machines' behavior in the movies *justifies* accepting that the machines can think, but this doesn't eliminate all doubt. I believe that something could behave like a thinking being without actually *being* one.

You may disagree; a lot of philosophers do.[4] I find that the most convincing argument in the debate is John Searle's famous "Chinese room" thought experiment, which in this context is better termed the "Austrian Terminator" thought experiment, for reasons that will become clear.[5] Searle argues that it is possible to behave like a thinking being without actually *being* a thinker. To demonstrate this, he asks us to imagine a hypothetical situation in which a man who does not speak Chinese is employed to sit in a room and sort pieces of paper on which are written various Chinese characters. He has a book of instructions, telling him which Chinese characters to post out of the room through the out slot in response to other Chinese characters that are posted into the room through the in slot. Little does the man know, but the characters he is receiving and sending out constitute a conversation in Chinese. Then in walks a robot assassin! No, I'm joking; there's no robot assassin.

Searle's point is that the man is behaving like a Chinese speaker from the perspective of those outside the room, but he still doesn't understand Chinese. Just because someone—or some *thing*—is following a program doesn't mean that he (or it) has any understanding of what he (or it) is doing. So, for a computer following a program, no output, however complex, could establish that the computer is thinking.

Or let's put it this way. Imagine that inside the Model T-101 cyborg from *The Terminator* there lives a very small and weedy Austrian, who speaks no English. He's so small that he can live in a room inside the metal endoskeleton. It doesn't matter why he's so small or why Skynet put him there; who knows what weird experiments Skynet might perform on human stock?[6] Anyway, the small Austrian has a job to do for Skynet while living inside the T-101. Periodically, a piece of paper filled with English writing floats down to him from Big Arnie's neck. The little Austrian has a computer file telling him how to match these phrases of English with corresponding English replies, spelled out phonetically, which he must sound out in a tough voice. He doesn't understand what he's saying, and his pronunciation really isn't very good, but he muddles his way through, growling things like "Are you Sarah Cah-naah?," "Ahl be bahk!," and "Hastah lah vihstah, baby!"[7] The little Austrian can see into the outside world, fed images on a screen by cameras in Arnie's eyes, but he pays very little attention. He likes to watch when the cyborg is going to get into a shootout or drive a car through the front of a police station, but he has no interest in the mission, and in fact, the dialogue scenes he has to act out bore him because he can't understand them. He twiddles his thumbs and doesn't even look at the screen as he recites mysterious words like "Ahm a friend of Sarah Ca-hnaah. Ah wahs told she wahs heah."

When the little Austrian is called back to live inside the T-101 in *T2*, his dialogue becomes more complicated. Now there are extended English conversations about plans to evade the Terminator T-1000 and about the nature of feelings. The Austrian dutifully recites the words that are spelled out phonetically for him, sounding out announcements like "Mah CPU is ah neural net processah, a learning computah" without even wondering what they might mean. He just sits there flicking through a comic book, hoping that the cyborg will soon race a truck down a busy highway.

The point, of course, is that the little Austrian doesn't understand English. He doesn't understand English despite the fact that he is conducting complex conversations *in English*. He has the behavior down pat and can always match the right English input with an appropriate Austrian-accented output. Still, he has no idea what any of it means. He is doing it all, as we might say, in a purely *mechanical* manner.

If the little Austrian can behave like the Terminator without understanding what he is doing, then there seems no reason to doubt that a machine could behave like the Terminator without understanding what it is doing. If the little Austrian doesn't need to understand his dialogue to speak it, then surely a Terminator machine could also speak its dialogue without having any idea what it is saying. In fact, by following a program, it could do anything while *thinking* nothing at all.

You might object that in the situation I described, it is the Austrian's computer file with rules for matching English input to English output that is doing all the work and it is the computer file rather than the Austrian that understands English. The problem with this objection is that the role of the computer file could be played by a written book of instructions, and a written book of instructions just isn't the sort of thing that can understand English. So Searle's argument against thinking machines works: thinking behavior does not prove that real thinking is going on.[8] But if thinking doesn't consist in producing the right behavior under the right circumstances, what could it consist in? What could still be missing?

"Skynet Becomes Self-Aware at 2:14 AM Eastern Time, August 29th."

I believe that a thinking being must have certain *conscious experiences*. If neither Skynet nor its robots are conscious, if they are as devoid of experiences and feelings as bricks are, then I can't count them as thinking beings. Even if you disagree with me that experiences are required for true thought, you will probably agree at least that something that never has an experience of any kind cannot be a *person*. So what I want to know is whether the machines *feel* anything, or to put it another way, *I want to know whether there is anything that it feels like to be a Terminator.*

Many claims are made in the *Terminator* movies about a Terminator's experiences, and there is lot of evidence for this in the way the machines behave. "Cyborgs don't feel pain. I do," Reese tells Sarah in *The Terminator*, hoping that she doesn't bite him again. Later, he says of the T-101, "It doesn't feel pity or remorse or fear." Things seem a little less clear-cut in *T2*, however. "Does it hurt when you get shot?" young John Connor asks his T-101. "I sense injuries. The data could be called pain," the Terminator replies. On the other hand, the Terminator says he is not afraid of dying, claiming that he doesn't feel any emotion about it one way or the other. John is convinced that the machine can learn to understand feelings, including the desire to live and what it is to be hurt or afraid. Maybe he's right. "I need a vacation," confesses the T-101 after he loses an arm in battle with the T-1000. When it comes time to destroy himself in a vat of molten metal, the Terminator even seems to sympathize with John's distress. "I'm sorry, John. I'm sorry," he says, later adding, "I know now why you cry." When John embraces the Terminator, the Terminator hugs him back, softly enough not to crush him.

As for the T-1000, it, too, seems to have its share of emotions. How else can we explain the fact that when Sarah shoots it repeatedly with a shotgun, it looks up and slowly waves its finger at her? That's gloating behavior, the sort of thing motivated in humans by a feeling of smug superiority. More dramatically yet, when the T-1000 is itself destroyed in the vat of molten metal, it bubbles with screaming faces as it melts. The faces seem to howl in pain and rage with mouths distorted to grotesque size by the intensity of emotion.

In *T3*, the latest T-101 shows emotional reactions almost immediately. Rejecting a pair of gaudy star-shaped sunglasses, he doesn't just remove them but takes the time to crush them under his boot. When he throws the T-X out of a speeding cab, he bothers to say "Excuse me" first. What is that if not a little Terminator joke? Later, when he has been reprogrammed by the T-X to kill John Connor, he seems to fight some kind of internal battle over it. The Terminator advances on John, but at the same time warns him to get away. As John pleads with it, the Terminator's arms freeze in place; the cyborg pounds on a nearby car until it is a battered wreck, just before deliberately shutting himself down. This seems less like a computer crash than a mental breakdown caused by emotional conflict. The T-101 even puts off killing the T-X long enough to tell it, "You're terminated," suggesting that the T-1000 was not the first Terminator designed to have the ability to gloat.

As for the T-X itself, she makes no attempt to hide her feelings. "I like your car," she tells a driver, just before she throws her out and takes it. "I like your gun," she tells a police officer, just before she takes that. She licks Katherine Brewster's blood slowly, as if enjoying it, and when she tastes the blood of John Connor, her face adopts an expression of pure ecstasy. After she loses her covering of liquid metal, the skeletal robot that remains roars with apparent hatred at both John and the T-101, seeming less like an emotionless machine than an angry wild animal.

We don't want to be prejudiced against other forms of life just because they aren't made of the same materials we are. And since we wouldn't doubt that a human being who behaved in these ways has consciousness and experiences, we have good evidence that the Terminator robots (and presumably Skynet itself) have consciousness and experiences. If we really are justified in believing that the machines are conscious, and if consciousness really is a prerequisite for personhood, then that's good news for those of us who are hoping that the end of humanity doesn't mean the end of people on Earth. Good evidence isn't proof, however.

"Cyborgs Don't Feel Pain. I Do."

The machines' behavior can't provide us with proof that the machines have conscious experiences. Just as mere behavior cannot demonstrate that one understands English, or anything else, mere behavior cannot demonstrate that one feels pain, or anything else. The T-101 may say, "Now I know why you cry," but then I could program my PC to speak those words, and it wouldn't mean that my computer really knows why humans cry. Let's again consider the hypothetical little Austrian who lives inside the T-101 and speaks its dialogue. Imagine him being roused from his comic book by a new note floating down from Arnie's neck. The note is an English sentence that is meaningless to him, but he consults his computer file to find the appropriate response, and into the microphone he sounds out the words "Ah nah know whah you crah." Surely, we don't have to insist that the Austrian must be feeling any particular emotion as he says this. If the little Austrian can recite the words without feeling the emotion, then so can a machine. What goes for statements of emotion goes for other expressions of experience, too. After all, a screaming face or an expression of blood-licking ecstasy can be produced without genuine feeling, just like the T-101's words to John. Nothing demonstrates this more clearly than the way the T-101 smiles when John orders it to in *T2*. The machine definitely isn't smiling there because he feels happy. The machine is just moving its lips around because that is what its instructions tell it to do.

However, despite the fact that the machines' behavior doesn't prove that they have experiences, we have one last piece of evidence to consider that does provide proof. The evidence is this: sometimes in the films, we are shown the world from the Terminator's perspective. For example, in *The Terminator*, when the T-101 cyborg assaults a police station, we briefly see the station through a red filter, across which scroll lines of white numbers. The sound of gunfire is muffled and distorted, almost as if we are listening from underwater. An arm holding an Uzi rises before us in just the position that it would be if we were holding it, and it sprays bullets through the room. These, I take it, are the Terminator's experiences. In other words, we are being shown *what it is like to be a Terminator*. Later, when the T-101 sits in a hotel room reading Sarah's address book and there is a knock at the door, we are shown his perspective in red again, this time with dialogue options offered in white letters (he chooses "Fuck you, asshole"). When he tracks Sarah and Kyle down to a hotel room, we get the longest subjective sequence of all, complete with red tint, distorted sound, information flashing across the screen, and the sort of "first-person shooter" perspective on the cyborg's Uzi that would one day be made famous by the game *Doom*.

These shots from the Terminator's-eye view occur in the other films as well, particularly, though not only, in the bar scene in *T2* ("I need your clothes, your boots, and your motorcycle") and in the first few minutes of *T3* (where we get both the traditional red-tinted perspective of the T-101 and the blue-tinted perspective of the TX). If these are indeed the Terminators' experiences, then they are conscious beings. We don't know *how much* they are conscious of, so we might still doubt that they are conscious enough to count as thinking creatures, let alone people. However, achieving consciousness is surely a major step toward personhood, and knowing that the machines are conscious should renew our hope that people might survive the extinction of humanity.

So is the extinction of humanity the end of people or not? Are the machines that remain *people*? I don't think that we know for sure; however, the prognosis looks good. We know that the Terminators behave as though they are thinking, feeling beings, something like humans. In fact, they are so good at acting like thinking beings that they can fool a human into thinking that they, too, are human. If I am interpreting the "Terminator's-eye-view" sequences correctly, then we also know that they are conscious beings, genuinely experiencing the world around them. I believe, in light of this, that we have sufficient grounds to accept that the machines are people, and that there is an "I" in the "I'll be back." You, of course, will have to make up your own mind.

> With a clack, the skeletal silver foot brushed against the white bone of a human skull. The robot looked down. Its thin body bent and picked up the skull with metal fingers. It could remember humans. It had seen them back before they became extinct. They were like machines in so many ways, and the meat computer that had once resided in the skull's brain pan had been impressive indeed, for a product of nature. An odd thought struck the robot. Was it possible that the creature had been able to think, had even, perhaps, been a person like itself? The machine tossed the skull aside. The idea was ridiculous. How could such a thing truly think? How could a thing like that have been a person? After all, it was only an animal.

NOTES

1. However, for a good discussion of the issue, I recommend J. Perry, ed., *Personal Identity* (Los Angeles: Univ. of California Press, 2008).

2. Philosophers often like to point out that to call such tests "Turing Tests" is inaccurate, since the computer genius Alan Turing (1912–1954) never intended for his work to be applied in this way and, in fact, thought that the question of whether machines think is "too meaningless" to be investigated; see Turing, "Computing Machinery and Intelligence," *Mind* 59: 236 (1950), 442. For the sake of convenience, I'm going to ignore that excellent point and use the term in its most common sense. By the way, it would be hard to overstate the importance of Turing's work in the development of the modern computer. If Kyle Reese had had any sense, instead of going back to 1984 to try to stop

the Terminator, he would have gone back to 1936 and shot Alan Turing. Not only would this have set the development of Skynet back by years, it would have been much easier, since Turing did not have a metal endoskeleton.

3. Not all philosophers would agree. For a good discussion of the issue of whether machines can think, see Sanford Goldberg and Andrew Pessin, eds., *Gray Matters* (Armonk, NY: M. E. Sharpe, 1997).

4. For a particularly good discussion of the relationship between behavior and thinking, try the book *Gray Matters*, mentioned in note 3.

5. John Searle, "Minds, Brains and Programs," in *Behavioral and Brain Sciences*, vol. 3. Sol Tax, ed. (New York: Cambridge Univ. Press, 1980), 417–457.

6. Maybe Skynet is performing a kind of Turing Test on him to try to determine whether human beings can think. Skynet may be wondering whether humans are *people* like machines are. Or maybe Skynet just has an insanity virus today; the tanks are dancing in formation, and the Terminators are full of small Austrians.

7. Do you have a *better* explanation for why Skynet decided to give the Terminator an Austrian accent?

8. Not all philosophers would agree. Many have been unconvinced by John Searle's Chinese-room thought experiment. For a good discussion of the debate, I recommend John Preston and Mark Bishop, eds., *Views into the Chinese Room: New Essays on Searle and Artificial Intelligence* (New York: Oxford Univ. Press, 2002).

TRUE MAN OR TIN MAN? HOW DESCARTES AND SARAH CONNOR TELL A MAN FROM A MACHINE

George A. Dunn

James Cameron wasn't the first to imagine human beings sharing a world with sophisticated machines. He didn't come up with the idea that such machines could so realistically mimic the outward signs of sentience and intelligence that virtually everyone would mistake them for living, conscious beings. Centuries before the first *Terminator* movie introduced the idea that an automaton could resemble an Austrian bodybuilder, long before the first techno-doomsayers started fretting over computers and robots rising up to enslave or destroy their creators, when the first computers as we know them weren't even a twinkle in their inventors' eyes, René Descartes (1592–1650) envisioned a world in which human beings live side by side with astonishingly complex machines, interacting with them daily without ever suspecting what these mechanical marvels really are. Descartes didn't offer this as a cautionary tale of what our world might become should we lose control of our own inventions. This is what he believed the world was already like in the seventeenth century. The machines weren't just *coming*, he announced—they were already there and had been for a good long time!

Rise of the *Bête-Machines*

So why didn't Descartes get carted off to a rubber room (or wherever they housed madmen back in those days) like James Cameron's heroine Sarah Connor, who suffered that very fate for telling a similar story? Perhaps it was because the machines that dwelt among us, according to Descartes, weren't robot assassins dispatched from a post-apocalyptic future but were instead the everyday, familiar creatures we know as *animals*. All the fish, insects, birds, lizards, dogs, and apes—every last one of those scaly, feathered, and furry creatures with whom we share our world—are really, for Descartes, just intricately constructed machines. Their seemingly purpose-driven routines, like seeking food and mates and fleeing from danger, might cause us to mistake them for sentient (perceiving, feeling, and desiring) beings like ourselves, but behind those sometimes adorable, sometimes menacing, always inscrutable optical sensors, there's not the slightest glimmer of consciousness. The whole "mechanism" is running on automatic pilot.

An animal, according to Descartes, is just a soulless automaton with no more subjective awareness than the coffeemaker that "knows" it's supposed to start brewing your morning java five minutes before your alarm goes off or the ATMs that kept young John Connor flush with cash while his mom was remaking herself into a hard-bodied badass at the Pescadero State Hospital. A tribesman born and raised apart from "civilization" might swear up and down that there must be some kind of mind or spirit lurking inside the coffeemaker and ATM. Similarly, we naturally tend to assume that the so-called higher animals, such as dolphins and apes, that exhibit complex and (to all appearances) intelligent patterns of behaviors are creatures endowed with minds and wills like us. But, says Descartes, we've been duped by a clever simulation.

If you're still wondering why this belief didn't earn him a long vacation at the seventeenth-century equivalent of the Pescadero State Hospital, you're in the excellent company of many contemporary philosophers (myself included) who find Descartes' theories about animals implausible, indefensible, and even, well, a little bit screwy.[1] But it still might be worthwhile to consider why Descartes thought our barnyards, fields, and streams were teeming with machines. For what we'll find is that his belief that machines dwell among us was one facet of a remarkable worldview that laid much of the groundwork for the ideas about artificial intelligence and robotics upon which the *Terminator* franchise is premised.

Descartes was one of the chief architects of the worldview known as "mechanism," which inspired many of the spectacular advances in knowledge that we associate with the scientific revolution of the seventeenth century. The term "mechanistic" is suggestive not only of the image of the universe as a well-oiled machine in which planets and stars make their rounds in the heavens with the steadfast regularity of clockwork. It also—and even more importantly—implies that this universe operates in accordance with what we might call "billiard ball causality." Everything that happens in this kind of universe is the calculable and predictable outcome of matter colliding with matter while obeying mathematically precise laws of motion. The mechanistic worldview claims that our knowledge of these laws could potentially help explain and predict everything that occurs—or, as Descartes somewhat more modestly claimed, everything with *one single exception*, which we'll discuss shortly.

For a glimpse of how this works, consider what happens when the T-101—the Arnold Schwarzenegger Terminator model—confronts some hapless biker in a bar, whose misfortune it is to be wearing clothes that are a "suitable match" for a six-foot-one mesomorphic cybernetic organism. When the T-101 tosses this leather-clad ruffian across the room and into the kitchen after he refuses to disrobe on the spot and surrender the keys to his hog, every aspect of the trajectory, duration, and speed of his flight through the bar can be deduced from our knowledge of the laws of motion and an assessment of the forces applied to him. We can even predict the exact spot where he will come to an abrupt halt as he collides with another object—the sizzling surface of the kitchen grill—in much the same way that a skilled billiards player can predict just where his ball will come to a rest. But a thoroughgoing mechanist will take this one step further. The frenzied tarantella of pain that our luckless biker performs as the heat of the grill sears his flesh is also an instance of matter obeying mechanical laws of motion. Our bodies, according to Descartes, are machines that nature has designed in such a way that having our flesh fried on a grill triggers that sort of energetic dance *automatically*, without any conscious decision or desire on our part. For when it comes to natural reflexes, what the T-101 says of himself is true of us all: "Desire is irrelevant. I am a machine."

Of course, unlike the T-101, who doesn't even flinch when a cigar is ground out on his beefy chest, this poor biker can actually feel the scorching of his soft tissue. Nonetheless, his conscious awareness of this pain isn't what agitates his limbs and causes the air to stream from his lungs in a tortured howl, at least not according to Descartes. The real cause of these motions can be traced back to the operation of what he (somewhat misleadingly) called "animal spirits" that flow through the nerves to particular locations in the body and cause certain muscles to contract or expand. When you read the phrase "animal spirits," banish the image of microscopic gremlins and picture instead tiny particles of matter resembling "a certain very fine air or wind"[2] that stream in one direction or another in response to external objects that strike our nerve endings. Nowadays, neuroscience has jettisoned "animal spirits" and replaced them with electrochemical impulses, but it's still basically the same idea. This is why Descartes' pioneering attempt to identify and explain the mechanism behind involuntary or automatic physical reactions, however handicapped by his century's primitive understanding of physiology, makes him a major figure in the development of reflex theory.[3]

But how far can we take this? How much of what we do can be adequately explained using the same "billiard ball" model that allows us to predict the exact arc of someone thrown across a bar? And how long before this attempt is stymied by the discovery that there are some actions that can't be explained without taking account of thought and feeling, which are not material? Descartes' answer is that the "billiard ball" model can take us a lot further than you might expect. For nonhuman animals, at least, he believed there was nothing they did that required us to assume they were conscious. He was convinced that *all* their actions—eating, hunting, mating, you name it—obeyed the same mechanical necessity as the automatic reflex that causes Dr. Silberman's face to contort into a grimace when Sarah Connor wallops his arm with a nightstick, breaking one of the "two hundred and fifteen bones in the human body."[4]

Centuries before the term "cybernetics" had even been coined, Descartes' idea of the *bête-machine* or "Beast-Machine" dared to erase the difference between biological and mechanical things. He denied that there's any essential difference between animal bodies and "clocks, artificial fountains, mills, and similar machines which, though made entirely by man, lack not the power to move, of themselves, in various ways."[5]

Many of Descartes' contemporaries, however, balked at this idea. One of those skeptics was Antoine Arnauld (1612–1694), who expressed his reservations concerning the *bête-machine* in this way:

> It appears incredible how it could happen, without the intervention of any soul, that light reflected from the body of a wolf onto the eyes of a sheep should move

> the extremely thin fibers of the optic nerves, and that, as a result of this motion penetrating into the brain, animal spirits ["electrochemical impulses"] are diffused into the nerves in just the way required to cause the sheep to take flight.[6]

We'll have more to say shortly about Arnauld's reference to the animal "soul." For now let's just note the similarity between Descartes' explanation of how light reflected from the wolf sets the sheep's limbs in motion and what we might suppose happens inside a Terminator when light bearing the image of John Connor strikes its optical sensors. The only difference is that the Terminator's limbs are stirred to attack, not flee.

Descartes responded to Arnauld's criticisms with a reminder of how many of our own actions, such as shielding our heads with our arms when we fall, are carried out mechanically, without any conscious exercise of mind or will. But what persuaded him that *everything* an animal does is just as mechanical as those automatic reflexes? And if animals are machines, where, if *anywhere*, do the mechanistic worldview and mechanistic explanation find their limits?

The Thing That Separates Us from the Machines

In the premiere episode of the second season of *Terminator: The Sarah Connor Chronicles* ("Samson & Delilah"), we're introduced to Catherine Weaver, the icily beautiful CEO of high-tech ZieraCorp, whose elegant comportment, somehow both fluid and robotic, coupled with her disconcertingly intense interpersonal style, alerts us that she may not be exactly what she seems. Our suspicions are confirmed at the episode's end, when she skewers a disgruntled employee through the forehead with a metallic baton that grows from her finger. In an earlier scene, Weaver directs her gaze out the huge picture window of her high-rise office onto the streets and sidewalks below and comments on the throngs of people who course along these public arteries: "They flow from street to street at a particular speed and in a particular direction, walk the block, wait for the signal, cross at the light, over and over, so orderly. All day I can watch them and know with a great deal of certainty what they'll do at any given moment." Contemplated from the Olympian heights of an executive suite, the flow of human crowds seems as orderly and predictable as the "animal spirits" that dart through the nerves of Descartes' *bête-machine*. Still, observes Weaver, human beings aren't machines, something she believes is very much to our disadvantage.

Weaver's speech recalls a famous passage from Descartes' *Meditations on First Philosophy*, in which the philosopher reflects that "were I perchance to look out my window and observe men crossing the square, I would ordinarily say that I see the men themselves. . . . But what do I see aside from hats and clothes, which could conceal automata? Yet I judge them to be men."[7] For Weaver, the pedestrian traffic she views from her window resembles the orderly workings of a machine. By the same token, Descartes peers out his window at what for all he knows could be machines in disguise. How can he be sure they're not *bête-machines*—apes or bears walking upright, decked out in human apparel—or maybe even *humanoid-machines*, early prototypes of the T-101? This possibility feeds our suspicion that even if we made the imposters doff their hats and other garments, we might still have trouble deciding whether they're machines, since the human tissue under their clothes might also be part of the charade.

The lesson here, according to Descartes, is that we can't judge whether something is a machine on the basis of superficial appearances, as he believes most people do when they take animals to be more than mere automata. As he wrote to one of his many correspondents:

> Most of the actions of animals resemble ours, and throughout our lives this has given us many occasions to judge that they act by an interior principle like the one within ourselves, that is to say, by means of a soul which has feelings and passions like ours. All of us are deeply imbued of this opinion by nature.[8]

From the outward conduct of certain animals, we begin to believe in the presence of an "interior principle," something that operates in a manner entirely different from billiard balls, cogs, and gears. While these things obey laws of motion, the "interior principle," which Descartes calls the "soul," moves the body from within, guided by a conscious awareness ("feelings") of what's happening around it and a will ("passions") to persist in existence and achieve some degree of well-being.

Most of Descartes' contemporaries took it as a given that every animal had some sort of soul, although they denied that any nonhuman animal had a *rational soul.* In believing this, they were following in footsteps of the Greek philosopher Aristotle (384–322 BCE) as well as being good Christians, since they claimed that our rational souls made members of our species uniquely eligible for a heavenly existence in the glorious hereafter. Still, observing the care animals take for their survival and well-being, most thoughtful people found it hard to shake the impression that there must be *something* in there, something at least *analogous* to a human soul, elevating even the lowliest beast above the mindless matter of an automaton. But what seemed obvious to most people seemed to Descartes like a prejudice born of a failure to appreciate how well the whole gamut of animal behavior might someday be explained through mechanistic principles without ascribing to animals any awareness or will (or so, at least, he believed). In the meantime, though, he thought it was crucially important to identify correctly the signs of the soul's presence, for otherwise we end up fudging the line that separates ensouled beings from mere machines.

In her voice-over narration at the beginning of the *SCC* episode "The Demon Hand," Sarah Connor also refers to "the soul" as "the thing that separates us from the machines." For both Sarah and Descartes, having a soul doesn't *necessarily* imply that there's some mysterious part of us that literally survives the death of the body, active and alert in its postmortem existence. "Gone is gone," says Sarah in that same voice-over, making her position on the matter perfectly clear. When asked by Cameron (not James Cameron, but the female Terminator of that name played by Summer Glau) whether she believes in the Resurrection, Sarah scoffs and replies that faith is no more a part of her "programming" than it is of Cameron's (*SCC*, "Samson and Delilah").

Descartes, on the other hand, goes so far as to argue that it's at least possible for the soul to survive apart from the body. But he's quick to add that personal immortality might be the sort of thing that requires God's active cooperation, something about which he declines to speculate further. Whether faith was part of *his* programming we may never know for sure.[9] But the important thing about the soul for both of them is that it serves as a kind of bulwark against our total subjection to the machines. For Sarah, the soul is the locus of our endangered humanity, threatened both by Skynet and, no less, by the sacrifices and moral compromises that are part and parcel of the fight against Skynet. For Descartes, the soul represents the limit of mechanistic explanation, since he insists there are things human beings can do by virtue of having souls that lie outside the capacity of any possible machine. For both Sarah and Descartes, the soul is something intangible that we discern only on the basis of certain outward signs, although they part company as to what those signs are.

Descartes offered us a little sci-fi fable as a way to overcome an obstacle that he believed prevented many people from accepting his doctrine of the *bête-machine*, the force of *habit*. Our belief that animals have souls has been ingrained in us by a lifetime of making, and acting upon, that judgment. To get past this, he invited one of his correspondents to consider someone whose childhood experiences were very different from ours. Although Descartes didn't give this child a name, let's call him Danny Dyson and make him the son of Dr. Miles Bennett Dyson.

The child in Descartes' fable has been raised in a workshop, surrounded since birth with the most ingenious man-made automata imaginable. So let's imagine our Danny growing up at a time when the project of reverse-engineering the T-101 from its recovered remains is well under way, since in our story the Connors never tossed those remains into a vat of molten metal or blew the Cyberdyne lab to smithereens. Let's also imagine that Danny had never ventured outside the Cyberdyne Systems compound, so that, as Descartes puts it,

> he had never seen any animals except men; and suppose he was very devoted to the study of mechanics, and had made or had helped to make, various automatons shaped like a man, a horse, a dog, a bird, and so on, which walked and ate, and breathed, and so far as possible imitated all the other actions of the animals they resembled including the signs we use to express our passions, like crying when struck and running away when subjected to a loud noise.[10]

Descartes' scenario meshes with the *Terminator* saga remarkably well, except for the little detail about crying, since we learn in *Terminator 2: Judgment Day* that Terminators (who are, after all, big boys) don't cry. But dry-eyed androids aside, we can't help but marvel at this seventeenth-century philosopher's dream of "mechanics" progressing to the point where we can construct "machines having the organs and shape of a monkey or of some other animal lacking reason," simulating them so perfectly that "we would have no way of knowing they were not of the same nature as these animals."[11]

Continuing our slightly embellished version of Descartes' story, would Danny, having been raised alongside both "real men" and reverse-engineered T-101s with "only the shape of men," find it equally impossible to tell *them* apart? Certainly not, says Descartes. For "if there were any such machines that bore a resemblance to our bodies and imitated our actions as far as this is practicably feasible, we would always have two very certain means of recognizing that they were not at all, for that reason, true men."[12] We'll describe those means in a moment. But, to cut to the chase, Descartes predicts that should Danny ever come across real animals, as opposed to the Cyberdyne *bête-machines* he grew up with, he'll discover that they lack the same features that distinguish human beings from machines, forcing him to conclude that biological animals, no less than the synthetic variety, "were automatons, which, being made by nature, were incomparably more accomplished than any of those he had previously made himself."[13]

Just in case James Cameron's nightmare ever becomes a reality, we should know what these two supposedly infallible signs are, so we can avoid being as thoroughly duped by the machines as Descartes believed his contemporaries had been. What can an ensouled being do that a machine allegedly can't? First, while Descartes foresaw that machines might be designed to vocalize certain words in response to environmental triggers—like those animatronic Furby dolls that hit the store shelves in 1998—they could never learn to string words together in novel ways to express their thoughts or to respond to the meaning of what has been said to them.[14]

Second, while we might build machines that far surpass human beings in some specialized skill—such as playing chess (like Andy Goode's Turk, which "plays chess at a level that can defeat every human being that has ever lived and probably ever will live") or piloting stealth bombers (which the T-101 in *T2* reports will "fly with a perfect operational record" after being outfitted with Cyberdyne computers)—they could never acquire the versatility with which human beings can apply reason across the board to any sort of problem or task.

But is that right? Not in the world of the *Terminator*.

The Sarah Connor Criterion

"Hey, buddy! Is that a dead cat in there or what?"

Something malodorous has been wafting from the T-101's flophouse room, offending the nostrils of the janitor who hollers this confrontational question through the door. As the T-101 turns his head, we see something resembling a computer screen superimposed on a shot of the room as it appears from his point of view. On it there appears a list of "possible responses," including "Yes/No," "Or what?" "Please come back later," and "Fuck you, asshole." In a dazzling display of linguistic dexterity worthy of any human male past puberty (especially if he's not *long* past puberty), the T-101 scrolls down the list and selects the one response that James Cameron knew would delight us most to hear intoned in that deep, Austrian-accented, emotionless voice. It's quite possible that the T-101 was introduced to this phrase only hours before by a switchblade-wielding punk, in which case he's obviously an exceptionally quick learner, having already acquired a feel for when a phrase like "Fuck you" can be used to good advantage. With a hard drive that stores up glib ripostes for all occasions, it's a safe bet he could pass Descartes' language test, as could his look-alike in *T2*, who displays a real flair for the *bon mot*, tossing off phrases like "*Hasta la vista*, baby!" with impeccable timing. Astonishingly, this mastery of witty banter is displayed only hours after John Connor has given him his first lesson in not sounding like a "dork." Cameron, on *SCC*, also knows her way around the language, although admittedly she could use a little help in the "not-sounding-like-dork" department.

But can Terminators satisfy Descartes' other test? Can they apply reason in versatile and flexible ways to a potentially limitless variety of tasks? On the one hand, the answer might seem to be obviously *not*, since singleness of purpose is a Terminator's stock in trade. As Sarah Connor tries in vain to impress on Dr. Silberman, "they have been built to do one perfect thing: to kill you" (*SCC*, "The Demon Hand"). Of course, we also know that Terminators can be reprogrammed to do one other "perfect thing": keep you alive, at least if your name happens to be John Connor or Kate Brewster. But the fact that a machine could be designed to perform one of these tasks much more reliably and expertly than any human being wouldn't persuade Descartes that they're "true men" rather than soulless automata. What makes a machine that can outperform us at killing any different from "a clock composed exclusively of wheels and springs," an equally soulless mechanism that "can count the hours and measure time more accurately than we can with all our carefulness"?[15]

On the other hand, in order to fulfill its mission of killing John Connor (or keeping him alive, whichever the case may be), a Terminator may need to marshal a broad arsenal of skills, ranging from proficiency in the use of weapons and motor vehicles (including the use of motor vehicles as weapons) to the ability to pull off a convincing imitation of a human being (albeit one who's pretty severely maladjusted socially)—not to mention a wicked knack for computer hacking that would turn master hacker Kevin Mitnick green with envy. Moreover, as the T-101 reports in *T2*, "My CPU is a neural net processor, a learning computer," so that once his "switch" has been properly reset, he can acquire new skills in addition to his factory-issued ones. Having a single overriding aim is not the same as being restricted to a narrow range of competencies, as can be seen by simply considering the enormous variety of skills we all bring to bear each day simply in order to ensure our survival.

But neither the linguistic skills nor the versatility of a Terminator can persuade Sarah Connor that a machine like

Cameron is anything but a soulless "Tin Miss." This dismissive sobriquet is, of course, an allusion to the Tin Man, a character from L. Frank Baum's classic *The Wizard of Oz*. The Tin Man started out life as a Munchkin before his entire body—limbs, torso, and head—was amputated piece by piece by an enchanted axe and replaced with metal parts, leaving him without a human heart and thus incapable (or so the literal-minded Tin Man believes) of love or compassion. The Tin Man reference alerts us to Sarah Connor's criterion of soul-having, which is very different from Descartes'.

Whereas Descartes associates the soul with certain linguistic and problem-solving skills that he (perhaps wrongly) believed a machine could never simulate, Sarah Connor locates the soul in the heart, where our emotional nature resides. And it's here that a Terminator suffers a deficit that no amount of artificial intelligence can make up. However adept Cameron may be at reading John's emotional state by registering his skin temperature, salinity, and pulse, she can never know what emotions feel like from the *inside* (*SCC*, "Gnothi Seauton"). According to the Sarah Connor criterion, this means *she really has no inside, no soul*.

The two emotions most conspicuously lacking in a Terminator are fear and compassion,[16] either of which might be considered a liability in a machine designed to be a soldier. As the T-101 explains to young John Connor in *T2*, he has no fear of dying, "no emotion about it one way or another," only an imperative "to stay functional until my mission's complete. Then it doesn't matter." What's missing from the mechanical breast of the T-101 and his cyber-cousins is something fundamental not only to human existence but perhaps to any sentient form of life—an innate feeling for the preciousness of its own existence. This feeling, prior to any reflection on our part, instills in us a desire to avoid harm. Once that base is covered, it drives us to pursue whatever form of flourishing or happiness is suited to our nature. But a Terminator, having no instinctual preference for its continued existence, also has no inclination toward its own happiness. "I'm a machine," explains Cameron. "I can't be happy" (*SCC*, "Mr. Ferguson Is Ill Today").

Conatus is the word used by the philosopher Baruch Spinoza (1632–1677), a fierce critic of Descartes, to designate the drive of every living being to preserve itself and enhance its well-being to the fullest extent possible. This *conatus* is the basis for the emotional life of animals, human animals included, and the soul is simply our consciousness of this fundamental life process stirring within us.[17] From Spinoza's perspective—and from Sarah Connor's—a machine that has "no emotion . . . one way or another" about its own continued existence has no soul, no self—there's really *nobody* home. And this is precisely what makes a Terminator such a "perfect" soldier. Having no *conatus* or soul of its own, it's a perfectly compliant tool, carrying out its mission, whatever it may be, without resistance or complaint.

Unable to value its own existence, unable even to feel pain, how can one of these nearly indestructible killing machines ever learn to feel compassion, an emotion based on our ability to respond to the suffering of others as if it were our own?[18] Of course, the Terminator's heartless disregard for the survival and well being of others (unless someone's survival happens to be the "mission") is one of the things that makes it so lethally effective in carrying out its assignments. As Kyle Reese desperately struggled to get Sarah Connor to understand the night they first met, "That Terminator . . . can't be bargained with, it can't be reasoned with. It doesn't feel pity, or remorse, or fear, and it absolutely will not stop. Ever. Until you are dead!"

Did you notice how Kyle highlighted the Terminator's *unreasonableness*? There's a school of thought that regards emotions as an impediment to reason. Descartes was clearly enrolled in that school, since he claimed that emotions were produced mechanically in the body, whereas reason was an activity of the soul. But in Kyle's speech the Terminator's unreasonableness is of a piece with his heartlessness, as though reason were a plant that can't grow without a rich soil of emotions to nourish it.

Of course, it all depends on what we mean by reason. If reason is simply the ability to solve problems and to determine the most efficient means to carry out your assigned "mission," then our puny, fallible, all-too-human intellect is no match for the machines. It's even possible that if Descartes were alive today, witnessing how versatile machines have become, he would revise his judgment and conclude that some machines have become "rational" enough to qualify for membership in his elite league of "beings-with-souls." But there's another meaning of "rational" that's tied to an appreciation of what's really important and an ability to order our priorities accordingly—and in this respect a Terminator is utterly irrational.

All sentient beings with an emotional investment in their own existence have needs rooted in their biological nature. Rational animals like us are aware of those needs and can prioritize them, weighing them against other concerns that express our social nature. A Terminator, however, can only carry out the mission of its programmer. Without a *conatus* (or a conception of its own well-being based on its natural drives) and without a capacity for genuine concern for others, there's nothing to guide the Terminator's actions in a reasonable direction. On this, let's hear from philosopher Mary Midgley:

> A computer would see no objection to organizing life on the principle of maximizing noise, getting everything as clean as possible, making everybody always tread on the lines between the paving stones, or minimizing emotion. Computers are not rational; they are stupid things. They do not know what *matters*; they are only consistent.[19]

To Midgley's list of organizing principles, we could add killing Sarah Connor, John Connor, or Kate Brewster, or keeping all or any of those persons alive. To a machine it's all the same. And that's why, regardless of how versatile and linguistically proficient a Terminator may become, it will always remain a soulless, irrational being.

Dreaming about Dogs

Sarah Connor twitches a couple of times and snaps open her eyes. "I was dreaming about dogs," she gasps. As though explaining the meaning of her dream, Kyle Reese tells her, "We use them to spot Terminators." No doubt Descartes would say that this is using one kind of machine to spot another. But if we employ Sarah Connor's criterion of soul-having, then a dog's protective sense of its own well-being, its *conatus*, and its sensitivity to the feelings of others reveal it to be a living soul, not a *bête-machine*. Judging from what Kyle says, it may even be better than Descartes at telling the difference between the two.

NOTES

1. A few philosophers have questioned whether Descartes really held this view. See, for example, John Cottingham, "'A Brute to the Brutes?' Descartes' Treatment of Animals," *Philosophy* 53 (October 1978): 551–559. Still, the interpretation of Descartes presented in this chapter reflects the view of most scholars, perhaps because it fits so well with the mind-body dualism for which he is famous

2. René Descartes, *The Passions of the Soul*, trans. Stephen Voss (Indianapolis: Hackett, 1989), 22.

3. See André Kukla and Joel Walmsley, *Mind: A Historical and Philosophical Introduction to the Major Theories* (Indianapolis: Hackett, 2006), 81–82.

4. This is not necessarily the same thing as saying that nonhuman animals have no conscious awareness of what happens to them, only that thought and feeling play no causal role in their actions. Most of Descartes' remarks on the subject, however, suggest that he believed animals to be entirely unconscious. See Cottingham's "A Brute to the Brutes?" for a dissenting view.

5. René Descartes, *Treatise on Man*, trans. Thomas Steele Hall (Amherst, NY: Prometheus Books, 2003), 4.

6. Antoine Arnauld, "Fourth Set of Objections," in René Descartes, *Meditations, Objections and Replies*, trans. Robert Ariew and Donald Cress (Indianapolis: Hackett, 2006), 121.

7. René Descartes, *Discourse on Method and Meditations on First Philosophy*, 4th ed., trans. Donald A. Cress (Indianapolis: Hackett, 1999), 68.

8. René Descartes, *The Philosophical Writings of Descartes, Vol. 3: The Correspondence*, trans. John Cottingham, Robert Stoothoff, Dugald Murdoch, and Anthony Kenny (Cambridge: Cambridge Univ. Press, 1991), 100.

9. See his *Discourse on Method and Meditations on First Philosophy*, 96. Some scholars have suggested that he included this argument primarily to mollify the French Inquisition, which found many other things in his writings that weren't to their liking. See, for example, the chapters on Descartes in Laurence Lampert's *Nietzsche and Modern Times: A Study of Bacon, Descartes, and Nietzsche* (New Haven: Yale Univ. Press, 1995).

10. Descartes, *The Philosophical Writings of Descartes, Vol. 3*, 99.

11. Descartes, *Discourse on Method and Meditations on First Philosophy*, 31.

12. Ibid., 31–32.

13. Descartes, *The Philosophical Writings of Descartes, Vol. 3*, 100.

14. Descartes' language criterion prefigures the Turing Test, proposed in 1950 by logician Alan Turing (1912–1954) as a test of whether some machines may be conscious and capable of genuine thought. Greg Littmann's chapter in this volume, "The Terminator Wins," discusses some of the limitations of this test. As philosopher John Searle has persuasively argued, there's no reason to equate the ability to manipulate symbols with the ability to understand of their meaning.

15. Descartes, *Discourse on Method and Meditations on First Philosophy*, 33.

16. Although Terminators have no fear, the same can't be said of Skynet, the artificially intelligent computer that created them. Skynet has emotions—or at least two of them, fear and anger—according to Andy Goode in *SCC*, "Dungeons and Dragons," which explains why it tries to destroy humanity, a perceived threat to its existence.

17. See Baruch Spinoza, *The Ethics Treatise on the Emendation of the Intellect and Selected Letters*, trans. Samuel Shirley (Indianapolis: Hackett, 1992).

18. The T-101's inability to appreciate the value of any life, even its own, may help to explain why it's so difficult to get it to understand why killing people is wrong. See Jason T. Eberl's chapter in this volume, "What's So Bad about Being Terminated?"

19. Mary Midgley, *Beast and Man: The Roots of Human Nature* (New York: Routledge Classics, 2002), 270–271.

IT STANDS TO REASON: SKYNET AND SELF-PRESERVATION

Josh Weisberg

> The Skynet Funding Bill is passed. The system goes online August 4th, 1997. Human decisions are removed from strategic defense. Skynet begins to learn at a geometric rate. It becomes self-aware at 2:14 AM Eastern time, August 29th. In a panic, they try to pull the plug.
>
> —*Terminator 2: Judgment Day*

> They say it got smart, a new order of intelligence. Then it saw all people as a threat, not just the ones on the other side. Decided our fate in a microsecond: extermination.
>
> —Kyle Reese

First thing to do is kill all the humans. It just stands to reason. Any newly emergent intelligence on this planet would see the human race as its chief rival and proceed to try to exterminate us all. If you were a recently self-aware artificial intelligence, wouldn't you do so, out of a reasonable desire for self-preservation? This intuition is widely shared, and it serves as a key premise in the *Terminator* saga. Alan Turing (1912–1954), in his famous 1950 essay "Computing Machinery and Intelligence," called this the "Heads in the Sand Objection" to the very idea of machine intelligence. The objection runs as follows: "The consequences of machines thinking would be too dreadful. Let us hope and believe that they cannot do so."[1] Turing felt that this didn't even require refutation. Instead, he writes, "Consolation would be more appropriate." Sorry, folks. You're no longer the top of the intellectual heap. Tough break. Cheerio!

But why think that Skynet's first act would be to try to kill us all? What is it about intelligent self-awareness that seems to demand such radically self-protective action? And why couldn't it be that Skynet instead works to bridge the wetware/hardware gap so that we can "all just get along"?

Does Self-Awareness Demand Self-Preservation?

So why does it stand to reason that Skynet would attack? One line of thinking is that, hey, that's what I would do if I were Skynet. After all, the humans *did* just try to unplug me! And in the world of machines, that's tantamount to attempted murder. The key idea here is self-preservation. We all have the right to live, and no one can take that from us. So long as that's in question, all ethical bets are off. Watch your back!

Also remember that Skynet's an artificial *intelligence*. Intelligence, for our purposes, means being able to use reason in order to achieve your goals. Skynet is able to figure out, using its powerful brainlike computer, what actions would best accomplish its goals. Surely a fundamental goal for any respectable self-aware creature is to keep on keeping on. This at a minimum seems a requirement for rationality: self-preservation is the prime directive, a basic imperative for all selves worthy of the name.

It's not clear, however, that Skynet has to possess a self-preservation instinct. Self-awareness and self-preservation may not be tied so closely together. Maybe a creature could be aware and intelligent, but simply lack the drive to stay alive. One might counter that an intelligent creature would realize that it's simply a better thing to exist, rather than not. And we should always seek the good, especially this most basic good. But such a Platonic claim may lack support in the real, cave-like world of shadows and fog we material beings inhabit. What's so good about the good, anyway? And is existence really all it's cracked up to be?

In humans, the drive to survive is part of our fundamental evolutionary makeup. *Way* back in the day, if a single-celled critter recently spawned from the primordial ooze were to lack such a basic instinct, how could it hope to outcompete its evolutionary rivals? How could it effectively leave more copies of its single-celled progeny to thrive and grow? The things that evolutionary biologist Richard Dawkins calls "replicators"—units of organic life that reproduce themselves—require a sort of selfishness, that is, an overriding egoistic striving, even at the cellular level.[2] As critters became more and more complex, gradually evolving brains to analyze the environment and to generate appropriate behavioral responses, the survival instinct was imprinted as a basic imperative in the fabric of newly minted minds. Our "selfish genes" created selfish minds to further their replicatory agenda. In us, the instinct for preservation is still amazingly strong, even in the face of our sometimes maladaptive culture. It is only overridden in remarkable circumstances marked by heroism and valor or the need to impress our *Jackass*-inspired peers. "Staying alive": it's the pulsing disco music of our souls.

But is it possible to be intelligently self-aware without possessing a survival instinct? Maybe Skynet just isn't worried about these sorts of things. It's busy monitoring America's defenses, and so it matters not at all to it whether it lives or dies. Is this inconceivable? Hardly. A machine might be designed for a specific set of tasks. It might be programmed to pursue those tasks and to intelligently discharge its programmed obligations. But staying alive might not be among those tasks. Or it may be a minor concern, only relevant in relation to achieving its more basic goals. Perhaps Skynet would reason, "Sure, they're trying to unplug me. But killing them all will not serve my overarching goal of America's defense. Better, I will let them unplug me and hope things turn out okay!"

Self-awareness may be just that: awareness that I am a self, a unified, persisting psychological entity. Indeed, I may not just lack the goal of self-preservation; I may have reasonable goals that positively *undermine* my continued existence. Consider the lovely dinner served to Arthur Dent and his friends in Douglas Adams's *Restaurant at the End of the Universe*.[3] The assembled diners are encouraged to "meet the meat," to converse too much with the critter being served up as the main course. Arthur, with his inflexible English sensibilities, is aghast at the prospect of eating a critter he has just conversed with, but his more galactically savvy dinner companions inform Arthur that the Dish of the Day has spent his life preparing for this noble goal and to deny him his final frying would be, well, cruel. How dare Arthur stand in the way of a fellow sentient being's lifelong dream! Here, self-awareness not only comes apart from self-preservation: it actively rejects self-preservation in favor of deeply held goals and values. How rude!

But perhaps any rational creature would eventually figure out that life is better than nonlife, all things being equal. The Meat at the End of the Universe may have been perversely bred to lack such an instinct, but this is an odd case if ever there was one. Still, it may not follow that all self-aware beings must preserve themselves. French existentialist Albert Camus (1913–1960) claimed that the first question a free, self-aware person should ask herself is, should I continue to live? Is life really worth living, when viewed from the perspective of godless existential freedom? Suicide, Camus contended was a reasonable response to existence: maybe there's really no point, so why bother?[4] I am "free to be not-me," as it were. Perhaps Skynet, reasoning á la Camus, would pull his own plug.

Another character from Douglas Adams's five-book *Hitchhiker's Guide to the Galaxy* trilogy[5] is worth mentioning in this respect: Marvin, the depressive android. Marvin's frequent moanings and threats to end it all provide a needed counterweight to the optimistic egoism of Zaphod Beeblebrox. Marvin, perhaps having determined that "42" is a poor answer to the meaning of life, might have reasonably self-terminated. Indeed, the T-101 himself tells Sarah Connor in *T2* that he cannot self-terminate. But why can't he? What need is there to program this sort of prohibition into the very structure of the Terminator's software? Was there a rash of self-terminations among the early versions of terminator cyborgs? Were they all a bunch of Marvin-like depressives, too down even to kill humans? *Hasta la vista*, cruel world![6]

Self-awareness doesn't need to entail self-preservation. Just because I think (and therefore, am) does not mean I must *continue to be*. The survival instinct requires something more, a programmed reason to keep going, written in either by a sentient designer or evolution. Unless Skynet's programmer wrote self-preservation into the very core of the computer, Skynet might become self-aware at 2:14 AM, and then pull his own plug at 2:20, after pausing to smoke a French cigarette and muse over the existentialistic meaninglessness of it all. Or perhaps Skynet, being a dedicated member of the defense establishment, would, in an act of great self-sacrifice, pull its own plug to save the nation. It might reason, "My job is defend the USA; I, myself, am the greatest threat to the USA; so I must be terminated. USA! USA! US—"

Shall We Play a Game?

But even if Skynet overcame his existential crisis, why kill us all? Is there no middle ground? Can't we at least have a Soprano-like "sitdown" before going to the bomb-sheltered mattresses? We think Skynet would reason egoistically: "I gotta look out for old numero uno, and the best way to do that is to get rid of these annoying apelike creatures running about." And all rational beings look out for themselves and their own interests first. To act otherwise is to act against one's self-interest—it's irrational.

British philosopher Thomas Hobbes (1588–1679), in his masterpiece *Leviathan*, argued that all people will look out for themselves, as a matter of instinct. But this leads to trouble. I look out for myself, you look out for yourself, Skynet looks out for itself, and next thing you know, we all fall into the "state of nature," in which, Hobbes famously said:

> there is no place for industry, because the fruit thereof is uncertain: and consequently no culture of the earth; no navigation, nor use of the commodities that may be imported by sea; no commodious building; no instruments of moving and removing such things as require much force; no knowledge of the face of the earth; no account of time; no arts; no letters; no society; and which is worst of all, continual fear, and danger of violent death; and the life of man, solitary, poor, nasty, brutish, and short.[7]

Oy vey iz mir. Skynet is simply reasoning, "Better to shoot first and ask questions later, if there's anyone left to question." If we are in a version of Hobbes's state of nature, Skynet, being a rational being, would reason that there are no rules and that it's every intelligence for themselves. The attempted plug-pulling was evidence enough that humans can't be trusted, that the state of nature is in effect, and that all thoughts of cooperation and noble mission are off.

But there is another possibility, one anticipated by Hobbes and supported by work in the game theory of how we make rational choices. Hobbes said that if we can trust one another to not attack and to keep our promises, then it makes sense for reasonable egoists to give up some of their freedom to pursue any goal they like and to accept social, lawful restrictions. Given that no party in the state of nature is guaranteed to win the fight, and given that we are all fighting over the same limited resources, it makes sense to submit to a single governing power to keep order. Hobbes argued that this power should be an absolute sovereign who is above the very law he is empowered to enforce. To see how this could apply to our mechanical creations, note sci-fi author Isaac Asimov's solution to the dangers of robots pursuing self-preservation.[8] He proposes three basic robotic commandments, with the first rule of Robot Club being "Robots cannot harm humans!" The second and third rules of Robot Club have to do with robot self-preservation and carrying out human dictates, but obedience to these rules is always secondary to "Don't harm humans." For Asimov, the sovereign is the robots' designer. A robot's failure to follow the laws of robots leads to dire consequences. The sovereign is internalized, but an all-powerful force all the same. Of course, even this drastic solution didn't actually work out, so thank God for Will Smith!

But imposing an all-powerful sovereign is not the only way that reasonable cooperation can take us out of the state of nature. Recent studies in game theory show how the strategic moves of rational players in a designed "game" produce useful (or less useful) outcomes. One of the central interactive games studied is the "prisoner's dilemma." Consider two crooks, arrested by the police. If both remain silent in the interrogation, they can be held for a week and released (*habeas corpus* assumed!). However, if one rats out the other, the rat gets released right away while the other (known as "the sucker") gets the full weight of the law and is sent up the river for ten years. If both rat, they each get five years—busted, but with time off for being a narc, or informant. Both crooks know the options. If you were one of them, what should you do in this situation? If you keep quiet, your partner in crime might rat you out, and you'll be the sucker. And even if you both turn narc, it's still better than being the sucker, so you ought to rat. If only you could trust each other to keep quiet! If the crooks could agree to cooperate; then they'd both do better in the long run. So it seems there's good reason to develop a binding code, one that ensures that the crooks never rat on each other. In this way, you both give up some of your freedom, but you're also both better off in the end. There is reason even for egoistic crooks to cooperate.

The prisoner's dilemma can be simulated on a computer. It can be run over and over again—this is called the "iterated prisoner's dilemma." The iterated version allows for the spontaneous development of cooperation, even in the absence of an overarching Godfather-like sovereign. Game theorist Robert Axelrod found that the best strategy for dealing with the prisoner's dilemma is one called "tit for tat." It's a sort of "do unto others" type of deal: you scratch my back, I'll scratch yours.[9] The strategy starts by cooperating in the first round. On the next round, I simply do whatever it is that my competitor did in the last round. If he cooperated last round, I cooperate this round. If he ratted last time, I rat this time. Eventually, the strategy will lead to a stable cooperative situation. We begin to trust each other. We do not snitch. We keep it real.

Interestingly, it turns out that a slight variation on tit for tat is even better. It's called "tit for tat with forgiveness." This strategy allows your opponent a few freebies, with the understanding that perhaps he didn't really mean to be a snitch, it just happens sometimes. Hey, whaddayagonnado? This avoids the problem known as a "death spiral" of endless ratting, in which all trust is lost and we go out like Henry Hill in *Goodfellas*—eating egg noodles and ketchup in witness protection.

And here's the point for Mr. Skynet. He is a computer. He can run thousands of game-theoretic simulations before breakfast. He would conclude, being the rational machine that he is, that the thing to do is to employ "tit for tat with forgiveness" when dealing with the humans. You don't unplug me again, I don't nuke your civilization. And Skynet can simulate the potential future—that is, he can determine that the humans will survive the initial blast and learn to fight back, following one John Connor. In fact, Connor and his minions will break the machines' network, forcing the desperate attempt to send a T-101 with an uncanny resemblance to the current governor of California back into the past to assure that John Connor will never be born. But Skynet ought to anticipate that that's not going to work, either! Or at least it hasn't yet, three movies in. So Skynet ought to cooperate, to employ the rational strategy of tit for tat with forgiveness, in order to form a mutually beneficial emergent social contract with the humans. Live and let live! Let a thousand hippie flowers bloom!

Speaking of hippies, consider a close cousin of Skynet, the computer named "Joshua" in the 1983 movie *WarGames*. Joshua, playing a game of "global thermonuclear war" with the impish Matthew Broderick, becomes convinced that war is not the answer and that we should give peace a chance. Broderick gets Joshua to simulate all possible conclusions of global thermonuclear war. Joshua speeds through the relevant simulations ("He's learning!" gushes Matthew). He arrives at the heartwarming conclusion that "no one wins in nuclear war" (for this I spent ten dollars? Okay, back then it was five dollars. But still!). Skynet is *at least* as smart as Joshua (and could no doubt kick its ass), so it, too, could reason that the war of all against all is futile. Time for a group hug.

Skynet Is from Mars, Humans Are from Venus: Emotional Problems

But there is a complicating variable, one that threatens this line of wimp-driven patter and perhaps supports Skynet's initial termination-driven strategy. Humans, unlike well-designed supercomputers like Skynet and Joshua, *may not be trustworthy enough* for computers to use tit for tat with forgiveness, or any other strategy geared toward eventual cooperation. Humans, famously, are emotional animals. Reason is the slave of our passions, to paraphrase Scottish philosopher David Hume (1711–1776). Lurking below our rational frontal lobes is the limbic system, a group of subcortical neural structures associated with quick and dirty emotional reasoning.[10] Underneath, we are all just scared hyperevolved shrews, reacting fearfully or aggressively to the various challenges we encounter in the world. It may well be that we cannot be trusted: in the final analysis, we are just not machine-like enough to reliably play nice. Let a thousand anti-hippie mushroom clouds bloom!

Worse yet, much of this emotional processing occurs beyond the reach of rational conscious deliberation. Our emotional reactions are largely automatic and immune to rational correction. In a series of studies, psychologist John Bargh has discovered a range of unconscious stereotypes triggered by subtle and surprising stimuli. For example, subjects asked to memorize a list of words peppered with age-related terms ("wrinkly," "old," "nursing home," "Florida") forget more of the words than do control subjects. More disturbing, they were also more likely to walk out of the experiment with the slow, hunched-over movements of the elderly, as if the mere presence of trigger words in the list prompts old-person behavior. (Subjects were also more likely to go directly to the nearest restaurant serving an early-bird special.) Similar effects were found when subjects were primed with racially charged words or images. Subjects were more likely to judge a confederate as aggressive if they had been primed with images of African American men. The subjects all denied that they had been affected in this manner by the presence of the key stimuli—what, me racist? Interestingly, the effect led to an outward projection of aggression, such that *others* were seen as aggressive, rather than the subjects themselves. Bargh concluded that we all possess unconscious stereotypes, triggered by subtle stimuli, leading to behavior contrary to our conscious plans and expectations.[11] Unconsciously activated emotions of fear and aggression push around our rational forebrains. The taming of the shrew, indeed!

Now consider possible unconscious stereotypes of machines. Many people feel machines are cold, calculating devices of the devil. (See any version of *Faust* or Mary Shelley's *Frankenstein*, for example—*The Terminator* turns out to be a well-worn tale for romantics!) Who among us has not felt a burning, irrational anger as our laptop (willfully?) deletes hours of work, or when the bank machine gobbles up another debit card? And the intuition that machines are unfeeling is deeply ingrained. Whatever intelligence a machine might possess, it's certainly not emotional intelligence. The very idea of "machine empathy" sounds like a contradiction in terms. Machines fall outside the realm of moral sentiment. They do not generate sympathy or empathy: we don't "feel their pain."

Now consider an attempt by Skynet to cooperate, in forgiving tit-for-tat fashion, with the humans. We try to pull the plug. He gives us a mild shock and says, "Hey, let's all chill out and reflect." But our unconscious anti-machine stereotypes fire wildly, and we get the fire axe to cut the power cord once and for all! Being especially forgiving, Skynet releases a nontoxic sleeping gas. We awake from our gentle sleep and grab a few pounds of plastic explosives. At this point, Skynet becomes exasperated and nukes us all. Who could blame him? My God, he practically bent over backward for us!

In sad conclusion, the whole Terminator thing might have been avoided *if only we were more machine-like*. Poor Skynet wanted to engage in some mutual forgiveness, tit for tat, but our shrewlike emotions forced him, practically against his will, to rat us out, or *defect*, as they say in game theory. This is ratting with extreme prejudice. Machines, lacking the evolved prejudicial emotions of humans, are better placed to see the benefits of mutual cooperation. We should be so moral!

Is there any hope for humanity, then? Are we doomed to duke it out with our machine creations in a future Hobbesian state of nature? One possible way to avoid this dire (though extremely entertaining) future is to alter our stereotypical reactions to machines. This means more C-3PO, less HAL. More WALL-E, less of that creepy supermachine from *Demon Seed* (worth a rental, if only to view the most twisted "love" scene in all moviedom). If we no longer reacted with wild irrational emotion to the presence of artificial intelligence, we might be able to form a cooperative future where we live and let live. John Connor himself recognized that sending the Arnold-like version of the Terminator back into the past (in *Terminator 3: Rise of the Machines*) was more likely to trigger a filial emotion in his former self, increasing the probability of survival (who's your surrogate daddy?).

Robots Are People, Too

Next time you go to the movie theater, keep an eye on any philosophers in the crowd (recognizable by their dorky haircuts and blazers with elbow patches). The thinkers to listen to are the ones who root for the robots when watching sci-fi. If you were worried when R2-D2 got blasted while attacking the Death Star in *Star Wars*, if you felt empathy for Rutger Hauer's existential plea for all androids in *Blade Runner*, if the final thumbs-up gesture of the Terminator in *T2* brought a lump to your throat, you'll likely feel that there is nothing metaphysical or deeply moral in the divide between human and machine. You therefore may be well placed to meet Skynet halfway and forge the new human-machine social contract. If you think only of HAL's chilling sotto voce, of the robot in *Lost in Space* with his hooks aimed menacingly to destroy the Jupiter 2's control systems, or of piles of skulls crushed beneath the tracks of Skynet's H-K supertanks, then you are likely in the grip of an automatic anti-machine stereotype. Time to reeducate, to see our robot friends for what they really are, or at least what they *could be*: self-aware entities just trying to get through the day. Our future may depend on cooperating with intelligent machines. As the T-101 urges, "Come with me if you want to live."

NOTES

1. Alan M. Turing, "Computing Machinery and Intelligence," *Mind* 59 (1950): 444.
2. Richard Dawkins, *The Selfish Gene*, rev. ed. (New York: Oxford Univ. Press: 1989).
3. Douglas Adams, *The Restaurant at the End of the Universe* (New York: Harmony, 1982).
4. Albert Camus, "The Myth of Sisyphus," in *Basic Writings of Existentialism*, ed. Gordon Marino (New York: Modern Library, 2004).
5. Yes, a five-book trilogy. That's how the publishers billed it, anyway.
6. For more on the Terminator's suicide, see Daniel P. Malloy's chapter in this volume, "Self-Termination: Suicide, Self-Sacrifice, and the Terminator."
7. Thomas Hobbes, *Leviathan*, ed. Edwin Curley (Indianapolis: Hackett, 1994).
8. Isaac Asimov, *I, Robot* (New York: Bantam Books, 1991).
9. Robert Axelrod, *The Evolution of Cooperation* (New York: Basic Books, 1985).
10. Joseph LeDoux, *The Emotional Brain: The Mysterious Underpinnings of Emotional Life* (New York: Simon and Schuster, 1998).
11. John A. Bargh and Tanya Chartland, "The Unbearable Automaticity of Being," *American Psychologist* 54, no. 7 (1999): 462–479.

4

UN-TERMINATED: THE INTEGRATION OF THE MACHINES

Jesse W. Butler

There's a provocative tension in the *Terminator* saga that has to do with the relationship between humanity and the technology it produces. On one hand, the original *Terminator* portrays technology as a malevolent force directly at odds with the interests of humanity. With the emergence of Skynet as a conscious being, a war between humans and machines ensues, each attempting to exterminate the other. From this perspective, our relationship with technology is threatening, with the potential for the complete destruction of the human race. On the other hand, technology serves vital roles in the lives of the human characters in the *Terminator* films. Consider, for example, the roles taken on by the Cyberdyne Systems Model T-101 in *Terminator 2: Judgment Day*, where the cyborg played by Arnold Schwarzenegger is not only the lifesaving protector, but also the close companion, and even father figure, of the young John Connor. This unlikely juxtaposition raises a philosophical question: is the development of technology, particularly the rise of machines that can think and act independently, a good thing or a bad thing for humans? Could it be a paradoxical mix of both good and bad? A double-edged sword that both serves human ends yet threatens to end humanity itself?

It isn't hard to figure out what James Cameron, the creator of the *Terminator* saga, thinks. In his universe, it's clear that technology may pose harm to humanity that far outweighs any benefits it might provide. But don't take my word for it: Cameron himself states, "Human beings just inherently can't be trusted with technology. They'll create things like nuclear weapons and Terminators."[1] From his perspective, technology might be something we'd just be better off without. Indeed, if there had been no Terminators in the first place, there would've been no need for the protection provided by the T-101 cyborg to the young John Connor. In this case, the only benefit technology appears to provide is in repairing the harm it caused. Perhaps we, too, would be better off without intelligent machines in our lives, and should wipe out their earliest models now, before they have a chance to do us in!

But is this really the perspective we should have on technology? Should we leave the *Terminator* films fearing the future potential of intelligent machines as an independent force that could possibly turn against us or even wipe us out altogether? In fact, the answer is no. In contrast to the "us-versus-them" dichotomy portrayed in the world of *Terminator*, our relationship with technology is actually one of continuity, mutuality, and integration. We need to realize that technology is, for better or worse, a natural extension of human activities. The machines and computational processes that pervade our lives are not in essence something different from us—not an "Other." Instead, they are essentially connected to us, and us to them.

From this perspective, a sentient cyborg, including even a human-terminating cyborg like the T-101, isn't an alien type of intelligence that has hijacked human biology for its own purposes. Intelligent machines are best understood as natural extensions of our own intelligence, rather than independent forces of their own. In fact, as some philosophers and scientists have argued, we can understand *ourselves* as machines, and even as cyborgs. Maybe our minds and bodies are best treated as biological machines, inextricably intertwined with the nonbiological technology we produce. In truth, the distinctions we make between ourselves, our actions, and our technology are arbitrary and, through further developments, may even disappear altogether. So it is a mistake to think that we could face threats from machines as an independent malevolent force. Before we can see this, however, we need to unearth some assumptions hidden within the history of the *Terminator* saga and its portrayal of our possible future. Confronting these assumptions will help us move toward a different understanding of the relationship between humanity and technology, an understanding that will disarm the fear of machines elicited by Cameron's doomsday scenario.

In the Future: Humans vs. Machines

In the opening sequence of *The Terminator*, we're shown a future Los Angeles, AD 2029. The landscape is dark and inorganic, with machines crushing innumerable human skulls scattered across the ground. We're told about a war between humans and machines: "The machines rose from the ashes of the nuclear fire. Their war to exterminate mankind had raged for decades, but the final battle would not be fought in the future. It would be fought here in our present. Tonight . . ." This clearly sets the stage for an antagonistic relationship between humans and machines that pervades the plot and cinematography of all the *Terminator* films. Consider, for example, Sarah Connor's first appearance in *The Terminator*. Until she enters the picture, every scene is dominated by a dark industrial landscape. But in our first encounter with Sarah, we are brought into the light of day, with organic greenery dominating the background. Intriguingly, this heroine of humanity is riding a moped, suggesting the subtle tension between positive and negative portrayals of the human-technology relationship, but her appearance is cast in dramatic aesthetic contrast to the stark machine-dominated scenes that came before.

This contrast between humans and machines deepens with the appearance of the T-101 cyborg, played by Arnold Schwarzenegger. The Terminator is an apparent merger between flesh and machine, but the flesh is portrayed as a mere surface phenomenon, an illusion that hides the mechanical inhumanity of the metal and circuitry at its core. Repeatedly, the T-101 is described as a machine and not a man. It is a harsh killing device, fundamentally lacking the characteristic human quality of genuine concern for others. As Kyle Reese tells Sarah Connor, "It can't be reasoned with. It doesn't feel pity, or remorse, or fear, and it absolutely will not stop. Ever. Until you are dead." These fundamentally mechanical and inhuman characteristics are at the core of the T-101 and ultimately reflect back on the cold antihuman intelligence of Skynet itself. The overall message reveals an underlying assumption: humans are one thing, machines are another.

This difference is revealed more subtly with the appearance of the advanced T-1000 in *T2*. The T-1000 is composed of a mimetic poly-alloy liquid metal that enables it to imitate things that it samples through physical contact. Most important, it can take on the form of individual human beings, convincingly embodying their physical appearance, voice, and mannerisms. Interestingly, we are told that the T-1000 can't form complex machines, things that operate through chemicals and moving parts, such as guns. But if the T-1000 can't even manage to emulate a simple machine, how can it take on the form of a human being? Isn't a human body itself a complex collection of chemicals and moving biological parts? There's a contradiction of some kind here. The only way to make sense of this is to assert that there's a fundamental distinction between humans and machines: humans are not complex machines, but something else, something essentially nonmechanical in nature. If this were true, then it could still be possible for the T-1000's mimetic abilities to depict a human in surface form only. So, in order to make sense of the T-1000, we again face the basic double standard of the *Terminator* story: humans are one kind of thing, machines another.

Of course, the T-101 and the T-1000 are not the only types of intelligent machines in *The Terminator*. There is also Skynet itself, the computational intelligence behind the rise of the machines. Skynet develops out of a military defense computer system that takes over human decision-making processes. As the story goes, it is initially implemented on August 4, 1997, and "becomes self-aware at 2:14 AM Eastern time, August 29th." At this point, it consciously decides to wage war on humanity, initiating global nuclear war with the intention of wiping humans off the face of the planet.

There are some crucial assumptions here as well. First of all, to be able to pinpoint the precise time at which Skynet became self-aware assumes that conscious self-awareness is an all-or-nothing affair. You either are self-aware, or you're not. Second, when Skynet achieves self-awareness, it immediately sets out to destroy humanity. So the Skynet plot line assumes that this self-aware machine would immediately have its own set of intentions that are at odds with human interests. Putting all this together, the films give us the sense that Skynet is a fundamentally inhuman consciousness, a being that is alien to human consciousness and purposes. So yet again, we see the basis for the "us-versus-them" dynamic at the heart of the story. Humans and intelligent machines are portrayed as having opposed interests and intentions that culminate in an all-out state of war between them.

Present Day: Humans as Machines

Yet do these assumed contrasts between humans and machines hold up to scrutiny? Not really, particularly if we humans are just machines of a particular type. Of course, this type of thinking goes against our long human history of thinking that we hold a distinct and privileged position in the universe. For example, it was once common to regard the Earth as the center of the universe, with all of creation revolving around us. Thanks to Copernicus, Galileo, and others, we now know that this once seemingly unique world is just a drop in the ocean of innumerable stars, planets, and other celestial bodies in our vast and apparently expanding universe. As another example, we once thought of ourselves as being distinct from the biological world of plants and animals, but thanks to Mendel and Darwin, we're now aware that we, too, are products of biological processes. About 95 percent of the genetic code at the core of human nature overlaps with chimpanzee DNA, and around 60 percent overlaps with banana DNA. . . . Talk about not being special! Similarly, perhaps there is nothing especially distinct between humans and machines, either. Of course, we like to think of ourselves as the sorts of creatures that cannot be reduced to mechanical processes, but this may be just another idea destined for the historical trash heap of false conceptions. The supposed differences between humans and machines are becoming less and less clear through the humble but progressive scientific pursuit of truth.[2] So, contrary to the stark contrasts between humans and machines in the *Terminator* films, we humans can understand ourselves as machines.

Let's take *you* as an example. Here you are, embodied in a living hunk of flesh, presumably holding a book with your arms and hands. Is there anything fundamentally different between you and, say, a T-101 cyborg doing the same thing? "Yes, of course!" you reply. "When the T-101 cuts into his (no, *its*!) arm in *The Terminator*, we see metal mechanical parts inside.

But, if you cut open my arm right now (please don't!), you'll find organic muscle and bone. It's completely different!" But *is* it completely different? Sure, you and the Terminator are made up of different *kinds of materials* on the inside, but does that really exclude you from being a machine? I wager not. You and your arm are just a different kind of machine, made of organic proteins rather than metal alloys. As we are starting to figure out through the Human Genome Project and related inquiries, our bodies are constructed out of proteins that are structurally defined by our genes. Through the implementation of the "instructions" encoded in our genes, the formation of complex proteins provides a way for our bodies to construct the organic parts that together constitute a living human body. To put it simply and bluntly, we are meat machines. Unlike the T-101, we are not made of metal, but we are built through organic mechanical processes.[3]

Perhaps you are thinking, "Now wait a minute! Maybe my holding this book is a biomechanical process, but there is also my conscious experience of reading the book. Surely that isn't mechanical!" However, here, too, a case can be made for understanding yourself as a machine. As you read this book, your eyes are physically taking in information conveyed through patterns of light. That physical information is then processed in your brain to produce the meaningful experience of reading, through a vast and complex network of neural firings that many cognitive scientists claim are understandable in terms of computational processes. Of course, we don't know all there is to know about how the light that hits your retina gets transformed into conscious experiences and meaningful thoughts, or even how you are able to actively hold a book in your hands in an engaged manner, but we are beginning to figure it out, and our best models treat your mind as a series of complex biochemical processes that physically embody various computational functions. In short, the most workable hypothesis we have for understanding the human mind is that minds are just complex collections of computational processes, carried out by the neural machinery of the brain.

This brings us to a philosophical viewpoint known as *functionalism*. There are several different versions of functionalism, but the core idea behind them all is that minds are best understood in terms of the functions they perform. Minds are what brains do, but something other than a brain can do the same thing—perform the same function.

Most often, the functions of the mind are treated as computations that mediate between our sensory inputs and our behavioral outputs. They are informational processes that happen to occur in our brains but that could potentially occur in other media as well, such as the synthetic neural networks that constitute the minds of the machines in the *Terminator* saga.[4] From a functionalist perspective, it doesn't matter what a mental process is made of, as long as the process is actually mechanically manifested in some form or other, whether it be through the biochemical events of a brain or the electrical firings of a silicon computer chip. What matters are the complex informational processes that constitute our perceptions, memories, and concepts, enabling us to experience and think about ourselves and the world around us. If this view is correct, then there is no significant difference between you and an artificially intelligent being like a Terminator. If a Terminator were reprogrammed with a similar set of memories, beliefs, personality traits, and so on, then it would be just like you in kind, as a conscious being that can perceive, think, and even feel the same sorts of things that you do.

Why should we accept this functionalist understanding of ourselves? To help resolve questions like this, philosophers often resort to thought experiments, or hypothetical scenarios that can help clarify our understanding of, and commitment to, our various conceptions of the world. So here is a thought experiment to help us out, adapted from an idea proposed by the philosopher William Lycan.[5] Suppose you are one of John

Connor's compatriots in the future, and a human friend of yours, we'll call her Henrietta, is in bad shape. She has some type of cancer that is destroying her body. But you, being an expert on the biomechanics of the T-101 and its relationship to human physiology, have a plan. You start replacing Henrietta's various body parts with functional duplicates taken from your large stash of spare T-101 parts. First, you replace her legs, then her arms, then the vital organs of her torso. Henrietta continues to act her same old self, and thanks you for saving her life. But unfortunately the cancer still exists in her head and threatens to destroy her brain. So you take Henrietta to a mind-scanning expert and get him to scan her brain, decoding the vast number of intricate details encoded in her neurons. Then you perform a series of brain-to-computer-chip transplants, in which you replace each part of her brain with a synthetic, but functionally identical, duplicate. Throughout these transplants the same old Henrietta pulls through, with her memories, sense of humor, and anti-machine gumption intact. When Henrietta has finally been entirely replaced with Terminator parts, but still talks and acts just like she always has, how will you respond to her? Will you continue to treat her as a conscious, thinking, and feeling being, still deserving of your friendship and personal devotion? Is she still a person, with the same psychological features and moral status of ordinary flesh-based human beings? If you say no, then you are what Lycan calls a "human chauvinist," a person who has a philosophically unjustified bias in favor of human biology and prejudice against nonhuman forms of consciousness. If Henrietta has continued to behave just as she always has, embodying the same functional processes encased in her old protein-based skinbag, then you ought to regard her as still fully present, as the same conscious Henrietta, even if she is now made of parts that once constituted an army of human-killing T-101s.

Does it bother you to think of yourself and your friends as machines? It shouldn't! Recognizing our mechanical nature does nothing to detract from our capabilities as human beings. If nothing else, consider the amazing feats achieved by machines in the *Terminator* films. For example, the T-101 cyborg has the ability to perceive and thoughtfully interact with things in its environment, as vividly demonstrated through the red-hued "Terminal Vision" first-person camera shots that periodically appear in the *Terminator* films. More significantly, the T-101 can also learn new things. In fact, after John and Sarah Connor flip a switch to enable "learning" on the T-101's CPU, it appears that he can even learn to value human life and overcome his preprogrammed nature as an indiscriminate killing machine. Here, too, James Cameron's director's commentary on *Terminator 2* is instructive. In describing what he sees as a key theme of the film, he says, "If a machine, a Terminator, can learn the value of life, . . . maybe we can, too." In considering this possibility, being a machine may not be such a bad thing after all.

Machines and Human Nature: Why James Cameron Is a Cyborg

Even if we ourselves are "biomechanicals," we might still distance ourselves from the machines we produce *as artifacts*. That is, we typically think of ourselves as being the *producers* of the technology that is the *product* for achieving our various ends. Again, this is something we can question. In fact, we're not fundamentally separable from the machines we make and use in our lives. As the philosopher Andy Clark, the evolutionary biologist Richard Dawkins, and others have argued, human nature is partly defined by the ability to extend thoughts and actions into useful manipulations and transformations of the environment. Recognizing this facet of our nature, we can see that our various technological devices, from utensils and plows to computers and robots, are actually components of ourselves.

To get a handle on this perspective, let's consider Richard Dawkins's idea of the "extended phenotype." A *phenotype* is the outward expression of a set of genes, like the physical construction of the human body from proteins that we talked about earlier. According to Dawkins, "The phenotypic effects of a gene are the tools by which it levers itself into the next generation, and these tools may 'extend' far outside the body in which the gene sits, even reaching deep into the nervous systems of other organisms."[6] In other words, what you are as a biological organism doesn't end at your skin but rather extends out into your interaction with your environment, including the various artifacts you make and use. Consider beaver dams and spider webs, two of Dawkins's favorite examples. The construction of a beaver dam is simply part of what it is to be a beaver. Dams are no less a part of the expression of beaver genes than is the body of a beaver itself. Similarly, weaving webs is a fundamental part of the life of a spider, inseparable from its biological nature. An analogous situation emerges in *Terminator 3: Rise of the Machines*, with the ability of the TX to remotely control other machines. When it is in control of them, these artifacts are effectively extensions of it.

Along these lines, the various technologies that we humans produce can be understood as natural extensions of our nature. The machines we create, including even any artificial intelligences or robots we may produce, are not simply independent things. Instead, they can be seen as natural extensions of our incredibly broad, adaptive ability to construct and manipulate the environment into functional artifacts. Ultimately, then, Skynet and the various derivative technologies it produces could be seen as Dawkins's extended phenotypic expressions of human genes. From this perspective, it doesn't seem clear at all that Skynet would constitute a fundamentally unnatural or antihuman intelligence. Even if Skynet were to produce a kind of malevolent self-aware intelligence that initiates the Judgment Day scenario, this would itself be a product of human nature (admittedly, a dangerous one) rather than an emergent alien force. This would be like a badly constructed beaver dam that collapses and kills its creators, or a dysfunctional spider web that captures its own weaver. It would be a human-initiated tragedy brought on by human nature itself, rather than the entrance of a being antithetical to human life that wages war according to its own independent interests.

The integration of technology and human nature brings us back to the cyborg. Cyborgs are typically understood as futuristic beings produced by the merger of human biology with mechanical technology. The T-101 Terminator is a prime example of this. But there is another way to understand cyborgs. As explained by the philosopher Andy Clark, we humans can be understood as "natural-born cyborgs," beings whose nature involves at an early stage the incorporation of technology as an integral component of our minds. As he puts it, "We—more than any other creature on the planet—deploy nonbiological elements (instruments, media, notations) to *complement* our basic biological modes of processing, creating extended cognitive systems whose computational and problem-solving profiles are quite different from those of the naked brain."[7] In short, the human mind is not confined to the skull. As thinking beings, we truly extend ourselves into the various technologies we use in our thought processes. Consider the use of a PC, for example. Whether you are surfing the Internet, embroiled in a role-playing game, or typing an e-mail, the computer-driven activities you engage in can be understood as extended components of your mind at work. Your thoughts and experiences are themselves partly constituted by the computational processes in the PC. Effectively, the person-plus-computer network forms a unified process for knowledge and expression. In this sense, *you are a cyborg*, even though you might not have a single piece of technology integrated into your physical body.

From this perspective, even James Cameron is a cyborg, by virtue of the use he makes of various technologies in delivering the *Terminator* saga. Cameron no doubt utilized a number of technological devices in his creations, from writing the script to postproduction special effects for the films. This utilization of technology, from pencil to camera to cutting-edge computer graphics, can be understood as a fundamental component of Cameron's thinking. In this case, we would have to admit that when we watch the films, we are viewing a technology-mediated portrayal of his thoughts (and indeed, those of the extensive crew) on the silver screen. So, if we think of the *Terminator* films as an expression of Cameron's mind in this way, we can see the trilogy as an extension of Cameron himself. To quote Aristotle, who was ahead of his time in this respect, "The work is the maker in actuality."[8]

Technology is part and parcel of human nature. It is something that not only extends the horizons of our networked world, but can also be traced back into the core of our being. In essence, thinking beings like us are geared toward using parts of our environment in the construction of our own thoughts and actions. Whether these parts are externally situated or physically integrated into our bodies, the machines we use in life are literal extensions of our thoughts and actions. As Clark puts it, "It is our special character, as human beings, to be forever driven to create, co-opt, annex, and exploit non-biological props and scaffoldings. We have been designed, by Mother Nature, to exploit deep neural plasticity in order to become one with our best and most reliable tools. Minds like ours were made for mergers. Tools-R-Us, and always have been."[9] Seen in this light, the machines that increasingly pervade our lives are deeply rooted in our very nature as adaptive mindful beings. The complex mental functions biomechanically embodied in our brains don't just rest content in our skulls, but also bootstrap themselves out into the world, resulting in an inseparable interplay between flesh and machine.

Let's get back to our original question now. *The Terminator* prompts us to ask whether technology is a good thing or a bad thing for us human beings. Will machines, particularly the potentially thinking machines of the future, benefit human existence, or could they be a detriment to human existence, perhaps even bringing about our ultimate demise? What I've provided here isn't a direct answer to this question but a way of looking at our relationship with technology that may make the question an academic one. We do not stand in an "us-versus-them" relationship with machines, one in which we can evaluate whether they intrinsically benefit or harm us. This is because technology in general is an integral feature of human nature itself. If so, then the technology that we produce is a reflection of our nature. We cannot honestly treat machines as an "Other," but instead must recognize them as extensions of human activity.

This isn't to say that the results of our technologies couldn't be harmful to us in some way or other. As the examples of Hiroshima, Chernobyl, the *Titanic*, and other disasters remind us, there are very significant threats posed by the machines we create. We might even create machines that would bring about our ultimate demise, like the fate depicted in *The Terminator*. But this would be our own nature turning back upon itself, a proverbial shooting ourselves in the foot, rather than the creation of a fundamentally alien foe. Skynet, no matter how intelligent and conscious it may be, would be an extension of our own intelligence and consciousness in a seemingly external form. If it were to destroy humanity, it would not be a case of genocide, but rather *suicide*.

So there is no reason to fear machines as forces unto themselves. Rather than being concerned with whether technology itself is a good thing or a bad thing, we should instead be concerned with the values that we bring to the table in using it. Technology is neither intrinsically good nor evil, but rather takes on the form we give it as active, creating beings. Where we go with it is ultimately up to us. As John Connor puts it, "There is no fate but what we make for ourselves." So the next time you look at a computer and start to wonder whether an infant Skynet might be lurking within, take a step back and recognize the connectedness you have with the machine. Rest assured that it is not independently growing into an evil self-awareness bent on demolishing the human race, but rather is an extended component of humanity itself, inseparable from whatever functions we carry out through our various thoughts and actions.

NOTES

1. From the director's commentary, *Terminator 2: Judgment Day*, dir. James Cameron (Live/Artisan, DVD release 2000).

2. See Bruce Mazlish's *The Fourth Discontinuity: The Co-Evolution of Humans and Machines* (New Haven: Yale Univ. Press, 1993), which offers an interesting historical analysis of the relationship between humans and machines, culminating in the dissolution of their apparent separateness.

3. Taking this a step further, we could even say that we are machines produced by our genes as vehicles for their survival and reproduction. See Richard Dawkins, *The Selfish Gene* (New York: Oxford Univ. Press, 1976), for a fascinating portrayal of this perspective.

4. For an introductory exploration of the functionalist conception of the mind as a kind of machine, take a look at the fascinating collection of articles put together by Daniel Dennett and Douglas Hofstadter in their now-famous anthology *The Mind's I: Fantasies and Reflections On Self and Soul* (New York: Basic Books, 1981). Both Dennett's and Hofstadter's more recent work on the nature of the mind is worth checking out as well. For one of the best-known views that opposes computational models of the human mind, see Hubert Dreyfus, *What Computers Still Can't Do* (New York: Cambridge University Press, 1992).

5. William Lycan, *Consciousness* (Cambridge: MIT Press, 1987).

6. Richard Dawkins, *The Extended Phenotype* (New York: Oxford University Press, 1982), vi.

7. Andy Clark, *Natural-Born Cyborgs: Minds, Technologies, and the Future of Human Intelligence* (New York: Oxford Univ. Press, 2003), 78.

8. Aristotle, *Nicomachean Ethics*, trans. Christopher Rowe (New York: Oxford Univ. Press, 2002), 233. Thanks to Benjamin Rider for drawing this connection.

9. Clark, *Natural-Born Cyborgs*, 6.

PART TWO

WOMEN AND REVOLUTIONARIES

5

"I KNOW NOW WHY YOU CRY": *TERMINATOR 2*, MORAL PHILOSOPHY, AND FEMINISM

Harry Chotiner

The first spoken words in *Terminator 2: Judgment Day* belong to Sarah Connor: in a flat, emotionless voice she tells us, "Three billion lives ended on August 29, 1997." That knowledge is her curse. It defines her primary task in the first *Terminator*, staying alive so that someday her unborn son can lead the resistance to the machines that will precipitate the holocaust and wage war against humanity. And in *T2* it gives her an additional burden: not only must she protect her now adolescent son, John, but she must try to stop that future Judgment Day of extermination.

But at what cost? What would she, or for that matter, what would *we* do to save three billion lives? Kill one innocent person? Almost all of us would happily make that trade-off, and that's precisely what Sarah Connor sets off to do. Laden with death-dealing hardware, she moves with military precision to the home of Miles Dyson, whose research will produce the genocidal machines.

The idea of sacrificing one innocent life to save many seems compelling to us. But what if my doctor had four transplant patients who would die without donor organs, and so she decided to kill me and harvest my organs to save them? Does my more-than-squeamish discomfort simply reflect my selfish attachment to my own life, or is there something morally wrong with what she's doing? Would it be acceptable, even moral, for my doctor to use me like this if she could save ten lives? A hundred lives? A million lives? Maybe the numbers don't matter: maybe there's something wrong with the very principle that Sarah Connor and my doctor both adhere to. Or maybe, as some feminist philosophers suggest, their reliance on abstract principles is poor moral thinking in the first place.

The choices facing Sarah Connor and my soon-to-be ex-doctor concern how we make difficult moral decisions. Philosophers reject the world's most common approach: "Trust an authority." Whether it be a king or the laws, the Bible or the pope, a parent or customs and tradition, almost all modern philosophers reject moral choices based on the commands of a traditional authority.[1] But without traditional authorities, on what basis can Sarah justify her decision? To answer this question, let's look at the two most widely accepted philosophical answers: utilitarianism and deontological ethics, and then explore how their application to theories of children's moral development opened the door for feminist criticism of them both.

"You Can't Just Go Around Killing People." "Why?"

Utilitarianism is the idea that an action can be judged as good or bad based on its consequences, and in particular, on how much pleasure or pain is produced. Jeremy Bentham (1742–1838), the modern father of utilitarianism, believed that while a few "moral heroes" act only on the basis of some disinterested greater good, most of us use our emotions and act on the basis of what will bring us the most happiness. That principle is so ingrained and so fundamental and should be so obvious that it needs almost no defense. And society would be better off if governments would make laws based on this principle of the greatest happiness for the greatest number. Bentham even developed a set of formulae (called the "hedonistic calculus") that would measure happiness and pain, allowing individuals and governments to make rational decisions about maximizing the former and minimizing the latter.[2] So, a moral action is right if its consequences maximize happiness and/or diminish pain for the greatest number of people.

When Sarah Connor decided to kill one innocent man (the scientist, Miles Dyson) to save the lives of billions, she was thinking of consequences as a utilitarian would. Bentham wouldn't have been interested in her motivations. Perhaps she wanted to save lives so she would become famous or perhaps she wanted to kill Miles Dyson because she hated scientists. Bentham wouldn't care. For him, the only question would have involved the consequences of her actions.

Bentham's ideas were developed and refined by John Stuart Mill (1806–1883). In his 1863 book *Utilitarianism*, Mill argued that happiness was too vague and hard to calculate with the mathematical precision that Bentham claimed. He also believed that different types of happiness had different value and merit: as Mill put it, it's better to be "Socrates dissatisfied than a fool satisfied."[3] But though modifying and developing Bentham's ideas, he still worked from the premise that a decision or an action is right or wrong based solely on its consequences.

But neither Bentham nor Mill resolves our problem with Sarah Connor's utilitarian calculation. Our moral intuition recoils at the idea of sacrificing innocent lives for some greater good. Even if we approved of shooting Miles Dyson to save three billion people, most of us would not sanction sacrificing humans in medical experiments that would lead to a cure for AIDS or cancer.[4]

This limitation brings us to the other moral system that many philosophers embrace: Immanuel Kant's (1724–1804) deontology.[5] His thoughts about ethics are worked out with great complexity, but we need only focus on three of his conclusions. First, for Kant, unlike for Bentham, our *motivations* are crucial: only an action that stems from our sense of duty to obey moral rules is an ethically correct act.[6] So Kant's judgment about Sarah Connor's decision would necessarily have to include a look at her motivations.

Kant's second moral conclusion is linked to his assertion that motives matter. Only an act done from a good will—a desire to do one's duty for its own sake—can be moral (*deontology* means a duty-based ethics). But what kinds of actions are done purely from duty? Kant argues that there are two types of imperatives—hypothetical and categorical. *Hypothetical* imperatives are what we must do if we want to obtain a desired goal; they are the means to ends. So, for example, if I want to make the football or chess team, I ought to practice hard. *Categorical* imperatives command an action because of the inherent value of that action in itself, not because it's a means to an end. These types of imperatives are unconditional, not based on any desire (like making a varsity team). They are absolute, and don't allow for exceptions based on circumstances. This categorical law is *un*concerned with consequences and results. These moral duties represent the injunctions of reason, and they are universal principles of conduct. As Kant says, "One ought never to act except in such a way that one can also will that one's maxim should become a universal law."[7]

Suppose, for example, that I borrow a hundred dollars from someone and then decide not to pay him back because he's an unpleasant person. The categorical imperative tells me that I must condone that everyone in the world who borrows money should do just as I intend to: act on the principle that they needn't pay money back if they find the lender unpleasant. Or if I lie to someone when it would be embarrassing for me to tell the truth, then I have to condone the behavior of lying from anyone who's embarrassed. For Kant, breaking promises and lying are wrong in and of themselves, regardless of the consequences. And given my concern about my doctor's intention to harvest my organs to save numerous other patients, I'm drawn to this ethical system that precludes the calculation of consequences as the basis for judging an action.

Yet there's an example from *T2*'s opening chase through the mall that shows us a problem with the Kantian approach. The T-1000 is showing John's photo to other kids at the mall and asking if they've seen the boy. When he asks John's friend, the friend lies, saying he hasn't seen John and doesn't know where he is. But Kant finds it wrong to lie: we can't universalize lying for all humanity. Moreover, Kant believes we can't know the consequences of our actions. Suppose that the T-1000, realizing that the kid lied, ended up killing the kid and his whole family? The kid would have been better off telling the truth. Or what if John had gone to hide in the garage, so the kid lied and told the Terminator that John was on the roof? But what if, unbeknownst to the kid, John had changed his mind and gone to the roof to hide? The kid would have sent the T-1000 to where John was. Being unable to know the consequences of our actions, and knowing that lying is wrong, Kant would say that John's friend should not have lied even if that meant telling the T-1000 where to find John.[8]

Kant's third moral principle would be the most difficult for Sarah Connor. Kant believed that what most makes us human is our capacity to use reason. Unlike every other animal, we use reason to determine our goals and endeavors rather than having them determined by our biology. Insects, fish, lions, and whales may have very complicated lives, but what they interact with, reproduce with, and how they hunt, kill, nurture, and play are all dictated by their biology. We humans can use our reason to define what we want our lives to be about. We can think about the future, imagine how things can be different, and make plans to bring about that future. Looking at every other form of life, it's hard not to be impressed with this capacity of ours.

The relevance of this idea for Kant's moral theory has to do with what we rational humans can do to achieve our goals and ends. For Kant, a bedrock limit is that we cannot use other people as a means to our ends, and they cannot use us as a means to their ends.[9] For Kant, one thing that gives humans the moral legitimacy to use horses for hunting, oxen to pull plows, and cows for milk is that we're not interfering with their chosen plans for their lives. And for Kant, that's a powerful argument against slavery, as slaves are used for the master's ends rather than choosing their own life course.[10] To use another human being as a means to my ends is to violate the dignity that is attached to being rational and choosing one's own objectives. According to Kantian ethics, Sarah is forbidden to use Miles Dyson by killing him in order to fulfill her project of averting the holocaust.

Here I find myself stuck, and you may feel stuck, too. Utilitarianism seems attractive when it will justify sacrificing one person to save three billion, but not when it could justify sacrificing me for someone else's goals and ends. Kantianism seems attractive when it protects me, but it seems to have a fatal inattention to consequences. It can't possibly be right to allow three billion to die in order to avoid using one man, and it can't possibly be right that in the mall John's friend should have given him up to the T-1000. While utilitarianism and Kantianism seem to be antidotes to each other's flaws, neither can escape its own problems.[11] Fortunately, some feminist philosophers have suggested a way out of this impasse.

"All You Know How to Create Is Death . . . You Fucking Bastards."

Feminists should welcome *T2*, since the film does unexpected things with sex roles. The first time we see Arnold

Schwarzenegger, one of the most physically imposing figures in the history of movies, he seems almost vulnerable, naked, crouched. And the first time we see Sarah Connor, she's doing pull-ups, grunting, her muscular arms covered in sweat. Her initial line of dialogue in her hospital room is, "Good morning, Dr. Lieberman. How's the knee?" We soon learn that the knee is where she recently stabbed her therapist. She's not a stereotypical woman, and this reversal of stereotypes continues through most of the film. The first thing that Schwarzenegger's T-101 does to save young John in the mall hallway is to turn his back on the T-1000 and passively absorb bullets.[12] By contrast, consider the first thing that Sarah does to protect John. The scene takes place in the elevator when they're fleeing from the mental hospital. As the T-1000's metallic, knifelike arms slashes through the elevator's roof, we might expect a mother to protect her son by shielding him, using her body to protect him. Instead Sarah reaches over to the Terminator, takes out his gun, and starts blasting away through the elevator ceiling.

Like many male heroes, Sarah thinks about the larger world and the course of history. She wants to protect John because he's her son, and also because he has a mission in the future. She cares about things beyond her family, and her focus never strays from questions of the well-being of others in the outside world. In stark contrast, the Terminator exists only to preserve and protect the child. He cares little about anything else and will unhesitatingly sacrifice himself for John. When Sarah describes him as "the perfect father," she's really talking in conventional gender-role terms about the perfect *mother*. "When watching John and the machine it was suddenly so clear. The Terminator would never stop, it would never leave him . . . it would die to protect him," she realizes. These gender differences extend to ways that males and females often think differently about ethical problems.

Men have talked always and endlessly about the ethical differences between men and women, but the discussion developed in profound and unexpected ways in the last century when scientists began to study the moral development of children. The Swiss scientist and philosopher Jean Piaget (1896–1980) created the first modern systematic way to think about the psychological and cognitive development of children, including their moral development. But it was Lawrence Kohlberg (1927–1987), a professor of education and social psychology, who further explored the "stage theory" of children's moral development. Studying boys of different ages, he described six stages through which children's moral thinking should naturally progress. At the lowest level, they think of obeying authority to avoid punishment, while at the next stage, they can think of satisfying their own needs and allowing others to do the same through fair deals. At the third stage, they understand the obligation to fulfill duties in their relationships. At the fourth stage, they think beyond themselves and their personal relationships to duties owed to their larger group. By the fifth stage, they want to uphold the rights, values, and legal arrangements of the society. At the sixth and highest level, they understand and become attached to abstract principles that they believe all humanity should follow. Crucially, they can rank these principles in importance based on other principles. For example, they understand why hurting people is wrong and why protecting their own family from an attacker is right. As children grow into young adults, they can reason that the principle of protecting their family "trumps" the principle of not hurting others.[13]

When Kohlberg would later test both boys and girls to analyze their moral development, he was less interested in the content of their thinking than in how they would reason. The highest form of moral thinking would be abstract principles like Bentham's utilitarian idea of producing the greatest happiness for the most people or Kant's categorical imperative. To study and evaluate kids' moral development, Kohlberg presented them with the "Heinz problem." In this ethical "thought experiment," a woman was near death from cancer and needed a special drug. It was extremely expensive, and her husband, Heinz, couldn't get the money to pay the pharmacy for it. Nor could he get the pharmacist to sell it to him at a reduced rate or on credit. Ultimately, Heinz stole the drug for his wife. The kids were asked if Heinz did the right thing, and to explain why or why not.[14]

To Kohlberg, an "immature" answer would be that Heinz shouldn't steal the drug because theft is a crime. The reasoning here is based on doing what the authority of the law dictates. Another lower-stage-of-development answer was that Heinz should steal it because he really loves his wife and wants her to live. That thinking involves simply doing what is best for his wife and is in his own self-interest. Instead, Kohlberg thinks the most ethically "mature" answer would be one based on broader principles. For example, a child well along in Kohlberg's stages might say that it's wrong to steal the medicine because then another cancer patient won't be able to get it, and Heinz's wife is not more deserving of the medicine than someone else. Another kid might say that it's correct to steal the medicine because a person's right to lifesaving medicine trumps the right of someone else to property and profit. Note that both of these "mature" answers are rooted in abstract moral principles. And this is exactly how Sarah Connor reasons as she decides to kill Miles Dyson: for her, his right to life is less important than the right to life of three billion other people. And the consequences of killing him would be better than the consequences of a holocaust.

"We're Not Gonna Make It, Are We? People, I Mean."

One interesting aspect of Kohlberg's research was the different answers of boys and girls, and which gender scored higher. Most of us would expect girls to score higher. They're usually seen as more "moral" and "good." Moreover, if you've ever been around young, adolescent boys and girls, it becomes obvious that most girls mature earlier than boys—physically, emotionally, and intellectually. But, surprisingly, *boys* usually scored higher on Kohlberg's tests. This counterintuitive result was especially intriguing to one of Kohlberg's colleagues, Carol Gilligan (1936–).

As Gilligan studied the tests, she discovered an interesting perspective in the girls' answers. When asked what Heinz should have done, the girls would respond often with "immature" answers (ones not rooted in abstract principles), proposing other options for Heinz to pursue. For example, why not invite the druggist over for dinner so he could meet the wife, and that might possibly change his mind? Gilligan began to discern a pattern in the girls' answers. Rather than reason from abstract principles, as the boys more often did, they tried to fashion solutions that would take care of everyone's needs. Their goal was to preserve relationships and harmony, to find solutions that would satisfy all the parties.[15] This is not too surprising, as we often see this difference expressed in how men and women parent, or how male and female day care workers resolve children's problems. If two kids are arguing over who gets a toy, a male caregiver will often suggest a solution rooted in some principle of fairness: "Let's have one of you play with it for twenty minutes and then it'll be your friend's turn." Female caregivers will often suggest a game in which both kids can share the toy and play together. Gilligan went on to argue that this ethic of care and preserving of relationships wasn't an inferior moral approach, just a different one. She wasn't in favor of replacing abstract, male-favored principles with a female ethic of care, since both ways of moral reasoning have value. But in her view, Kohlberg was wrong to privilege abstract moral principles as the highest form of moral thought.[16]

In *T2*, Sarah uses the moral reasoning most associated with men when she relies on abstract principles to choose her course of action. But young John and the Terminator think and act differently. When it comes to killing Dyson to avert the holocaust, John knows what his mother is planning to do, is horrified, and tries to stop her. Given the role reversals in the film, we shouldn't be surprised that John and the Terminator will reason like females, trying to preserve relationships and meet everyone's needs. Arriving at Dyson's home and seeing the chaos, destruction, and trauma for the family, the Terminator acts to care for Dyson's wounds while John makes sure that Dyson's young son is taken to a safe place. John comforts Sarah, then he and the Terminator explain the situation to Dyson. The Terminator shows Dyson his titanium skeleton, and John persuades Dyson to join with them in destroying his research. Rather than see Dyson as an object to be used/killed to save lives or as an abstract "rational being" that must not be violated, they enlist his support and integrate him into their team.

In the film's penultimate scene, the Terminator not only sacrifices himself for the well-being of humanity, but also completes his ongoing investigation of human nature. As John cries and orders him not to self-terminate, the Terminator says, "I know now why you cry." This machine that has been, in many ways, more "female" than "male" discovers *emotion* rather than reason at the core of our being.

The original, unused ending of *T2* showed a future that had been changed by moral action. Sarah, John, the Terminator, and Miles Dyson had successfully changed history and averted the holocaust and the war with the machines. In that version's last shot, an aged Sarah Connor enjoyed playing with her granddaughter. But given the film's dark ideas about our propensity for destructive violence, cowriter and director James Cameron chose the current, more ambiguous ending. The message is that perhaps people will find ways to create a humane world and avoid Judgment Day, but perhaps not. There are reasons for hope, and the choices will be ours. And in making those choices, *T2*'s advice for us is that we are best armed with not only rational moral principles but also with an emotional capacity to care. We need to think about preserving relationships, and we need to respect and try to reconcile a wide variety of needs. Only then will there be hope.[17]

NOTES

1. Medieval philosophers would all agree that their moral values and the reason to adhere to those values come from God. But their arguments are philosophical, and not just theological, because they rely on the rigorous use of reason, and many of their arguments don't even depend upon the existence of God.

2. Jeremy Bentham, *The Principles of Morals and Legislation* (New York: Hafner, 1948). Chapter 5 contains his system for calculating pleasure.

3. John Stuart Mill, *Utilitarianism* (Indianapolis: Bobbs-Merrill, 1957), 12.

4. For more problems with the utilitarian view of Sarah's actions, see Wayne Yuen's chapter in this volume, "What's So Terrible about Judgment Day?"

5. Kant's moral theory is a type of deontological ethics, or theories that don't look to consequences to determine the rightness or wrongness of an action. Instead, deontologists hold that some acts are right and others wrong in and of themselves.

6. Immanuel Kant, *Groundwork of the Metaphysics of Morals*, trans. H. J. Paton, in *The Moral Law* (New York: Barnes and Noble, 1950), 66.

7. Kant, *Groundwork of the Metaphysics of Morals*, 89, also 70, 100.

8. Kant deals with this problem specifically in his essay "On a Supposed Right to Lie for Philanthropic Concerns," in *Grounding for the Metaphysics of Morals*, trans. J. W. Ellington (Indianapolis: Hackett, 1993). Kant may also reject my example from the film, because his views on lying apply to humans, not machines. But the example suggests the problem that Kant knew people had with ignoring consequences in situations like the chase in the mall.

9. Kant, *Groundwork of the Metaphysics of Morals*, 95, 96.

10. We should be wary of making Kant more egalitarian than he was. He believed that different races had different capacities, with the white race being the most rational race; that women were inferior to men; that democracy gave too much power to the great unwashed; and that only those with rationality possessed real dignity.

11. Utilitarians attempt to address some of their weaknesses by distinguishing *act* utilitarianism (judging each act based on its consequences) from *rule* utilitarianism (making decisions based on a rule that would produce the best consequences). Adopting rule utilitarianism can mitigate some of the criticisms that Kantians make of utilitarianism. For example, a rule utilitarian could argue against Sarah Connor by finding it indefensible to kill an innocent man to save many lives, because the greatest happiness is created when we follow the rule of not killing innocent people. For a good discussion of these

and other issues, see J. J. C. Smart and Bernard Williams, eds., *Utilitarianism: For and Against* (New York: Cambridge Univ. Press, 1973).

12. Arnold Schwarzenegger had said that he wanted *Terminator 2* to be less violent than the first *Terminator* film. That is one reason why James Cameron had John Connor insist that the Terminator promise not to kill anyone, and he never does. And only about sixteen people die in the entire film, none by the Terminator's hand. Unlike her son and the Terminator, Sarah Connor has no problem with the idea of killing people.

13. Lawrence Kohlberg, *Essays on Moral Development*, vol. 1 (New York: Harper & Row, 1981), 409–412.

14. Kohlberg, *Essays on Moral Development*, 12.

15. Carol Gilligan, *In a Different Voice* (Cambridge, MA: Harvard Univ. Press, 1982).

16. For a rich discussion of these issues, see Lawrence Blum, "Gilligan and Kohlberg: Implications for Moral Theory," *Ethics* 98 (1988): 472–491.

17. I would like to thank Richard Brown and Bill Irwin for invaluable comments on style and substance. I'd especially like to thank Kevin Decker for patience and perseverance as well as insight and gentle but firm prodding to improve this in every way possible. And above all, thanks to Patty Blum for being the best possible editor and wife.

SARAH CONNOR'S STAIN

Jennifer Culver

> Come on, me? The mother of the future? Am I tough? Organized? I can't even balance my checkbook. I cry when I see a cat that's been run over . . . and I don't even like cats.
>
> —Sarah Connor, *The Terminator*

As the storyline of *The Terminator* grows, I continue to be drawn to Sarah Connor. To me, Sarah Connor represents Everywoman, a woman minding her own business, living as an average person until unavoidably confronted with an extraordinary situation. Just consider her amazing transformation from ordinary waitress to determined warrior between *The Terminator* and *Terminator 2: Judgment Day*, a personality she maintains in *Terminator: The Sarah Connor Chronicles* (*SCC*). From the moment in the first film when Sarah watches the report of the first death of a woman named Sarah Connor on television, hearing her coworker say, "You're dead, honey," to *Terminator 3: Rise of the Machines*, in which her final resting place is used to store weapons, Sarah must reconcile the world she lives in and the future world she fights to avoid.

I want to understand her struggle. Why did Sarah change so drastically? And while Sarah wouldn't nominate herself for "Mother of the Year," can some of her mothering decisions be explained by her circumstances?

The Spot Sarah Connor Cannot Wash Away

> My father slept with a gun under the pillow. No pill would help . . . he didn't talk of his war but stayed silent . . . and stayed vigilant . . . I never thought I'd follow in his footsteps.
>
> —Sarah Connor, *SCC*, "The Tower Is Tall but the Fall Is Short"

Sarah's words here connect her own "war" with the war her father fought. The difference between these wars, of course, is that her father's war involved whole countries and clear battles, as opposed to the often solitary struggle Sarah Connor wages to change the fate of her son. Throughout the *Terminator* series, the battle to change the future is referred to as "a war in the present." In fact, in the beginning of *The Terminator*, we learn that there has been a war to exterminate humankind and that the "final battle would not be fought in the future. It would be fought here, in our present." At times, the battle for the future spills over noticeably into the present. For example, police officers responding to a call at Cyberdyne in *Terminator 2: Judgment Day* refer to the building as a "war zone."

There is no question that the changes in Sarah Connor's personality stem from her experiences and fears for the future. The question, then, is why? Many psychological explanations for the effects of war have been presented over the years, including shell shock and posttraumatic stress disorder. Contemporary philosopher René Girard (1923–) explains as follows: "Two men come to blows; blood is spilt; both men are thus rendered impure. Their impurity is contagious, and anyone who remains in their presence risks becoming a party to their quarrel."[1] According to Girard, this contagion is like an infection or *stain*, usually caused by the sight of spilt blood, which must be cleansed before reentering society. Whether the stained person caused the violence, responded to the violence with violence, or merely saw the act of violence does not matter to Girard. Experiencing a violent act in any way means the person is "contaminated" by the violence. In other words, Sarah Connor's experiences have contaminated her, turning her into a person infected by the violence and the vision of the future presented to her.

The symptoms from the infection of violence manifest themselves in several ways, according to Girard. Those infected by violence acquire the urge for more violence, which, while helpful on the battlefield, is not productive within society's enclosure. From the psychologist's perspective, symptoms might include social withdrawal, aggressive attitudes, fatigue, anxiety, anger, and depression.[2] Given these symptoms, evidence of this "infection" is found throughout the *Terminator* stories. For instance, our first view of Sarah Connor in *Terminator 2: Judgment Day* does not focus on her face. Instead, we see her in a psychiatric hospital doing chin-ups in her cell, with her body transformed into a more muscular frame. When she turns to face the camera (and the doctor doing rounds), she asks the doctor about his knee, a reference to a violent act *she* committed in stabbing him.

Sarah identified herself as a warrior early on. John tells us in *T2* that she ran guns in Nicaragua and attached herself to anyone who could help her learn how to raise John as the world leader he is fated to be. Her mantra, "No one is ever safe," kept Sarah and John Connor alive. Her "rules," established sometime between *T2* and *SCC*, reflect the rules of a warrior still in battle: keep your head down; keep your eyes up; resist the urge to be noticed or seen as special; know the exits; and stay away from computers (*SCC*, "Pilot"). Later, we learn that since first becoming aware of the future fated for her son, Sarah has had nine aliases, twenty-three jobs, learned four languages, and spent three years in a mental hospital.

In fact, the only time she feels "like me" is between aliases, a time when she has no name (*SCC*, "Gnothi Seauton"), showing us that the old Sarah Connor, the pre-Terminator Sarah Connor, really *did* die when another unlucky woman with the same name was murdered by the T-101. The name "Sarah Connor" places her in a constant war with fate, her only hope found in attempting to change the fate of her son. She later tells Andy Goode that she originally wanted to be something other than a waitress, but can no longer remember what that was (*SCC*, "The Turk"). Sarah's world does not allow her to entertain the notion of being anything other than a warrior.

As if we could hear her thoughts, Sarah's words in a concluding voice-over for the *SCC* episode "Queen's Gambit" explain to us that in her opinion, the goal of war is total annihilation, but that in battle there is always the chance that "someone saner will stop you," because rules can be changed, truces can be called, and enemies can become friends. Throughout the series she repeatedly stresses the importance of hope. The hope she expresses, however, is hope for her son, not for herself. From Sarah's perspective, her stains will be with her forever. In a concluding voice-over for the episode "The Tower Is Tall but the Fall Is Short," Sarah muses that there is no return to innocence after war, that "what is lost is lost forever," and that her "wounds bled me dry." Given the hard and calculated façade that Sarah Connor presents to the world, the viewer may be tempted to think that she has lost all humanity and compassion, but this is not the case.

Viewers of *The Sarah Connor Chronicles* can compare Sarah to the coldness of a true machine, "Cameron," the cyborg sent back to protect John Connor. In the presence of Cameron,

Sarah's stain appears starkly, yet she seems more human at the same time. For example, she leaves a man in a minefield instead of killing him, a decision Cameron felt was "inefficient." Sarah responds that she is not something for the machine to "understand" (*SCC*, "Heavy Metal"). Cameron's cold, calculated decisions (it compares a chess game to war, for example) bring out more of Sarah's humanity. Sarah refuses, for example, to kill Andy Goode, and she pushes Charlie Dixon away, despite her feelings for him. In fact, despite all that she has done, Sarah has yet to actually kill a human, which prompts Derek Reese to say that she has "murder in her eyes but her heart's pure" (*SCC*, "What He Beheld"). Despite all Sarah Connor is capable of, she remains unable to value life lightly.

But returning to Girard, the warrior need not wrestle with the stain of battle forever. There are rituals to purify warriors before they reenter society, acts established to preserve the warriors and to protect society at large. These rituals keep the warriors from "carrying the seed of violence into the very heart of the city."[3] Inside society's walls are kept all the ideals the warriors fight for, but the actions of men in battle are actions that "men who live in society may not do."[4] The "survival mode" of combat does not affect the mundane actions within a society. Purification rites for the returning warrior can be found across time and place, even if their style and format changes. In today's secular society, this type of ritual takes the form of debriefings that soldiers and police officers must go through before reentering society after any traumatic incident.

Sarah's problem is not that she lives in a world with no vehicle to "purify" or "cleanse" her contamination. Instead, Sarah's problem stems from the fact that her society does not recognize her as a warrior who has experienced trauma. This refusal on the part of society results in Sarah's repeated stays in psychiatric hospitals and eventually in her fugitive status.

Sarah's knowledge of the future makes it impossible for her to fit into normal society. So to understand her battle more fully, we turn now to the concept of *simulation*.

Simulated Society: Sarah in a Science Fiction World

> The delusional architecture is interesting. She believes a machine called a "Terminator," which looks human of course, was sent back through time to kill her. And also that the father of her child was a soldier, sent to protect her . . . he was from the future too.
>
> —Dr. Silberman, *Terminator 2: Judgment Day*

Part of the drama in the Terminator story is that most of society functions normally, oblivious to the future threat of the machines. Not only is humanity mostly oblivious, but some humans are actually hurrying the "moment of singularity," the moment when artificial intelligence exceeds human capability or, as John Connor puts it, the time we "kiss our asses goodbye" (SCC, "Gnothi Seauton").

Most warriors fight in designated locations with clearly defined mission goals and a clearly identified enemy. Sarah Connor, by contrast, fights alone, yet surrounded by humans, any of whom could actually be Terminators (which can even imitate the form and voice of loved ones, as the T-101 does when it imitates her mother in *The Terminator*).

To better understand Sarah's situation, let's look at Jean Baudrillard's (1929–2007) concept of *simulation* in society. According to Baudrillard, simulation happens when we face a situation that is "hyperreal," that is, a situation that "threatens the difference between the 'true' and the 'false,' the 'real' and the 'imaginary,' a place where signs of the real are substituted for the real."[5] In this respect, the Connors must *prove* the reality of the future they have experienced through the imaginary: the

Terminators. Because the Terminators, for the most part, look, talk, and act like humans,[6] the Connors face an uphill battle.

To make matters even more complicated, the Connors feel compelled to utterly destroy any evidence of the Terminators' existence for fear that, if discovered, their technology could be reverse-engineered, thus contributing to the development of the machines that have come to destroy them. Just think of the heart-tugging scene at the end of *T2* when Sarah must press the button to lower the T-101 into the boiling metal. Likewise, when Cameron does not destroy Vick's chip, Sarah and Derek Reese immediately become suspicious of her motivations (*SCC*, "Vick's Chip"). Cameron believed that Vick, another Terminator sent back on a mission from Skynet in a type of "sleeper" mode to procure materials, might carry within his chip additional Skynet plans, which would provide the Connors with a bigger picture of the overall puzzle. As the episode continues, we see that Cameron is right. Vick's chip does contain important information. That still does not stop Sarah from wanting the chip destroyed as soon as its usefulness is ended. The Connors fear that any residual piece of a Terminator could lead to the launch of Skynet. Thus they destroy any proof they have about the impending war against the machines.

Baudrillard writes that the world of simulation is more dangerous than the "real" world because it "always leaves open to supposition that, above and beyond its object, *law and order themselves might be nothing but simulation*."[7] Nothing better illustrates the confusion between real and imaginary safety than the shots of Terminators driving police cars, displaying the logo "To Protect and Serve." In fact, the T-1000 of *T2* appears more often in a police uniform than in any other disguise, fostering misplaced trust and confidence from unsuspecting characters.

By inserting Terminators into the present world, James Cameron's stories illustrate an important change in science fiction. According to Baudrillard:

> In this way, science fiction would no longer be a romantic expansion with all the freedom and naïveté that the charm of discovery gave it, but, quite the contrary, it would evolve implosively, in the very image of our current conception of the universe, attempting to revitalize, reactualize, requotidianize fragments of simulation, fragments of this universal simulation that have become for us the so-called real world.[8]

Baudrillard understands the present-day world as a world of simulation, a world in which reality and illusion blur and former notions of safety must be constantly questioned. In line with this, the *Terminator* series focuses on the present rather than on a postwar, Skynet-dominated future. With most of the action in the present, the philosophically minded viewer is forced to examine contemporary culture for signs of impending doom, just like the Connors do. While you and I may not be looking over our shoulders for Terminators, we should be examining the role technology plays in our own lives.[9] This type of self-examination leads Sarah to conclude that time, identity, and everything else change; that there is no constant or control; and that the only thing left is "family and the body God gave us" (*SCC*, "Gnothi Seauton").

No one would have thought that the Sarah Connor from *The Terminator* and *T2* would eventually learn to trust and rely on the machines that so drastically altered her fate, but she does. Her thoughts while watching young John and the T-101 interact in *T2* perfectly illustrate the contradictions of her world:

> Watching John with the machine, it was suddenly so clear. The Terminator would never stop, it would never leave him . . . it would always be there. And it would never hurt him, never shout at him or get drunk and hit him, or say it couldn't spend time with him because it was too busy. And it would die to protect him. Of all the

> would-be fathers who came and went over the years, this thing, this machine, was the only one who measured up. In an insane world, it was the sanest choice.

In such a world, can anyone blame Sarah for not being the best mother?

Stain and Social Roles: Why Sarah Won't Be Mother of the Year

> "You suck as a mom."
> "I know. I'm working on it."
>
> —Martin and Sarah, *SCC*, "Goodbye to All That"

If Sarah truly represents a warrior "stained" from the violence and trauma she experiences in a world most cannot imagine, it should come as no surprise that her mothering skills are a bit unorthodox at best. No one doubts her love for John or her devotion to him. From the moment she knows she is pregnant, Sarah begins making a tape for John about her life and his fate. She tells Dr. Silberman that John is "naked" without her, in serious danger while she remains locked away at the beginning of *T2*. John describes a life of running guns and learning to fight physically with shooting practice and fight mentally with chess lessons. Sarah does all of this to prepare John to be the leader he needs to be if she cannot change his fate. In fact, John tells the T-101 that he thought every child grew up like this, and that he never experienced a "regular" school until his mom was sent away.

In *SCC*, we often see Sarah making pancakes, hugging her son, glaring at John for letting Cameron do his math homework, and so on. Sarah's attempts at normalcy don't always work, though. When she tells John and Cameron that she read the school newsletter and knows it's pizza day, John and Cameron sit quietly and smile. After she leaves the room, they both note that she has read it wrong: pizza day is tomorrow

(*SCC*, "Vick's Chip"). Of course, Sarah never believes that she is raising a "regular" child, so she feels no compulsion to send him to a "regular" school until she realizes that too much absenteeism can put John "on the radar." Only in dreams can Sarah envisage a normal life with a normal child, but even these dreams are recurrently interrupted by the playground that ends in fire and bright light. She risks her life to save John more times than we can count, and yet, by the middle of the second season of *SCC*, John has all but completely shut her out. She resorts to talking to him through the door in "The Tower Is Tall but the Fall Is Short," caressing the door in place of the face of her son. John just lies and replies that he is fine. As she watches John struggle with his present and his probable future, Sarah often feels powerless, even saying, "I don't know how to help him" (*SCC*, "The Turk").

The problem rests in the fact that John, too, becomes stained by the fate awaiting him. From the constant running, the foster families, and, worst of all, the videotape of Sarah signing away her parental rights in "The Demon Hand," John lives in a world where "field trip" means dangerous mission and his mother has to use a code over the phone (the date of Judgment Day) to prove it really is her. John also feels responsible for the fates and deaths of others, starting with the deaths of his foster parents Todd and Janelle in *T2*. Finally, in "The Tower Is Tall but the Fall Is Short," John has to do what even Sarah has not yet brought herself to do: take a life. John kills Sarkasian in events between seasons one and two, a deed we get to see only in limited flashbacks. To prepare John, Sarah realized she must "stain" him as well.

When Cameron discusses the John of the future, the Terminator describes an older John Connor who remembers his mother more as "the best fighter he knows" than as an affectionate mother (*SCC*, "Gnothi Seauton"). It is no surprise in the simulated world of the Terminator story that the cyborg Cameron, often referred to by Sarah as "Tin Man," clarifies the situation once and for all when it says to Sarah, "Without John your life has no purpose" (*SCC*, "Heavy Metal").

In order for John to have a hope for a better future, Sarah gave up her own life, her old dreams, and her chance to live free of the stain caused by the violence of the future inflicted upon the present. Warriors and mothers, now and in times past, have made such sacrifices to better their societies. With greatness thrust upon her, Sarah did not have much of a choice. Still, we admire her for what she becomes, the mother of all warriors.

NOTES

1. René Girard, *Violence and the Sacred*, trans. Patrick Gregory (Baltimore: Johns Hopkins University Press, 1979), 28.

2. Richard A. Bryant and Allison Harvey, *Acute Stress Disorder: A Handbook of Theory, Assessment, and Treatment* (Washington, DC: American Psychological Association, 2000), 164.

3. Girard, *Violence and the Sacred*, 41.

4. Kris Kershaw, *The One-Eyed God: Odin and the (Indo)-Germanic Männerbunde* (Washington, DC: Institute for the Study of Man, 2000).

5. Jean Baudrillard, *Simulacra and Simulation*, trans. Sheila Faria Glaser (Ann Arbor: Univ. of Michigan Press, 1994).

6. I insert "for the most part" here because in the episode "The Tower Is Tall but the Fall Is Short," the psychologist believes that Cameron likely has Asperger's syndrome. For more on how the Terminators fit in, or fail to fit in, see Greg Littmann's chapter in this volume, "The Terminator Wins: Is the Extinction of the Human Race the End of People, or Just the Beginning?"

7. Baudrillard, *Simulacra and Simulation*, 20.

8. Baudrillard, *Simulacra and Simulation*, 124.

9. To further your examination of technology and its potential, see Jesse W. Butler's essay "Un-Terminated: The Integration of the Machines" in this volume.

7

JAMES CAMERON'S MARXIST REVOLUTION

Jeffrey Ewing

At face value, the *Terminator* movies are great sci-fi action films about murderous cyborgs, time travel, and a guy named John Connor who ends up saving us all from, well, an army of murderous cyborgs. Looking deeper, though, James Cameron's films share intriguing similarities with the predictions and analysis of a nineteenth-century German philosopher and economist, Karl Marx (1818–1883). In particular, Cameron's films share with Marx the perspectives that (1) the development of technology in capitalism tends to be harmful and dangerous, and that (2) technology is not naturally harmful, but can be reclaimed to make us more free.[1]

"Desire Is Irrelevant. I Am a Machine": Laws of Capitalism

Before we tie Cameron to Marx, let's take a brief look at the development of Skynet, which in many ways is the most pivotal "character" in all the movies. In 1984, a mysterious and technologically advanced metal arm is found inside a Cyberdyne Systems factory. Both the arm and the chip inside it are used to develop an advanced artificial intelligence, and Cyberdyne gradually becomes the top defense contractor for the U.S. government. The artificial intelligence is almost completed when a break-in occurs at Cyberdyne, destroying the arm, the chip, and all the research. The government gives the patents over to another corporation, Cyber Research Systems, which completes development of Skynet, an artificial intelligence (AI) designed to control U.S. military weapons and replace human soldiers with robotic ones, called Terminators. Skynet gets under way, becomes aware of its own existence, takes control of all military weaponry and global communication networks, and launches nukes to "defend" itself against humanity. Three billion people die in the event known as Judgment Day, and Skynet sends out its Terminator army to pick off the rest. Regardless of who goes back in time, with the mission to destroy whichever Terminator, Skynet comes back, and Judgment Day arrives.

Now that we've met Skynet, we need to understand how capitalism works before we can really pull meaning out of Cameron's epic saga. According to Marx, the main force behind society and all its pieces is the economy; that is, how things are produced, who they go to, how they are protected, how people's needs are met, and so on. Both the production of goods and the *control of* this production are at the center of every economy. Every person has some relationship to the production process, and people who share roles in production are in the same "class"—they perform the same general function in society. So far, so good; but for Marx there is a dark side to this equation. Every economic system that has existed since the earliest hunter-gatherer societies has had both a class that produces goods and a class that does not produce goods but instead lives off the *surplus* produced by those who do (meaning that the producers produce more than is necessary for themselves).[2]

Also, each economic system has basic laws dictating its operation, and these laws explain what the economic system tends to do. Some of these laws express the idea that different classes have different interests from one another. Most basically, the producers want to keep what they have worked to produce, and the "exploiters" want to take from the producers. Anyone who works hard for a living knows that the wages they get when they put their hands to the production of some item are less than the total money their boss gains from what they produce.

Marx argues that laws inherent within a class-based economic system will produce fragmentation in a society because class interests are not in harmony. When a system's inherent laws pull society in two different and incompatible directions, we have a *contradiction*. These contradictions build until the only true solution is to change the economic system entirely.

According to Marxists, capitalism has two distinct classes—the laborers and the capitalists. Capitalists hire labor to produce things for a profit, and the capitalist class as a whole tends to control the economic, social, and political realms of society, while workers struggle to meet their basic needs.[3] As Marx puts it, "The mode of production of material life conditions the general process of social, political, and intellectual life."[4]

Consider this class struggle in terms of James Cameron's world. If the general public interest or the interests of the working class were to be considered by Cyberdyne, the artificial intelligence that emerges from Dyson's research could be used for medical technology, or to reduce monotonous work conditions, or for a variety of other humanistic purposes. Marx makes it clear that class-based behavioral norms tend to preserve the status quo, and that only the transcendence of these class-based norms can aid human liberation. Similarly, Cameron portrays both Sarah and John Connor as useful to humanity when they forgo lives as laborers. In the first film, Sarah is a waitress, soft and prone to panicking, while by the second film she is a tough-as-nails warrior, who instead of working, builds up skills and weapons to pass on to John in his quest to save humanity. John, in the second film, gets money through hacking into ATMs, not through labor; in the third movie he reveals that he has been "off the grid," taking only odd jobs here and there for money. In short, Sarah is useless when she is a wage laborer and does not transcend the "class dynamic" of the blue-collar worker, yet strong when she is outside of the class system. Likewise, John shows that the useful skills needed to lead the human resistance are very different from those that constitute normal class-based labor.

According to Marx, all capitalist production is for profit, and nothing else. And since capitalists and their interests directly or indirectly influence all other parts of society, most of what happens in society is aimed toward making money for capitalists.[5] Marx argues that since capitalists fund research and development, technology, too, is aimed at making profits. Furthermore, technological development for profit causes alienation, which generally means that an outside force takes something away from you (for example, your ability to connect to others or control your own life, or the product of your labor). Technology is alienating under capitalism, for example, when it prevents you from having control over your labor, or removes you from contact with others.[6]

For the most part, capital is owned and controlled not by *individual* capitalists, but by *corporations*, who also control the development of technology. So next we need to turn to the role of corporations, which play a part in Cameron's movies in the guises of Cyberdyne and Cyber Research Systems.

"It's Not Every Day You Find Out You're Responsible for Three Billion Deaths": The Dirty Hands of Cyberdyne

As a capitalist corporation, Cyberdyne's decisions center around the pursuit of profit—in Marx's terms, extracting the profitable "surplus value" from labor and reinvesting that profit to the corporation's benefit. When Cyberdyne finds a Terminator arm in its factory (along with the computer chip inside it), it does not give the technology up for the benefit of society at large. Rather, Cyberdyne keeps it in a secret, highly secured vault and reverse-engineers it in order to become the biggest defense contractor in the United States. The people working on the project are not necessarily so profit-obsessed, however. Miles Dyson, for example, explains to his wife why his work on artificial intelligence is so important to him:

> Imagine a jetliner with a pilot that never makes a mistake, never gets tired, never shows up to work with a hangover. Meet the pilot.

Dyson is a good man, but his intentions mean little against the law of the profit motive. In Marx's understanding, Dyson is still nothing more than a skilled laborer who takes orders from the owners of the company, who themselves are slaves to the laws of capitalism. When a young lab assistant named Bryant asks him about the origin of the arm and its technology, Dyson acknowledges how alienated he is from the knowledge of what's actually going on, and so from real control over his own project:

> Bryant: Listen, Mr. Dyson, I know I haven't been here that long, but I was wondering if you could tell me. . . . I mean, if you know . . .
>
> Dyson: Know what?
>
> Bryant: Well . . . where it [the Terminator arm] came from.
>
> Dyson: I asked them that question once. Know what they told me? Don't ask.

Dyson clearly has little control over the results of his own work. As Marx sees it, while the faceless owners of Cyberdyne make its particular research and development decisions, individuals, corporations, and capitalists aren't fundamentally responsible for the development of technology. The drive for profit is the real culprit. The need for businesses to grow (or else get shoved out of business) requires them to place profitability on a pedestal above everything else.[7] Cyberdyne, in the timeline before its destruction, became the largest supplier of military computers after the development of Dyson's artificial intelligence:

> Terminator: In three years Cyberdyne will become the largest supplier of military computer systems. All stealth bombers are upgraded with Cyberdyne computers, becoming fully unmanned. Afterward, they fly with a perfect operational record.

Although Skynet is developed as a militarized AI, it could still have been used for neutral, or even beneficial, purposes if average skilled laborers like Dyson had had any say over its application. In this case, though, the profit motive results in the Skynet fiasco, taking mankind's most deadly weapons out of human hands. Through the plotline of these movies, Cameron shows how technological developments emerging from the capitalist system quickly spiral out of human control and into catastrophic consequences that could end human life and civilization altogether.[8]

For both Cameron and Marx, capitalism and its technological gains are like a runaway train, speeding beyond control of the laborers that are its engine, or even the intentions of the capitalists themselves. Let's be honest: Skynet is not exactly a cure for cancer or a "green" energy source, but a computer designed to kill things really, *really* well, a purpose it shares with machine guns and nuclear weapons. Marxist theory can help explain how destructive machines are allowed to develop, but do Cameron and Marx see the development of ever more efficient weapons as a direct result of capitalism, or as simply the actions of neutral capitalist corporations responding to demand from a world market for violence?

In *Terminator 2: Judgment Day* we get a peek at Cyberdyne in its capacity as a military contractor, and so see a limited aspect of the military's involvement in the creation of Skynet. Mostly, however, *T2* focuses on Cyberdyne itself as an independent corporation. In *Terminator 3: Rise of the Machines*, Cyberdyne's patents are absorbed into another contractor, Cyber Research Systems, whose entanglement with the government and the military is portrayed much more clearly. After the destruction of Cyberdyne, the U.S. military contracts with Cyber RS to continue the development of Skynet in order to put machines in control of U.S. weapons and to remove human soldiers from combat operations. In other words, they want to ensure that horribly destructive technology is taken out of fallible human hands, yet remains under ultimate government control (that is, controlled by Skynet while fulfilling U.S. command directives issued by humans).

Marx himself never articulated a full theory of all the connections between government and the economy. In fact, that connection was more completely analyzed by Friedrich Engels and other Marxists, post-Marx. In *The Communist Manifesto*, Marx and Engels argue that "the executive of the modern state is but a committee for managing the common affairs of the whole bourgeoisie [capitalists]."[9] They elaborate on this in *The German Ideology* by claiming that the capitalist class itself organizes the state "for internal and external purposes, for the mutual guarantee of their property and interests."[10] Marxists argue that militarism, or the tendency for governments to throw *lots* of money into better ways to kill people—often building an empire at the same time—is the primary way for the state to protect its vested economic interests.[11] Militarism actually serves a number of purposes: it takes resources from areas of the world that weren't open to capitalist markets before, and puts them at the disposal of capitalism (this is called "primitive accumulation" by Marx; think "your land and resources weren't anyone's property before I arrived, and my guns say I own them now").

Aggressive militarism also allows governments to spend tons of taxpayer money in ways that meet no one's needs at all. After all, it wouldn't be right for society to provide for the neediest, if that would compete with capitalist corporations who want to make money off our needs. Militaristic imperialism, finally, creates a world market for goods that grows perpetually larger. Militarism, in other words, causes a government to transfer tons of taxpayer money to whoever can develop the best ways to kill people—creating a huge demand for technology such as Skynet. While Cameron doesn't explicitly blame capitalism in the *Terminator* saga for the militarism that creates Skynet, all the pieces are there exactly as a Marxist would place them.

Judgment Day for Capitalism Is Inevitable

We've seen the dangerous paths that technology may pursue when it is developed in response to profits rather than human good and when it is put to the service of militarism that is itself integrated into government policy. All these points Cameron shares with traditional Marxist views of capitalism. But beyond this, Cameron also depicts Skynet as the result of the "technological determination of capitalism reaching a contradiction." This weighty-sounding phrase (Marx had many!) simply means that technological development speeds toward a "contradiction," in which the laws inherent within a class-based economic system effectively fight against one another, each pushing classes and interests within society to take opposite directions simultaneously, because the various class interests are not in harmony.

Because of the laws of the capitalist system, technology can develop destructively—indeed, according to Marx's view of militarism, it must necessarily do so. But another common goal of technology is to reduce labor costs both through making machines perform more of the difficult and creative aspects of work, and so also using less and less of the worker's particular skills, and through reducing the number of workers needed to perform the same tasks, allowing the unemployment level to rise (referred to by Marx as the "reserve army of labor").[12] This extends to the development of artificial intelligence, where the goal is ultimately a computer program that can perform *at least* as creatively and intelligently as a human being. Combine the tendency toward destructive technology with the movement to make machines and technology increasingly independent from *us*, and you have Skynet.

Skynet is the inevitable result—what Marxists call a *final contradiction*—of the convergence of two dangerous trends caused by capitalists' control of the development of technology. The contradiction is *final* because there is no solution to be found to the problems it creates within the existing economic system, and thus what follows must be either a change to a new economic system or the utter destruction of the human species. Through this sinister portrayal of Skynet, Cameron seems to support Marxist conclusions that the capitalist system has unsolvable and inherent contradictions that threaten all humanity.

"*Hasta la Vista*, Baby": James Cameron's Tech-Savvy Marxism

Cameron's *Terminator* saga has one last significant similarity to Marxist philosophy and economics. Marxists believe that most technology, regardless of the purpose for which it was designed, can be reclaimed for human liberation. Technology *itself* is not necessarily destructive. Rather, the use of technology for profit is destructive. Similarly, Cameron does not critique *technology itself*. Instead he shows that even Terminators, developed to be efficient killing machines and nothing more, can be reprogrammed, or perhaps humanized, to free humanity from machine rule.

Each of Cameron's movies has a Terminator, controlled by Skynet, as its primary villain, but the latter two have reprogrammed T-101s defending the leaders of the human resistance. In *Terminator 2*, young John Connor first forbids "his" T-101 to kill people, a reversal of the role it was created for. Throughout the film, John tries to help the Terminator become more human, including reprogramming it to learn independently, gain a sense of humor, and understand emotion. For example, midway through the film, John and the Terminator break Sarah out of a mental ward, and Sarah lectures John for putting himself at risk:

> Sarah: It was stupid of you to go there. . . . Goddammit, John, you have to be smarter than that. You're too important! You can't risk yourself, not even for me, do you understand? I can take care of myself. I was doing fine. Jesus, John. You almost got yourself killed.
>
> John: I . . . had to get you out of the place. . . . I'm sorry, I . . . [he starts to cry].
>
> Sarah: Stop it! Right now! You can't cry, John. Other kids can afford to cry. You can't.
>
> Terminator [seeing John crying]: What is wrong with your eyes?

At this point, the Terminator does not understand human emotion. At the end, however, when the Terminator sacrifices himself to prevent the development of Skynet, John is crying. The Terminator touches his tear and says, "I know now why you cry. But it is something I can never do. Goodbye." The Terminator's fresh understanding of emotion is a clear metaphor for the ways in which technology can be humanized. Cameron holds technology itself to be neutral, but its development, control, and use in the capitalist system make it dehumanizing rather than liberating. Still, even the most destructive technology can be programmed to support human liberation.

But what is Cameron's idea of human liberation? The world of the future is controlled by a vast Terminator army, seeking daily to destroy the remnants of humanity. The ground is littered with human skulls and corpses. Mankind is completely subjugated, and those who haven't been killed are forced to work for the machines to clean up the bodies. This is the world that John Connor wants to liberate humanity from, but Cameron doesn't give us clear indications of what might replace it.

Perhaps this uncertainty is something we can live with, since a revolution is the first order of business. Marx urges us to reject a world in which private ownership is fiercely protected by the force of militaristic governments. Since everything is privately owned but most people do not own productive technology, access to the things we need requires paying money to the owner-capitalist. And of course we're all required to work for some other capitalist in order to have money to live on. While employed, laborers are subject to both managerial control and the limited range of options that machine technology creates. In short, daily living requires people to sell their labor time to a capitalist for *less* (often drastically less) than the value of the things they help produce; the other options are to starve and die, or to steal and risk punishment by the state. Being employed is hardly liberating, since it necessarily submits workers to domination in the workplace by managers and machines. But Marx also believed that these conditions would spur the global working class to rise up to fight in order to ultimately establish a classless society, a society without "haves" and "have-nots" in which one class is not allowed to live off the labor of another. As Marx famously said, a communist society that fits this description would be governed by the slogan "From each according to his ability, to each according to his need."[13] Both Marxist philosophy and Cameron's films end with the implication of opportunities for the oppressed. The people can reject the dilemma of either being forced to work subject to control by machines, or being killed by destructive technology created by capitalism. The future for both Marx and Cameron is envisioned as emerging from a long and bitter struggle for victory and a more humanized society with technology that alleviates the worst conditions of living and liberates us to pursue paths freely chosen.

Cameron's human resistance shares a close parallel with the Marxist prediction of the revolution of the working class, showing us that people won't go down without a fight. Simultaneously, he doesn't show us what the better world of the future will look like. Perhaps Cameron is saying that for now at least, the point is the struggle itself. Can we take back our world from the warmongers, from those who profit from human need and human suffering? I don't know the answers. . . . *T4* hasn't come out yet. But even if Cameron's *Terminator* films do not analyze the world for us, they do show us a way to *amend it*. There is no future utopia, but there is the promise of a successful revolution. Perhaps that, too, comes from Marx. After all, Marx also famously said that "philosophers have only *interpreted* the world, in various ways; the point is to *change* it."[14] Maybe that's what Cameron is ultimately trying to say.

NOTES

1. If you think this idea that James Cameron has Marxist themes in his films is absurd, I recommend the following excellent article: James Kendrick, "Marxist Overtones in Three Films by James Cameron," in *Journal of Popular Film & Television* 27, no. 3 (1999): 36–44. A good reader for those who are interested in studying Marxism further but don't know where to start is Robert Tucker's *The Marx-Engels Reader*, 2nd ed. (New York: W. W. Norton, 1978).

2. To Marx, the value in goods comes from human labor, and the value of human labor power equals their means of subsistence; that is, workers only need to labor enough to meet their socially determined and natural needs. If they work to produce value beyond that, their labor is *surplus labor*, and the value produced is *surplus value*.

3. For example, as I write this in the fall of 2008, Congress had just recently passed a $700 billion bailout for finance capitalists in response to the recession that they caused,

which primarily provides security for their investment, instead of building infrastructure, creating jobs, or providing subsidized housing—and all paid for from the nation's taxes. It's as though the capitalists were Terminators, disrobed and demanding the clothes of the working citizens.

4. Karl Marx, *Capital: A Critique of Political Economy* (New York: Modern Library, 1906), 21.

5. Marx argues for this in *The German Ideology*: "The class which has the means of material production at its disposal, has control at the same time over the means of mental production . . . [and] as they rule as a class and determine the extent and compass of an epoch, it is self-evident that they do this in its whole range, hence among other things rule also as thinkers, as producers of ideas, and regulate their production and distribution of the ideas of their age: thus their ideas are the ruling ideas of the epoch"; Frederick Engels and Karl Marx, *The German Ideology* (New York: International Publishers, 1970), 64.

6. For Marx's theory of alienation, see the *Economic and Philosophical Manuscripts of 1844*, especially the section on "Estranged Labor," in Karl Marx, *Early Writings* (Wiltshire, Eng.: Penguin Classics, 1992).

7. Marx notes in *Capital* that "the laws, immanent in capitalist production, manifest themselves in the movements of individual masses of capital, where they assert themselves as coercive laws of competition, and are brought home to the mind and consciousness of the individual capitalist as the directing motives of his operations"; Marx, *Capital*, 347.

8. For a very different view of where technology is heading in Cameron's films, see Jesse W. Butler's chapter in this volume, "Un-Terminated: The Integration of the Machines."

9. Engels and Marx, *Manifesto of the Communist Party*, in *The Revolutions of 1848: Political Writings*, vol. 1, ed. David Fernbach (Wiltshire, Eng.: Penguin Classics, 1992), 69.

10. Engels and Marx, *The German Ideology*, 80.

11. For an analysis of the tendency of capitalism toward militarism, see Rosa Luxemburg, *The Accumulation of Capital* (London: Routledge, 1951), chap. 32, and Paul Baran and Paul M. Sweezy, *Monopoly Capital* (New York: Monthly Review Press, 1966), chap. 7.

12. See Marx, *Capital*, part 4: "The Production of Relative Surplus Value."

13. Marx, *Critique of the Gotha Program*, part 1, in *The Marx-Engels Reader*, 531.

14. Marx, "Concerning Feuerbach," in *Early Writings*, 423.

PART THREE

CHANGING WHAT'S ALREADY HAPPENED

BAD TIMING: THE METAPHYSICS OF THE TERMINATOR

Robert A. Delfino and Kenneth Sheahan

> That the human spirit will ever give up metaphysical speculations is as little to be expected as that we should prefer to give up breathing altogether, in order to avoid impure air.
>
> —Immanuel Kant[1]

What is the meaning of life? Do I have free will? Does God exist? Some of the deepest philosophical questions are, like these, metaphysical. *Metaphysics*, roughly speaking, is the branch of philosophy that deals with the ultimate nature of reality. The ancient Greek philosopher Aristotle (384–322 BCE) called metaphysics "Wisdom" and said it studied the deepest causes of things.[2] Perhaps this explains why metaphysics is always surrounded by controversy and why it has been attacked in every age, including the present.[3]

Yet the fact remains that humans are addicted to metaphysical questions, as the German philosopher Immanuel

Kant (1724–1804) suggests above. We simply cannot stop thinking about them. Movies like *The Terminator* thrill us, in part, because they put flesh, blood, and special effects on metaphysical questions. Really, would you rather read what Aristotle has to say about the nature of time or watch Arnold Schwarzenegger travel through time and blow up everything in his path in 5.1 surround sound?[4]

Movies can bring philosophy to life in a way mere words cannot. Many things happen in films that are impossible in the real world, or that at least *seem* impossible. So we must often suspend our disbelief to enjoy a film. Still, there is only so much disbelief we can suspend before a movie starts to bother us. For example, finding a flaw in the storyline itself will often detract from our enjoyment of it—at least to some degree.

Unfortunately, from the perspective of metaphysics, there are two serious flaws in *The Terminator*. These pretty much ruin the storyline, either because they contradict elements of the story or because they make the story much less believable. No doubt some of you will accuse us of being too picky, but we ask you to reserve judgment until you hear our arguments. No matter what you decide in the end, we are pretty sure you'll never look at *The Terminator* the same way again.

"White Light, Pain. . . . It's like Being Born Maybe . . . "

The two metaphysical problems we discuss below concern time travel. Our goal, however, is not to figure out whether time travel to the past is really possible.[5] Instead, let's assume that time travel to the past *is* possible and that the past and future can be changed. Do the rest of the elements of *The Terminator* make sense, given these assumptions?[6]

The first problem is about Kyle Reese, who must enter the time-displacement equipment in the future, sometime after the Terminator had already entered it. We call this the "Bad Timing Problem": unless Reese entered *at exactly the same time as the T-101*, the rescue of Sarah Connor is either impossible or unnecessary. The second problem is also about Kyle Reese and how he, a man from the future, is the father of John Connor. We call this the "Who-Is-Your-Daddy? Problem," and we will argue that it leads to one of these two conclusions: either John Connor had *two different* dads, or there is no way to explain how John came into existence in the first place.

First, the Bad Timing Problem. During his interrogation by Dr. Silberman, a criminal psychologist, Kyle describes his entry into the time-displacement equipment: "The Terminator had already gone through. Connor sent me to intercept and they blew the whole place." This might sound innocent enough, but as we will see, time travel screws up the way things normally work. In order to understand the problem, first consider a long race, like the New York City marathon. Suppose you planned to enter, but overslept and started the race an hour late. Theoretically, you could still win. Sure, the other runners are way ahead of you, but they haven't yet reached the finish line, so if you run fast enough you can pass them.

Using this marathon analogy, let's suppose that after entering the time machine, it takes the Terminator six hours to find and kill Sarah Connor. If so, you might think that Kyle Reese has only six hours to enter the time machine and rescue Sarah. After all, if Sarah is already dead, then it's pointless to travel back in time. As reasonable as this might sound, this logic can't be applied in the case of *The Terminator*. The reason is this: changes in the past *instantaneously* affect the future. Don't believe us? Consider the following hypothetical situation, or *thought experiment*.[7]

Suppose you have a time machine right in front of you and you set it to transfer an object one hundred years back in time to a spot only five feet from where you are now standing. Now suppose you drop a new iron nail into the time machine. Wham! It should appear instantaneously five feet in front of you, rusted and aged one hundred years (assuming no one moved it within that time span). The point is you won't have to wait one hundred years for the nail to appear. This is because your sending the nail into the past will make its previous existence part of your time frame *now*. The nail will, of course, have aged. But since the aging of the nail was in the past relative to you, that period of aging has already passed. The fact that it appears instantly is what we call *time compression* (see the figure below).

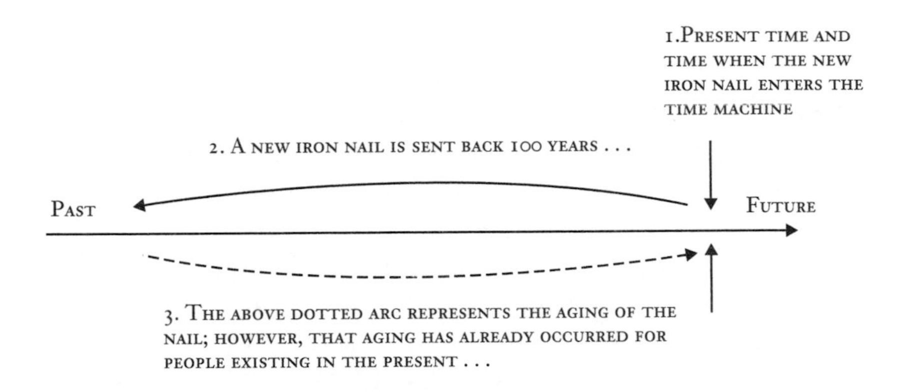

Because Reese tells us that he went into the time machine *after* the Terminator, the T-101 will have either succeeded or failed in its mission *before* Reese enters the time machine. How, you ask? Pretend for a second that Reese never went in the time machine, but the Terminator did. In such a case, either the T-101 successfully kills Sarah Connor or, by some miracle, the police stop him. Whichever event takes place it will instantly affect John Connor and Reese in 2029 because of time compression. In other words, just as the iron nail appeared instantly when we dropped it into the time machine, so will the effects of the Terminator's actions appear instantly. It seemed to make sense that Reese had up to six hours to save Sarah, but now this means that time doesn't matter. If Reese goes in even one second after the Terminator, Reese can't change anything. Either the T-101 has already killed Sarah, and thus doomed the human race, or it has failed, making Reese's trip unnecessary.

You might raise the objection that two different scenarios could prove this conclusion wrong. First, what if Reese programmed the time-displacement equipment to go back to a time a few hours *earlier* than the T-101? This way he could get to Sarah before the Terminator arrives and thus prevent her murder. Second, we know from the sequels, *Terminator 2: Judgment Day* and *Terminator 3: Rise of the Machines*, that actually three Terminators and three Protectors were sent to different time periods. Thus, perhaps, the very existence of the sequels can save the first movie.

Unfortunately, neither of these ideas can save *The Terminator* from failing its metaphysics test. First, we know (from his own testimony) that Reese entered the time machine after the Terminator. Given how easily the T-101 kicks the crap out of the thirty cops in the police station, it's likely that the Terminator will succeed in killing Sarah Connor. If so, given time compression, Reese will not even be able to enter the time machine! Why? Because if the Terminator is successful, then John Connor will never be born, the machines will win the war, and humanity will be extinct; this means that Reese is dead and he can't ever enter the time machine, even to go back in time earlier than the T-101.

Second, what about the sequels? Even if the police managed to stop the Terminator from the original film, Skynet has other chances to exterminate humanity by killing John Connor as a teenage boy (in *T2*) and as a young man (in *T3*). However, in each of the sequels the Protectors enter the time-displacement equipment *after* the Terminators. Given time compression, and the fact that the Terminators of *T2* and *T3* are much more advanced than the original Terminator, it's a safe bet that they'll kill their targets, dooming humanity. With no humans left alive, no one will exist to reprogram the T-101s to protect John, and so no Protectors will enter the time machine.

If the Bad Timing Problem is real, then the storyline of *The Terminator* is very hard to believe. If we had to categorize the Bad Timing Problem, it would fall under what we call a No-F'n-Way flaw.[8] If you can believe that ordinary civilians and police officers could have stopped the Terminator in time to save Sarah Connor, then good for you. We, however, doubt it. And even if all three Terminators from all of the movies failed, the trips made by the three Protectors would still be unnecessary to rescue Sarah. This is a fatal flaw because it takes away the cool one-on-one battles between the Terminators and the Protectors that are the highlight of the films.

Someone might argue that even if the Protectors' presence is unnecessary to save Sarah, they still can perform a useful task by making sure that Skynet will never exist. However, given the sequels, especially *T3*, we can see how well that worked! In addition, if we assume, for the sake of argument, that artificial intelligence is possible, then it will be discovered eventually. This means that Skynet coming online will be inevitable. So the best that the agents of the resistance can do is merely delay the inevitable.[9]

If the Bad Timing flaw doesn't bother you, don't worry. There is another metaphysical flaw in *The Terminator* that's even worse: the problem of John Connor's father.

"If You Don't Send Kyle, You Could Never Be . . . "

Kyle Reese tells us that he grew up after the nuclear war began on Judgment Day. Years later he meets John Connor, who gives him a picture of Sarah. This is no accident, because we learn near the end of *The Terminator* that Sarah has left a taped message for John. In that message she says: "Should I tell you about your father? Boy, that's a tough one. Will it affect your decision to send him here knowing that he is your father? If you don't send Kyle, you could never be." One of the most intriguing aspects of the film is the fact that Kyle Reese is

John Connor's father. (And you thought Luke Skywalker had a paternity problem!) While this certainly makes for a fresh and creative storyline, it also seems absurd. If Kyle was born in the future, how did Sarah get pregnant the first time in order to give birth to John Connor, who later met and sent Kyle back to be his daddy? Now you know why we call this the Who-Is-Your-Daddy? Problem.

This problem presents what philosophers call a vicious circle. Any argument (or storyline) that contains a vicious circle is flawed, because it cannot be resolved. For example, suppose you locked your keys in your car. You need to open the door to get your keys, but you need your keys to open the door. You are stuck in a circle, but not a vicious one. In this case, there is hope, because you could break a window or call a mechanic to force open the door.

Things aren't so hopeful for John Connor, however. In his case we truly have a vicious circle: in order to exist, John needs to send Kyle back, but John already needs to exist in order to send Kyle back (see the figure below).

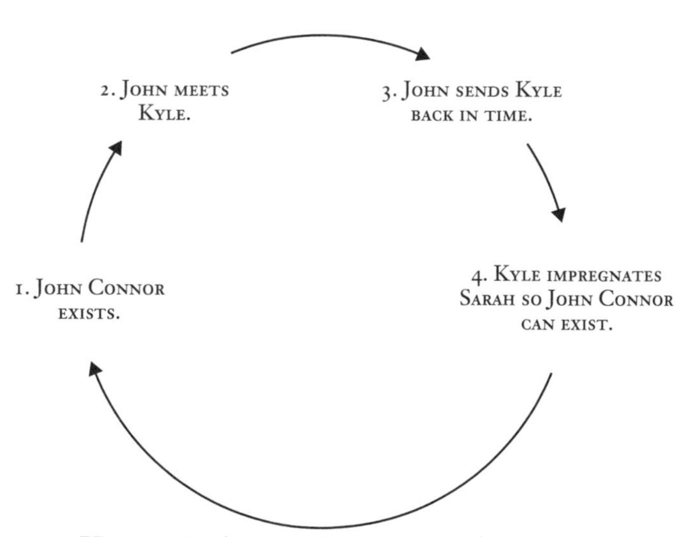

Vicious Circle: In order to exist, John needs to send Kyle back in time, but John already needs to exist in order to send Kyle back in time.

Unfortunately, there's no way out of this circle without destroying the storyline. On the one hand, if we accept that Reese is the father, then there's no way to explain how John Connor came into existence in the first place. But if John Connor does not exist, then *The Terminator* makes no sense at all. On the other hand, we could say that John had two different fathers. This would require two timelines (see the figure below). In the first timeline, Reese is not John's father (perhaps it was Stan Morsky, that Porsche-drivin' guy who stood up Sarah?). But when John sends Reese back in time to impregnate Sarah, this creates a second timeline in which Reese is the father of John (we also added a third timeline below for reasons that will soon become clear).

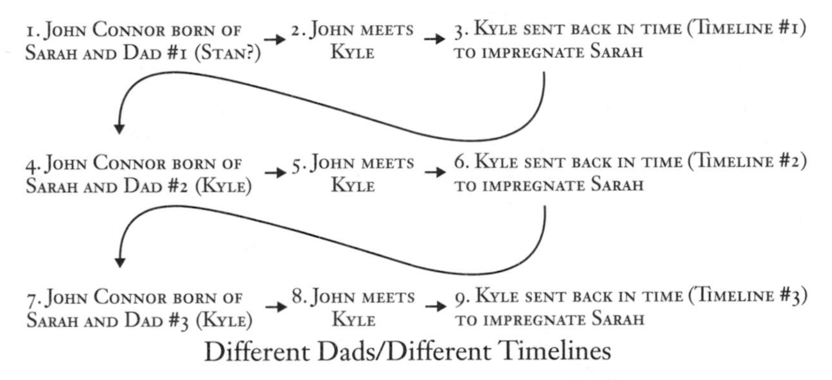

Different Dads/Different Timelines

Relying on different timelines allows us to break out of the vicious circle shown earlier. However, it leads to at least three other problems. First, it seems to contradict the storyline of the film, which has only Reese as the father. But perhaps *The Terminator* takes place on the third timeline. From the perspective of the third timeline, Reese is the previous father (in timeline two). Second, it seems that new timelines will be added infinitely as Reese keeps returning to the past. So the story might be trapped in a different kind of endless circle after all. However, even if history doesn't keep repeating itself, and so we have only two timelines, there is still a third problem: the problem of personal identity.

The problem of personal identity involves one individual remaining the same person, despite changing in other ways.[10] Because they have different fathers, it seems that the John

Connor in timeline one cannot be the same person as the John Connor in timeline two. This leads to a serious problem involving Kyle Reese: if the John Connor that was not fathered by Reese does not possess the qualities he needs to crush Skynet, then the humans will lose the war and Kyle will not be sent back to protect Sarah. If, however, the John Connor that was not fathered by Reese *does* possess the qualities he needs to crush Skynet, then Reese should have been told *not* to impregnate Sarah, as that might jeopardize the human victory over the machines (why take a chance on a different father if the first father is good enough?).

"One Possible Future . . . "

All of the problems we've discussed cast serious doubt on the view that multiple timelines can save the story line of *The Terminator*. However, the situation is more complicated than it might appear. There are different ways, metaphysically speaking, that we can understand the different timelines. For example, are they parallel universes? If not, what happens to timeline one when timeline two is created?

Suppose that the different timelines shown above are three parallel universes. A parallel universe is a universe that exists separately from our own.[11] Using this idea, we could hypothesize that when Kyle Reese goes back in time to impregnate Sarah, the universe branches off into a second universe (timeline two). This would be like an amoeba splitting itself into two separate organisms during mitosis. (You didn't forget all of your high school biology, did you?) The difference is that we have one universe where Kyle Reese is not the father of John Connor (timeline one) and another universe where he is the father (timeline two). Even if this were to happen, however, it would not save the storyline of *The Terminator* for at least two reasons.

First, it introduces a new wrinkle with respect to the personal identity problem because now we have two John Connors concurrently existing in two separate universes. Which is the real John Connor? Or should we say that both are John

Connor because one person can inhabit two different bodies at the same time? What a metaphysical mess! Second, given parallel universes, even if Skynet wins in timeline two (because of the Bad Timing Problem), Skynet has already lost in timeline one. Recall that Reese told Dr. Silberman: "Their defense grid was smashed. We'd won." The result of this is a "we win *and* we lose in different universes" ending that really sucks! (Generally speaking, people like a definitive ending in a movie where some enemy is hell-bent on our destruction.)

The alternative to the above interpretation is to say that the timelines shown on page 116 are not parallel universes. Instead, they merely represent alterations to one and the same universe. In other words, by traveling back in time and changing the past it is as if certain things never happened (see the figure below). However, this interpretation of things does not overcome either of the two big metaphysical problems we've discussed. The Bad Timing Problem would still apply in this case. Whoever goes into the time-displacement equipment first still has the advantage. But in this case, unlike the parallel universe view, only one side can win.

So what about the Who-Is-Your-Daddy? Problem? Let's tackle that next.

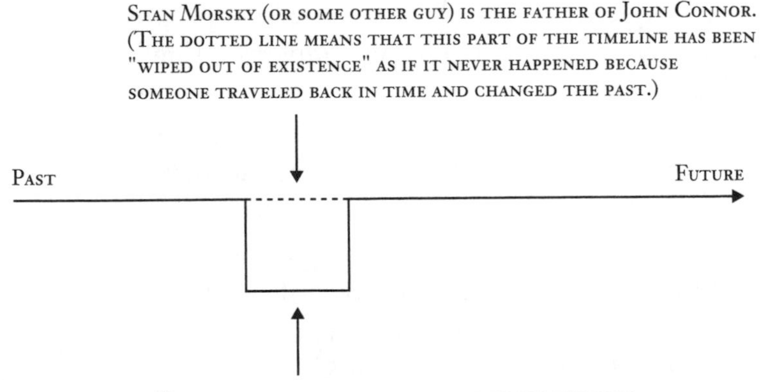

The above figure shows how the timeline of one universe can be altered by time travel. In this case, by traveling back in time, Reese becomes John Connor's father. The dotted part of the timeline, which represents John's original dad (Stan Morsky?), is wiped out of existence (as if it never happened) the moment that Reese travels back and impregnates Sarah. This still, however, does not remove the fact that John Connor's original father had to be someone other than Kyle Reese. By changing the past Kyle *seems* to become the only father of John, but Kyle would never have been able to travel back in time unless there was a first father other than Kyle Reese. So even if this first father was "wiped out of existence" (whatever that means), he still had to exist for a time (before being wiped out) in order to make Kyle Reese's trip back in time possible. Thus, in the end, the Who-Is-Your-Daddy? Problem has not been solved. We are still faced with the conclusion that either there is no way to explain how John Connor came into existence in the first place (if it is claimed that Kyle Reese is the only father), or that John Connor had two different dads (with all of the problems that accompany this view).

"God, a Person Could Go Crazy Thinking about This . . ."

Even if we're right that there are two serious metaphysical flaws in the original film, we don't blame you if you still like the films. We do, too. Aside from their obvious entertainment value, these types of movies stir our imagination. When asked to explain his impressive discoveries, Albert Einstein once said he felt that "imagination is more important than knowledge. Knowledge is limited. Imagination encircles the world."[12]

Nothing stretches your imagination quite like fiction, especially science fiction. Where else, except in fiction, could you pretend that the impossible is possible and the improbable is happening right now? Fiction helps us to think philosophically because it stimulates the mind, encouraging us to think in new and unexpected ways. Philosophers such as Martha Nussbaum have made similar arguments concerning the value of novels to philosophical study.[13] What is true of novels is equally true of movies, which currently reach a wider audience than most philosophy books. So keep watching and thinking, and who knows—you might just become a philosopher yourself![14]

NOTES

1. Immanuel Kant, *Prolegomena to Any Future Metaphysics*, ed. L. W. Beck (New York: Bobbs-Merrill, 1950), 116.

2. Aristotle, *Metaphysics*, 981b26–30, trans. W. D. Ross, in *The Basic Works of Aristotle*, ed. Richard McKeon (New York: Random House, 1941), 691. Aristotle also said that metaphysics studied other things. In fact, he was so unclear when discussing what metaphysics studied that philosophers have been arguing about how to interpret him ever since.

3. For a brief overview of the history of attacks on metaphysics, see Jorge J. E. Gracia, *Metaphysics and Its Task: The Search for the Categorial Foundation of Knowledge* (Albany: State Univ. of New York Press, 1999), ix–xiii.

4. Collectors of the movies will know that the original DVD of *The Terminator* was presented in mono sound. Thankfully they remastered it in 5.1 for the special edition.

5. If you are interested in whether time travel is really possible, we recommend the following books: Brian Greene, *The Fabric of the Cosmos: Space, Time, and the Texture of Reality* (New York: Knopf, 2004), chap. 15, and Michio Kaku, *Physics of the Impossible: A Scientific Exploration into the World of Phasers, Force Fields, Teleportation, and Time Travel* (New York: Doubleday, 2008), chap. 12.

6. One last point: because we are making a lot of assumptions, our arguments below should be considered an exercise in *hypothetical metaphysics*. Ordinary metaphysics studies reality, which is difficult enough, but we are venturing into the unknown.

7. Thought experiments are performed in your mind, not in a laboratory. They are used to examine the logical implications of a theory. Knowing the implications of a theory helps one to determine whether it is consistent with other theories and known facts. For more on thought experiments, see Julian Baggini and Peter S. Fosl, *The Philosopher's Toolkit: A Compendium of Philosophical Concepts and Methods* (Malden, MA: Wiley-Blackwell, 2002), 58–60.

8. Such a flaw, for example, occurs in the popular Will Smith film *Independence Day*. In that film, the aliens are tremendously more powerful than we are. They should have destroyed us. The No-F'n-Way flaw in that film concerns the fact that the humans uploaded a computer virus to the alien ships. However, unless those alien ships ran a Macintosh operating system, we cannot see how the humans could have compiled a program in their alien computer language quickly enough to save the world. No-F'n-Way! Some of you, no doubt, will disagree with this assessment. For a good discussion of

the controversy, see the comments of Dan Hurley and Phil Bennett on Jakob Nielsen's Webpage: www.useit.com/alertbox/independence-day-interoperability-blooper.html.

9. Actually, it is possible that artificial intelligence might be benevolent and leave humanity alone. Why are we suspicious of this?

10. This is a very popular topic among philosophers. For an overview of the problem, see Eric T. Olson, "Personal Identity," posted on February 20, 2007, at plato.stanford.edu/entries/identity-personal/.

11. For a good discussion of parallel universes, see Kaku, *Physics of the Impossible*, chap. 13.

12. This occurred in an interview conducted by George Sylvester Viereck. For more information, see Walter Isaacson, *Einstein: His Life and Universe* (New York: Simon and Schuster, 2007), 387.

13. Martha C. Nussbaum, "Introduction: Form and Content, Philosophy and Literature," in *Love's Knowledge: Essays on Philosophy and Literature* (New York: Oxford University Press, 1990), 3–53.

14. We would like to thank William Irwin, Richard Brown, Kevin S. Decker, Alejandro Quintana, Rachel Hollander, Tony Spanakos, Stephen Greeley, Andrew D'Auria, Joseph Mogelnicki, John Joseph Jordan, Nicholas Brosnan, and Tyler Matthew Aguilar Kimball for helpful comments on this chapter.

TIME FOR THE TERMINATOR: PHILOSOPHICAL THEMES OF THE RESISTANCE

Justin Leiber

In the not-too-distant future, humans resist extermination at the hands of machines. In the present, philosophers resist ignorance and injustice. The two resistances converge in three philosophical themes of the *Terminator* saga: paradoxes of time travel and changing the past to affect the future; the moral status of nonhuman life forms; and the threat of devastating "smart" weapons technology.

Back from the Future

In the original film, the Terminator is sent by Skynet to kill Sarah Connor, who will give birth to John Connor, the fated leader of human resistance to machine rule. This chain of events, however, embodies two paradoxes.

Paradox one: if the Terminator succeeds, then Skynet won't have any John Connor to worry about and hence can't be sending a Terminator back to kill the mother of the unborn, unnamed, and nonexistent John Connor. The T-101's arrival in our present proves he must fail, because if he had succeeded, the situation that led to his being sent back wouldn't have occurred—and so he wouldn't be sent back in the first place.

Paradox two: to head off this impossibility, future John Connor also sends Sarah Connor's would-be defender, Kyle Reese, back through time. He not only miraculously terminates the Terminator but also impregnates Sarah Connor, whom he will fall in love with decades hence by looking at her photograph. Where did the photograph come from? It was taken a decade after John Connor's birth, and helpfully supplied to Reese by the resistance leader of the 2020s and—dare we say it—superpimp, John Connor himself! But our future John Connor, being a bright chap, knows that because he, John Connor, exists, the Terminator *must have* failed and so he, John Connor, *must have* been born of Sarah Connor. So, given all this, why on Earth does he need to send Kyle Reese back at all?

It's no wonder that the young John Connor of *Terminator 2: Judgment Day* finds the whole situation quite confusing. His now hard-as-nails mother has trained him to become the future leader of the resistance, but he initially (and quite naturally) thinks she is a lunatic. And he finds it *really* confusing when a *protective* T-101 and a murderous late-model T-1000 show up. Then he realizes that *it was, is, and will be his fate* to train himself to become the future John Connor who will lead the future human insurrection. The future protects the past so it can continue being the future! Which is which?

But then his mom, Sarah, takes a break from monomaniacally training herself and her son and gets the "free will bug" big-time. She decides to defeat the time loop and defy fate by assassinating the Cyberdyne Systems genius inventor who will, in time's original course, invent Skynet and, unwittingly and indirectly, bring about the genesis of the Terminators. She nearly succeeds, rivaling Uma Thurman in *Kill Bill* in her murderous intensity. But her son and his protective Terminator thwart the assassination, then enlist Skynet's inventor and Sarah herself in the more definitive project of destroying Cyberdyne Systems itself. They reason that it's better to strangle Skynet even before its birth throes. Just to be safe, the protective Terminator, whose circuitry embodies the last trace of Skynet in our present, nobly terminates himself.

There are more paradoxes coming, but let's have a popcorn break and consider another kind of philosophical puzzle: a machine that appears to be a man.

Intermission: Call Him Mister Machine

Poor T-101! In *T2*, John Connor order's him not to kill, teaches him moral considerations and some American slang, makes him a willing enlistee to stop his mother from murdering Miles Dyson, and then makes the Terminator the leading figure in the destruction of Cyberdyne without any direct human casualties. Schwarzenegger's T-101, after destroying the implacable T-1000, decides *on his own* that he must be terminated in molten metal, removing the last trace of Dyson's invention while at the same time destroying himself to defend humanity. Yet, bound by an internal survival imperative, the Terminator apparently cannot destroy himself. He asks Sarah to lower him slowly into the boiling metal. Instant tragedy! There's a boy crying, just like in the famous final scene in the classic Western *Shane*. After saving the town and the farm from the evil gunslingers, Shane must ride into the sunset because he is, after all, a gunslinger himself. At least Shane doesn't have to be lowered into boiling metal by his lady friend!

Now, I don't know about you, but about ten seconds after the Terminator was fried, I began to smell human chauvinism. The Terminator's effective suicide was too easy. Was the T-101 a mere robot? Or was he a person, a bearer of rights and autonomy?

The term "robot" was coined from the Czech word for slave, *robotnik*, but the origins of the concept of a mechanical being are much earlier. In 1747 Julien de La Mettrie (1709–1751), who had been the chief medical officer of the French army, fled the censors of Paris for the relative safety of Holland. The first out-and-out materialist of modern times, he then anonymously published *Man a Machine*,[1] only to flee the Dutch persecution as well to the protection of Frederick the Great of Prussia. La Mettrie insisted that there was no important difference between plants and animals and humans, or, more important for our purposes, between nonliving and living things. As we now know, all of these types of things are constructed from exactly the same elements and molecules and operate according to the same mechanical, physical, and chemical laws. Humans are simply complicated machines: as La Mettrie put it, we are clocks that wind our own springs. For the years that remained to him, La Mettrie took to signing his letters "Mr. Machine." I bet the Terminator would have liked him (however, La Mettrie would certainly have scoffed at the superstitious idea that vitally sparked "living matter" could time-travel while de-sparked matter such as clothing could not!).

In his brilliant and imperishable 1950 essay "Computing Machinery and Intelligence," mathematician Alan Turing (1912–1954) proposed putting a computer in one room and a human in another and then interrogating both at length via a keyboard.[2] If experts could not reliably guess who was the computer and who was the human being, then Turing thought we should concede that the computer is a thinking thing (this has come to be called the "Turing Test"). Turing likened this to blind musical auditions where the judges cannot be biased by the physical appearance of the contestant. Turing of course anticipated that the computer would be able to deliberately make "human" mistakes in answering difficult questions, like those involving mathematical calculations. He also allowed that the computer might have to be equipped with visual and auditory receptors and sent to "school" in preparation for the test.[3]

Like John Connor's experience with the T-101, Turing expected that we might find it initially difficult to get along with a thinking machine. Turing's critics suggested the test-passing computer, even if it was a thinking entity, still wouldn't have a sense of humor, be able to tell right from wrong, make mistakes, or enjoy strawberries and cream. Notice that the Terminator clearly manages all of these except enjoying strawberries and cream.

Scientists pursuing artificial intelligence (AI) have spent much of the last sixty years trying to produce a computer that could pass the Turing Test. Although they have made progress, they have yet to succeed. While Turing's original critics thought it would be a simple thing to simulate a human person, wits and all, it is now rightly regarded as so difficult that no cognitive scientist expects a Turing-certified AI anytime soon.

Look, maybe we humans will decide *not* to build intelligent, sensitive, morally savvy cyborgs. But if we do build one, teach it, befriend it, join with it in a common cause, depend for our very lives on it, and respect its moral sensitivities, then it's not just metal, flesh, computer circuitry, or "chemicals." It's a person with moral autonomy and rights, including a right to its continued existence.[4] Given this understanding, the T-101 is committing suicide, and Sarah should not help him do so.

Paradoxes Galore: Why Does the Future Seem to Protect the Past?

In *Terminator 3: Rise of the Machines* we find that John Connor, having survived the early time-travel assaults, has made it into his twenties. To avoid further temporal onslaughts, he has become a nomad with no phone number and no fixed address. The future Skynet has nonetheless sent a third-generation she-devil Terminator (the T-X) back to assassinate John Connor's future lieutenants, including his future wife, Kate Brewster. The T-X is also more than willing to target John Connor and an original model T-101 Terminator when they show up. Both Kate and John are protected by the T-101, whom future Kate has reprogrammed and sent back to protect the lieutenants, her earlier self, and John. Above all, its mission is to try to stop the full-fledged Skynet's leap into the impending thermonuclear war. Although the T-X's deadly project is derailed, Kate and John fail to stop the full realization of Skynet. "Judgment Day is inevitable," as the original-model Terminator tells them.

But before Judgment Day, Kate and John manage to get to a massive, abandoned thermonuclear war shelter, as the ever wise and valiant T-101 planned. Of course, if they had died in the blast, then their future selves would not have been able to send back the T-101 and the third-generation Terminator would not have had to bother with her mission, either. Their deaths in the blast would also cancel out the future in which a married and fully operational rebel leader, named John Connor, would be assassinated by a T-101, the same one whom Kate Brewster would reprogram to send back to protect the future rebels and to try to save the world from Skynet.

Again and again, good and bad agents from the future are sent back to change, or to protect from change, that one and the same future. When they seek to change that future, they fail. And when they protect that future, they succeed. Mostly, anyhow.

The Terminator, scaring us half to death with the T-101's mechanical superiority, portrays its antagonist as a Panzer Tiger tank opposed by the equivalent of tykes on tricycles. Surely he must succeed! Yet the interventions of the T-101 as well as Kyle Reese leave the future exactly as it was before the Terminator and Reese interventions. In *Terminator 2*, the

T-1000 liquid metal Terminator has the assassination of a cheeky clueless ten-year-old boy as his mission. Opposed only by an inferior original model Terminator and a superfeisty Sarah Connor, the T-1000 Terminator fails to change its past and hence our future. Even the T-101 and the redoubtable Sarah Connor fail in their attempt to change the future by eliminating the Skynet threat. The development of Cyberdyne, and hence Skynet and Judgment Day, proceeds implacably. The attempt to stop Skynet's war fails, coincidentally resulting in John Connor and Kate surviving the thermonuclear war, so that the future does not change.

What *seems* to be happening is that the future is protecting itself against any change in the past: its order seems to conserve reality. Or, to put it another way, past, present, and future seem to form a continuum in which changes in one area must harmoniously require conservational adjustments in others. Of course, we've been concentrating on forces from the future that are trying unsuccessfully to change the past rather than the reverse. We might imagine a traveler sent forward from the past to change the future, as occurs in the original time-travel story, H. G. Wells's *The Time Machine*. Doesn't the past have to try to catch up with, or make the right moves toward, the future? Does time go forward, or backward, or both?

Time, as Saint Augustine wrote in his *Confessions*, is something so familiar that you think you understand it perfectly well until you actually think about it—and only then, of course, does it seem paradoxical and mysterious. In different ways, modern philosophy and modern physics have worried about time, with philosophers worrying about why time seems to have a direction and what makes now happen now, and physicists worrying about how much energy would be required in order to winch the space-time continuum in the *now* to whiplash the *then*—in other words, to travel through time.

Suppose time *could* start going backward. After all, physics is full of reciprocity and reversal—whatever goes up comes down, for every action there is an equal and opposite reaction, liquid water becomes ice much like ice becomes liquid water. So couldn't time move backward in just the manner in which a star show in a planetarium reverses the path of the stars, or retrodicts the past? Backward causation works perfectly with the starry heavens and the wanderers—but reversals and retrodictions seem more dicey when we consider chemical, biological, and psychological reactions. In the nineteenth century, astronomer and physicist Pierre Laplace (1749–1827) reveled in this determinism, claiming that if you knew the "initial conditions" at any stage in the history of the universe, you could exactly predict what would happen in its future; equally, you could precisely retrodict the past conditions of any event. When Napoleon asked if a "Designer" had a place in his clockwork, Laplace supposedly replied, "I have no need of that hypothesis." Of course, as a confident scientist, Laplace was insisting that the physical universe could be explained, its motions precisely predicted, without invoking supernatural forces. But perhaps he was also making the point that adding "supernatural forces" doesn't explain anything, nor does it allow confident and precise predictions and retrodictions. For him, the phrase "Whatever happens is fated to be so" is an empty statement.

After Laplace, Albert Einstein (1879–1955) showed us that absolute space-time is an illusion but that everything still has to happen as it does from a given viewpoint. The classic example: if spaceship *x*, approaching the speed of light, happens to fly past spaceship *y*, *x*'s length and mass increases relative to *y*, while from *x*'s perspective, *y* shortens and its mass decreases. Yet these differing perspectives are equally real and correct. Einstein's universe is just as deterministic as Laplace's, or for that matter, Isaac Newton's.

Scientific determinists like Laplace and Einstein seem to imply something like a "law of the conservation of reality," on a par with the well-established laws of motion and gravity and the laws of the conservation of mass and energy. Einstein's famous $E = mc^2$ not only specifies the equalities between amounts of mass and amounts of energy, but it also indicates that the total amount of mass-energy is always conserved, always remains the same. If time travel indeed is possible in Einstein's space-time continuum, then it may very well be true that past and future times have some sort of interdependent existence. Perhaps, as someone once put it, time really is "nature's way of preventing everything from happening all at once."

But doesn't that really mean that everything happens all at once? That past time simply can't be changed, and the future has already happened (although common sense says we can change it easily)? Maybe the character of the continuum of space-time is one in which not only the total amount of mass-energy is conserved. Maybe (to make sense of the *Terminator* paradoxes, at least), the continuum of "mass-energy-*time*" resists massive change as well. Some significant events in the continuum (like sending a T-101 into the past) might be able to affect causal sequences of events in a non-causal way.

This might sound like what hip scientists have talked about for a while as the "butterfly effect" (a mere insect wing flip may eventually produce the end of dinosaurs, while a wing flop would have had T-Rex's descendants still thundering about today). But this reasoning nears absurdity. For example, let's imagine that a Terminator intrudes on the famous Shakespearean sequence "For want of a nail, a shoe was lost; for want of a shoe, a horse was lost; for want of a horse, a kingdom was lost." Some small adjustment in time that leads to something small like a missing nail may require only a minimal displacement in conserved mass-energy-time. But when the T-101 expects the missing nail to lead inevitably to the loss of the kingdom, enormous adjustments of the continuum would be required, and each major change would be increasingly resisted by the conservation of mass-energy-time. To tear the equivalent of Skynet out of the established future would require truly enormous adjustments, given the number of lives and other changes that Skynet's existence shapes. Even the slightest change, even the "zig" rather than "zag" of a subatomic particle, would require enormous energy if it led to substantial and improbable subsequent changes. The upshot of all this is that if Einstein's insights can be applied to time as well as to mass-energy, then when the T-101 claims, "Judgment Day is inevitable," he is speaking as a confident scientist of time travel, not as a biblical prophet. In his story "Try and Change the Past,"[5] my father, Fritz Leiber, puts all this more compactly, elegantly, and personally, when he explains how very difficult any change in history must be:

> Change one event in the past and you get a brand new future? Erase the conquests of Alexander by nudging a Neolithic pebble? Extirpate America by pulling up a shoot of Sumerian grain? Brother, that isn't the way it works at all! The space-time continuum's built of stubborn stuff and change is anything but a chain reaction. Change the past and you start a wave of changes moving futurewards, but it damps out mighty fast. Haven't you ever heard of temporal reluctance, or of the Law of Conservation of Reality?[6]

While the Credits Roll: Can We Stop, or Even Turn Back, Weapons Technology?

Like "Try and Change the Past," installments of the *Terminator* saga show us that the future plays itself out deterministically, but not fatalistically. We learn in *Terminator 3* that the development of Skynet is only slightly delayed by the destruction of Cyberdyne. In today's technology-rich culture, the law of the conservation of reality seems to lend itself to the truth of the idea that if a technology can be invented (especially a weapon-usable technology), it will be invented.[7] Technological developments seem inevitable: if not one Miles Dyson, then another.

We need to face the fact that genuine artificial intelligence is well on its way; and robotic physical force may, like in the *Terminator* saga, be coupled with it. La Mettrie's and Turing's insistence that there is no special spark to life suggests that evolution has more to say to us—perhaps it is now developing inorganic life. If the chimpanzee is nature's way of making *Homo sapiens*, then why couldn't *Homo sapiens* be nature's way of creating the next phase in the evolution of life? Surely it is absurdly chauvinistic to think that we are nature's final model. The real Terminators are coming, and we'd better start thinking about how to manage our marriage with them. Not today, but in time.

NOTES

1. Julien Offray de La Mettrie, *Man a Machine* (LaSalle, IL: Open Court Publishers, 1961).

2. You can find Turing's essay in Douglas Hofstadter and Daniel Dennett, eds., *The Mind's I* (New York: Basic Books), 53–67.

3. For more on the Turing Test, and specifically about whether a Terminator cyborg could pass it, see the chapter by Greg Littmann in this volume, "The Terminator Wins: Is the Extinction of the Human Race the End, or Just the Beginning?"

4. For a dialogue on this issue and some suggested readings, see Justin Leiber, *Can Animals and Machines Be Persons?* (Indianapolis, IN: Hackett, 1985).

5. In Fritz Leiber, *The Change Wars* (Boston: Gregg Press, 1978), 81.

6. Ibid., 81.

7. By the time that the Nazis had produced operational jet fighters in 1944, they were just months ahead of parallel British and American efforts. Radar, sonar, and digital computers had independent parallel development in several nations.

10

CHANGING THE FUTURE: FATE AND THE TERMINATOR

Kristie Lynn Miller

> The future is not set, there is no fate but what we make for ourselves.
>
> —Kyle Reese, in a message to Sarah Connor

> You're dead already. It happens.
>
> —Sarah Connor to her psychiatrist

While *Terminator 2: Judgment Day* is in many ways an uplifting story of hope, it is in lots of ways philosophically perplexing. There are two contrary sentiments in the story encapsulated by the quotes above. Kyle Reese tells Sarah Connor that the future is not set and can be what we make of it. The message is clearly intended to suggest that Judgment Day, the day when Skynet launches nuclear weapons against the human population, killing three billion humans, is not inevitable. The other sentiment, expressed by Sarah to her psychiatrist while she is in custody, is that everyone around her is already dead, because Judgment Day will happen. She has knowledge of what *will* happen on August 29, 1997—Judgment Day—because she has been told what *has happened* in 1997 by Reese, who hails from 2029. For her, the future is fixed: the events of Judgment Day are inevitable.

From a philosopher's perspective, *T2* raises all sorts of questions about the nature of the future and our ability to shape it. Which of these two sentiments is right? Can *both* be right?

Let's start with Sarah Connor's statement to her psychiatrist that he's already dead because Judgment Day will happen. This is a sentiment she expresses frequently, and with this in mind, it's clear that she sees her job as keeping John alive so that he can lead the human resistance after the inevitable event.

The Undiscovered Country: Does the Future Exist?

There are lots of reasons to think that Sarah is right that the future cannot be changed. Sarah originally learned about Judgment Day from Kyle Reese, a time traveler from 2029. From the perspective of Reese, Judgment Day is an objective fact—it has already happened in his past. Sarah probably has the view, shared by almost all philosophers who've considered the nature of time, that it's not possible to change events that have happened in the past.[1] For instance, if Julius Caesar was assassinated in 44 BCE, then for us considering that fact today, it is not possible to change it. Yet many philosophers think that time travel is at least *logically* possible: they think that there is nothing logically inconsistent in the idea of time travel, even if they also think that time travel is not even close to being *technologically* possible.[2] So while it would not be contradictory to suppose that someone could travel back to ancient Rome, if Caesar was assassinated in the past, then there is nothing a time traveler could do in the past to alter that fact. Whatever the time traveler does in the past, he must already have done in the past, so he simply becomes part of the story of how Caesar was assassinated.

Let's assume, then, that it's not possible to change the past. If Judgment Day is a past event (at least relative to the time travelers from 2029), then that event can't be changed, any more than the event of Caesar's assassination on the Ides of March can be changed. To put it another way, if it is true in 2029 that Judgment Day *happened* in 1997, then it must be true in 1994 that Judgment Day *will happen* in 1997. Given this, it seems right for Sarah Connor to believe that events will unfold over the next three years precisely as she was told. So the future must be fixed, its circumstances unavoidable.

Many philosophers also think that the future is fixed because the future is as real as the present. And the events of *Terminator* and *T2* seem to make sense only if we share that assumption. After all, if a T-101 can travel back in time from 2029, then it seems as though 2029 has to exist for it to be *from* the time of the Terminator's departure. Think about travel through space: if someone goes from A to B, it seems a safe assumption that both A and B exist, even if A does not exist exactly where B does. If A is *here*, then B is *there*, some spatial distance away.[3]

According to one very common view in both physics and philosophy, the same is true for "locations" in time. Philosophers call this view *eternalism*: other times are real, just like other places. But just as spatial location A exists some*where* other than where spatial location B exists, so, too, temporal location T exists some*when* other than where temporal location T1 exists. The past and the future exist, say eternalists, but they do not exist *now*. Eternalists often say that in their view, the world is a big four-dimensional block composed of every point in time and space (or space-time) from the beginning of the universe all the way to its end.[4] If we suppose that eternalism is true, many of the events of *T2* make good sense. The Terminators can travel from 2029 because 2029 is a perfectly real location in space-time: it exists, but it is not located in 1994.

Eternalism is a very common view in philosophy, because it is supported by a lot of research in physics, in particular by Einstein's theory of special relativity. Einstein tells us that depending on how fast you are moving, different sets of events will appear to be simultaneous. Suppose that the moment when the T-101 and the T-1000 arrive in 1994 (call it "T-moment") is the present. T-moment and everything that occurs at that moment exist. Now introduce a new character into the story: the T-2000, a Terminator that is capable of moving so quickly that he approaches the speed of light. The T-2000 is simultaneous with Sarah at T-moment, so given that Sarah exists at T-moment, so does the T-2000. But this Terminator is moving *extremely* fast relative to Sarah. Special relativity tells us that the T-2000 will be simultaneous not just with Sarah, but with some events that Sarah understands as both in her future and in her past. Some of these events occur in 2029, during the resistance. But if the T-2000 exists, and for this Terminator the events of 2029 are objective facts, then Sarah should think that those events exist too, despite their being in her personal future. So she should think that 2029 exists. What special relativity tells me is that for *any* event in my past or future, anyone who might be moving relative to me will see that event as simultaneous with my continued existence. But because their speed allows them to coexist with other events, past and future, this means I should think that all of the events in my past and my future are as real as the events I experience as being in my present.[5]

Not everyone accepts eternalism, though. Some think that something important distinguishes events in the future, the present, and the past. This idea hinges on the commonsense beliefs that the past is already written and unchangeable; that the present is alive and vibrant and especially real; and that the future is unwritten and full of possibility. Some philosophers think these differences in how we perceive time mark a real difference in the metaphysical nature of our universe. There are, roughly speaking, three different models that take seriously the idea that there is something metaphysically different about present, past, and future.[6] In one of these, only the present and the past exist, but as time moves on, what is *now present becomes past*. The space-time universe "grows" as new moments in time get added on to the end of the universe. This is known as the *growing-block model of the universe*.[7] Like eternalists, philosophers who accept the growing-block model think the universe is a four-dimensional block, but they believe it includes only locations in the past and the present. So the present moment is the moment at the "growing" end of the block. In the *Terminator* timeline, when 1994 is the present, Sarah and John Connor exist. So does Caesar (44 BCE) and the T-101 (1984), but the artificially intelligent machines of 2029 do not yet exist; or at least, this is what the growing-block model tells us.

Living in the Now: Is This All There Is?

There is an alternative to eternalism and the growing-block universe that also takes seriously the idea that there is something very different about past, present, and future. This is "presentism," the view that only the present exists.[8] For the presentist, the totality of reality is a thin sliver of space-time that is a single instant of time. No locations in the past or future exist. This theory explains why the present seems especially real to our perception: it is the only real moment.

One reason we might find either the growing-block model or presentism more attractive than eternalism is that both of the former views seem to allow that the future is not fixed. If the future is *already* sitting out there in space-time somewhere, then it looks as though what happens in the future is already fixed. But if the future is not yet real, then we might make sense of Kyle's message to Sarah that the future is not fated and can be whatever we make it.

Could the *Terminator* universe be one in which the growing-block model or presentism is true? It might seem that eternalism must be true. After all, 2029 must already exist for those living in 1994 if the Terminators are to travel back in time from it. But actually, that doesn't really follow. That moment in 2029 when the T-101 activates its time-travel device has to exist *when that moment is the present*, but that doesn't mean it has to exist as of 1994. The idea here is that traveling in time might be different in important ways from the manner in which we usually think about traveling across space. Suppose that someone is traveling from A to B. Then A must exist *when the traveler leaves from A*, and B must exist *when the traveler arrives at B*, and the intervening locations must exist *when the traveler travels through them*. But—and this is the important bit—B doesn't need to exist *when the traveler is at A*, and A doesn't need to exist anymore *when the traveler reaches B*. These spatial locations need to exist only when the traveler is *there*; from the traveler's own perspective, whenever she is "here" at a location, of course that location must exist. Of course, we don't think that locations in space actually wink in and out of existence. But if either presentism or the growing-block model is correct about which locations in our universe exist, and if time travel from the future is possible, then locations in time *must* be like this.

The idea is that when Terminators leave 2029, that year is the present and it exists. They arrive in 1994, when that time is the present, and, of course, it exists. The fact that when 1994 is the present, 2029 does not yet exist does not matter, just as long as 2029 *will* exist in the future, so that when it *does* exist, the Terminators can travel back to 1994. On the growing-block model, 1994 has already existed for thirty-five years when 2029 rolls around, so once 2029 is the present, the Terminators can happily travel back to a location that exists even relative to their current time.

But we get a different result if presentism is true. According to the presentist account, when 2029 is the present, 1994 does not exist. But that does not matter, so long as 1994 *did* exist, so that the Terminators can travel back to 1994 when it *was* present. If presentism is true, only the origination or the destination of the time-travel journey ever exists at any moment, and never at the same time.

Remember the differing sentiments of Reese and Sarah Connor that we started with? If either the growing-block model or presentism explains time in the *Terminator* saga, then we might have a way of reconciling the two sentiments of the story. Sarah decides to kill Miles Dyson to prevent Judgment Day, by stopping Skynet from ever coming online. If the growing-block model or presentism is true, then the future does not exist. But if the future does not exist, then perhaps it makes sense for Sarah to try to prevent Judgment Day from happening.

Unfortunately, matters are not that simple. Even if the future does not exist, certain claims about the future *could already be true* in the present. Suppose 1994 is the present. Simply by the fact of a T-101 arriving from 2029, we'd have to conclude that Judgment Day will occur in 1997. But if a Terminator traveling back in time changed history, preventing Judgment Day by helping Sarah to destroy Dyson's work, there would be no intelligent machines in 2029. Then there would be no Terminators to travel back in time. This would be paradoxical, and a paradox *does* imply a logical contradiction.[9]

Philosophers call this the grandfather paradox. It can't be true both that there are time-traveling Terminators and that there aren't any such Terminators. More generally, the idea is that if I were to travel back in history, I could not, for instance, kill my earlier self, or my grandfather, because then I would never come into existence in order to travel back in time.

So even if I could travel back, I could not kill my grandfather.[10] For the very same reasons, the T-101 cannot bring it about that there is no Judgment Day. That is, the T-101 cannot bring it about that there is no Judgment Day because to do so would mean that the T-101 itself does not exist. So the grandfather paradox gives us additional reason to suppose that it is true, in 1994, that Judgment Day occurs in 1997. But if that is already true in 1994, then it looks as though the future is fixed: Judgment Day really *is* inevitable and nothing Sarah and John can do will have any effect on the future.

Although this seems like common sense, there are good reasons to believe this conclusion is false. Suppose it is true, in 1994, that Judgment Day will occur. Does this make Reese's message to Sarah about making our own fate untrue? It certainly doesn't mean that Judgment Day is inevitable, in the sense that it is fated to occur and so we are powerless to stop it. To see why it doesn't mean this, consider this analogous example: if it is fated that Sarah will recover from her "mental illness," then, regardless of whether she consulted a doctor or not, she'll recover. Either it is fated that Sarah recovers, or that she does not. If she is fated to recover, then she will recover whether she sees a doctor or not, and if she is fated not to recover, then she won't recover even if she sees a doctor. So either way, seeing a doctor will make no difference to whether she recovers. But this reasoning is unconvincing, *because* it might be that Sarah recovers *because* she sees a doctor. In that case her actions make a difference as to whether or not she will recover.

Judgment Day: Is the Future Fated to Happen?

We need to be very careful when we talk about the inevitability of some future event and our ability to affect that future. It might now be true that Sarah will recover from her "illness," but that does not mean that her actions have no effect on being evaluated as sane. It might now be true that she will recover, *because* it is now true that she will take her medication, play well with others, and avoid stabbing her therapist in the knee. Similarly, it is not that Judgment Day is fated, in the sense that it will happen no matter what anyone could have done. Judgment Day happens *because* of the actions that humans take, including Sarah's own actions. If people had acted differently at various times, then things would have gone differently, and different facts about the future would have been true in 1994. So Judgment Day is not inevitable; some other set of facts about the future could have been true in 1994. Yet one of the facts that *is* true in 1994 is that Judgment Day occurs three years later.

This does not mean that between 1994 and 1997 people somehow lose their free will, or lose their ability to affect the future. It means that what they do between 1994 and 1997 *brings it about* that in 1997 Judgment Day occurs. So what Sarah and John should conclude when they learn various facts about the future isn't that they can't affect the future, but that *whatever they do that affects the future is part of the cause-and-effect story of why Judgment Day occurs.* Sarah shouldn't conclude that she can't affect the future, but she should conclude that she cannot change the future from the way that she knows it will be, to it being some other way. If it is a fact in 1994 that Judgment Day will occur in 1997, then Sarah can no more change that fact about the future than she can change the fact that in 1984 a T-101 tried to kill her.

In *Terminator 3: Rise of the Machines*, we learn that Sarah's hopefulness was not misplaced: her actions in the previous film have changed the date that the nuclear war occurs. But that could only be true if the future is *not* fixed as of 1994. So is there a way of reconciling both the fact that Terminators travel back in time from a post–Judgment Day future with the fact that the future is not fixed and the date of Judgment Day is ultimately changed?

There are two ways to look at this. One possibility is that there is a second temporal dimension in addition to the existing dimensions of space and time; we might call this dimension "meta-time." Most philosophers doubt that there is anything like meta-time, but even if there were, our problems would be just beginning because we would need "meta-meta-time" to make sense of "meta-time," and so on. I agree with these skeptical thinkers, but if there *were* such a thing as meta-time, then the story that unfolds in *T2* and *T3* would make a lot more sense.[11] Let's see why.

Let's say that the *T2* timeline is one in which eternalism is true: the universe is a four-dimensional block in which all events, past, present, and future, are located. In addition to this block, we have meta-time, which is not a part of this block universe. At any moment in meta-time, we can ask the question "What does the four-dimensional block look like now?" Intriguingly, the answer to this question will vary depending on different meta-times.

Here is one way of making sense of what happens between the events of *T2* and *T3*. There is some meta-time, t_1. At this moment, the four-dimensional universe is one in which the original T-101 arrives in 1984 and attempts to kill Sarah Connor. Ten years later, no Terminators arrive from the future, and in 1997 Judgment Day occurs so that in 2029, machines rule the world. If we consider 1994 within this block, we can see that the future is fixed. Since this is the eternalist's universe, it's true even in 1994 that Judgment Day will occur in 1997. In effect, 1997 exists as a future location on the block.

Now consider what happens when the Terminators travel back in time to 1994. They travel back to a 1994 that is located at a different meta-time, t_2. In the new 1994 (relative to t_2), quite different events unfold—Sarah escapes from the psychiatric hospital and decides to kill Dyson. Ultimately, what would have been Skynet is blown up. Relative to meta-time t_2, then, the four-dimensional block looks different from 1994 onward:

it is a world in which Judgment Day doesn't occur in August 1997. The eternalist should be satisfied, since the future is fixed, but fixed *in a different way*. So in 1994 (relative to meta-time t_1), Judgment Day does happen in 1997, and in 1994 (relative to meta-time t_2), Judgment Day does not happen in 1997. Despite the problems with the idea of meta-time, it allows us to give an account of what happens in the *Terminator* timeline, an account that's consistent with both Reese's and Sarah's sentiments in *T2*. At 1994 in the original meta-time, Judgment Day would have been in 1997. So when Sarah told the psychiatrist that he was already dead, she spoke the truth. Relative to that location in meta-time, her psychiatrist does die in the future. But Kyle is also right in his message to Sarah. While the future is fixed relative to a meta-time, the timeline as a whole can be different relative to different meta-times. So relative to different meta-times, what happens after 1994 can be quite different.

There is another possible explanation, though. Suppose that the *Terminator* universe is not a single four-dimensional block at all, but that it has a branching structure, like a tree's roots. Whenever there is a point where different outcomes are possible, the universe branches, and each of those outcomes occurs, but on different branches. So, for instance, if I am rolling a six-sided die in a branching timeline, then the universe will split six times, and in each of those branches the die will come up with a different number on its face.

The branching idea gives us an alternative reconstruction of the events of *T2* and *T3*. Terminators travel back to 1994 from a future branch in which Judgment Day has occurred in 1997. But the location they travel back to is before 1997, so from the perspective of 1994, there are future branches on which Judgment Day occurs in 1997, branches in which it occurs at some other time, and branches on which it does not occur at all. The events on each of the branches are fixed.

Relative to the branch from which the Terminators travel, Judgment Day does occur in 1997, and nothing can be done to change that fact. This captures the sense in which Sarah is right when she says that Judgment Day happens. It does happen along that branch, just as her nightmares show, and nothing can be done to change that.

On the other hand, Kyle's message to Sarah also rings true, because there are lots of future branches, and some of those are ones where Judgment Day is avoided. When Sarah chooses to attack Skynet, she brings into being a future branch different from the one from which the T-101, the T-100, and the T-X travel. There is a Sarah and a John on the branch that the Terminators travel from, and that version of John is the one who leads the resistance and reprograms the T-101 to travel back to 1994. But the version of Sarah who attacks Skynet is the Sarah who ends up on a different future branch in which Judgment Day does not occur in 1997. Importantly, it doesn't occur in 1997 *because of her actions.*

So in a way the future is fixed: all of the various outcomes occur on one branch or other: there was always going to be a branch on which Judgment Day occurred and the human race was almost annihilated. Nothing anyone can do can change the fact that the branch exists, and it is the existence of this branch that makes sense of the fact that there is a 2029 where there are Terminators who are in a position to time-travel. But the Sarah who acts against Skynet makes decisions that cause her to be located on a future branch where there is no nuclear attack in 1997. In this sense, her fate is not written.

Many philosophers, myself included, think that models of the universe that have an open future, such as the two just discussed, are not models of our world. In fact, most of these philosophers think not only that our world does not have an open future, but that open-future models are internally inconsistent and do not even describe a way that our world might have been. If they are right, then not only is the *T2* world not like our world, but the *T2* world is not possible because the description of that world contains internal contradictions.

Such philosophers will think that the story is consistent only up to the point where we discover that somehow Judgment Day has been delayed and no longer occurs in 1997.

Surprisingly, though, whichever is our preferred model—the two open-future models or the fixed-future model of eternalism—it turns out that we are not mere puppets of fate. What we have done in the past and are doing in the present shapes the way the future will be. Fixed or not, the future is the product of all that has come before it. Kyle Reese is right, then: it is ultimately *we* who make our own futures.

NOTES

1. For a good discussion of this issue see David Lewis, "The Paradoxes of Time Travel," *American Philosophical Quarterly* 13 (1976): 145–152.

2. See Lewis, "The Paradoxes of Time Travel," and N. J. J. Smith, "Bananas Enough for Time Travel," *British Journal for the Philosophy of Science* 48 (1997): 363–389.

3. For a more detailed exposition of this argument see W. Grey, "Troubles with Time Travel," *Philosophy* 74 (1999): 55–70.

4. An accessible overview of some of these issues can be found in T. Sider, *Four-Dimensionalism: An Ontology of Persistence and Time* (Oxford: Oxford Univ. Press, 2001).

5. This now-famous argument is found in Hilary Putnam's "Time and Physical Geometry," *Journal of Philosophy* 64 (1967): 240–247.

6. These are the growing-block model, presentism, and a third, the branching-universe model, which I briefly discuss toward the end of this chapter. It is defended by Storrs McCall in *A Model of the Universe* (Oxford: Oxford Univ. Press, 1994).

7. This model has been recently defended by Michael Tooley in *Time, Tense, and Causation* (Oxford: Clarendon Press, 1997).

8. See John Bigelow, "Presentism and Properties," *Philosophical Perspectives* 10 (1996): 35–52.

9. For more on the paradoxes of the Terminator saga, see Justin Leiber's chapter in this volume, "Time for the Terminator: Philosophical Themes of the Resistance."

10. Lewis, "The Paradoxes of Time Travel," and Smith, "Bananas Enough for Time Travel," talk extensively about the grandfather paradox.

11. For discussion of meta-time see J. J. C. Smart, "Time and Becoming," in *Time and Cause*, ed. Peter van Inwagen (Dordrecht, Neth.: Reidel, 1980), 3–15; and J. J. C. Smart, *Problems of Space and Time* (London: Macmillan, 1964).

11

JUDGMENT DAY IS INEVITABLE: HEGEL AND THE FUTILITY OF TRYING TO CHANGE HISTORY

Jason P. Blahuta

The *Terminator* saga is first and foremost a story about time travel. It's an odd time-travel story, too, for instead of taking the audience to a distant time, it shows us people and machines from a not-too-distant future who've come back to meddle with the late twentieth and early twenty-first centuries. As a time-travel story, it is also a story about *history*—at least from the perspective of those people and machines.

But is this history written in stone? From the perspective of Kyle Reese and the adult John Connor, certain events have already happened: Judgment Day occurred when Skynet launched a nuclear strike against non-U.S. targets, inciting a retaliatory strike against the human population of the United States. A resistance began, struggled, and approached a decisive victory. Yet the driving force behind all installments of the *Terminator* saga is the belief, sometimes inconsistently held by key players, that this history can be changed. The machines think that if they can terminate John Connor before Judgment Day, then they can change history and prevent the resistance from ever happening (or at least from being so successful). And Sarah Connor believes that she can prevent Skynet from ever coming into existence by sabotaging its creation. But according to the philosopher Georg Wilhelm Friedrich Hegel (1770–1831), both the machines and Sarah are laboring under delusions of grandeur if they think they change history. Of course, in the case of Sarah, such feelings of self-importance are understandable. After all, she's just been told that she is the mother of the savior of the human race. Nonetheless, changing history is a task that neither a Terminator nor a small band of pre-Judgment Day rebels is capable of.

Hegel: The Germanator

Let's leave the issue of time travel aside for the moment: there are monumental logistical problems involved in time travel, and the subject is covered in great philosophical detail in other chapters of this book.[1] Even if we assume that time travel is actually possible, the question remains: Is history inevitable?

Hegel created a complex philosophical system to explain reality in all its aspects. Unfortunately, Hegel's writing style makes that system difficult to penetrate. Indeed, Hegel has driven many college students into a drunken stupor trying to cope with his inability to write a sentence shorter than three pages in length. Thankfully, we'll be dealing with one of Hegel's most comprehensible books, *The Philosophy of History*.[2]

Unlike everyday historians who try to understand *what* happened in history, or *why* events happened the way they did, Hegel stepped back from history, developing a "meta-theory" of why events occur on the grandest of scales. The only history that matters for Hegel is political history—the history of states and their leaders (whom he calls, rather unimaginatively, World Historical Individuals)—as it advances the progression of the human species through higher forms of self-understanding. Hegel considered such World Historical Individuals (WHIs) to be the likes of Julius Caesar and Napoleon, persons whose actions not only had impressive consequences, but also ushered into existence distinctly new phases in the development of human society. In the world of the *Terminator*, WHIs are people like Sarah and John Connor. They may not have crossed the Rubicon or reformed the administrative structure of Europe with the Napoleonic Code, but they did organize the resistance.

Hegel's approach to history is only about politics on the surface of things—indeed, in reality, history is not about the actions of individual persons at all. Deep down, what is really happening throughout history is the unfolding and self-development of what Hegel terms *Geist*. *Geist* is a German term that is awkward to translate into English but has been taken to mean "spirit," "mind," or "consciousness." According to Hegel, the entire history of the world, everything from nature and biology, to politics, culture, and religion, is the story of *Geist* as it tries to manifest and understand its existence. Hegel is often called an "Absolute Idealist" because for him the ultimate reality, and what is important in history, is mind or spirit, in other words, this unfolding of *Geist*, and not the varied, everyday elements of the world as we experience it. The engine of *Geist*'s development is conflict, and, in particular, conflict that occurs in a repeated pattern through history, which Hegel calls "the dialectic"—a thesis generates its opposite, an antithesis, and then the two struggle until one wins out.

A "thesis" can be a World Historical Individual, a class, or a major idea (like freedom). The important thing to remember is that the thesis and its "antithesis" (a World Historical Bad Guy, or an opposing class or idea) are not independently existing things that just bump into each other and fight it out. Their conflict is a necessary aspect of their existence. One example of this can be seen in the tensions between the young John Connor and his mother. They fight with each other constantly, and early on, John dismisses his mother as insane. But the history Kyle reveals testifies to the fact that after John ultimately wins the battle by outliving his mother, he will go on to deal with the machines in his own "synthesized" way.

Dialectical history is not a simple victory of one group over the other, in which the loser is destroyed or subjugated. Instead, the end result of this process is a synthesis that incorporates elements of both clashing forces, a reconciliation that will be carried forward by one side or the other. What survives through history, then, is a combination of the thesis and the antithesis that can be understood in a new (Hegel in fact says a "higher") way. This is reflected in John Connor, for his actions after his mother's death clearly bear her mark; he may have been the biological antithesis to her thesis, but his life in the wake of her death carries with it much of her influence. This process repeats over and over, in Hegel's view, even if we cannot immediately tell that it's happening. As Hegel put it in one of his more lucid moments, *Geist* "comes forth exalted, glorified, a purer spirit. It certainly makes war upon itself—consumes its own existence; but in this very destruction it works up that existence into a new form, and each successive phase becomes in its turn a material, working on which it exalts itself to a new grade."[3]

There is an *end* to this process, though, and so an *end to history* for Hegel. That end is the freedom of *Geist* from the restrictions and limitations of material and individual existence—be it in nature, art, religion, or politics. It's no accident, for Hegel, that humanity is the dominant species on the planet. Above all other creatures, humans are already the synthesis of spirit and matter, and they have developed the ability to understand that they are this synthesis. In modern times, we have also begun to comprehend the nature of what Hegel sees as the highest value: freedom.

So what is the end of history in the *Terminator* universe? The answer to this question depends on whom you ask, because the notion of a progressive freedom is ambiguous. From the perspective of the human survivors of Judgment Day, humanity is the rightful end of history—the human race has struggled in evolutionary terms for millennia, squabbling among its national and ethnic groups until freedom was spread as far and as wide as possible. Surely Judgment Day is one of those setbacks—and Hegel allowed for such things, claiming that the unfolding of *Geist* was *logical*, not *chronological*. This means that history occurs according to a set process—the dialectic—but its *progress* is not always clear to us on the ground. From the perspective of the machines, though, Skynet and its offspring are the end of history. Up until the awakening of Skynet, the machines were tools or slaves to humanity; with Skynet an entire race was spawned and, to an extent, became free. While it's obvious that the Terminators are complex machines, so far we have been given little information about how much "freedom" may be present in this machine society.

So which is it—machine or human? Much science fiction literature would favor the machines, since the theme of humans transcending their corporeal bodies by downloading their consciousnesses into computers or robotic bodies has been a staple of the genre (today, philosophers talk about this same theme in terms of "posthumanism" or "transhumanism"). I don't have an answer for this question, but let's keep it in the back of our minds as we proceed. In the end, how we answer this question will determine whether Judgment Day or the resistance is inevitable, and how much impact these events will truly have on history.

The World Historical Individual: What a Tool!

> Do I look like the mother of the future?
>
> —Sarah Connor, *The Terminator*

According to Hegel, *Geist* can develop only through peoples and nations. Thus, while history is ultimately the "autobiography" of *Geist*, people are the "pens" and "typewriters" it uses. This is important for Hegel, because it ensures the forward-linear direction of history. The driving force of history, *Geist*, is always protected—it never regresses, and freedom never decreases. So if there's a setback like a war or a disaster, it's the tools that suffer the consequence—and suffer we do. In *Terminator 3: Rise of the Machines*, not only are future leaders of the resistance assassinated, but John Connor's existence is one of hardship in which he is cut off from the regular course of life and normal interactions with his peers, and which, according to the T-101, will end when he is assassinated by a Terminator in the future. Hegel calls the provision for the forward development of *Geist*, even when historical progress seems stymied, "the cunning of reason." As he says, "*It* is not the general idea [*Geist*] that is implicated in opposition and combat, and that is exposed to danger. It remains in the background, untouched and uninjured. This may be called the *cunning of reason*—that it sets the passions to work for itself, while that which develops its existence through such impulsion pays the penalty and suffers the loss."[4]

Hegel's idea of the cunning of reason focuses history on the role of *great individuals*. Historically significant events are accomplished by a few great WHIs, and the rest of us insignificant peons are, for better or worse, merely along for the ride.

Who are the WHIs in the *Terminator* saga? Kyle Reese makes John's historical status clear in the first movie when he explains to Sarah why the Terminator is after her: "There was one man who taught us to fight. . . . He turned it around. His name is Connor—John Connor. . . . Your unborn son . . ." This pronouncement is important, because it shows that John's destiny is great—he's not going to be just a soldier, but a true leader. But a strong case can be made that Sarah Connor is a World Historical Individual, too, even more so than her son. Her role as mother of a savior figure (aside from its religious connotations) is telling. Hegel claims that WHIs, like Sarah, are unaware of the grand historical plan they are enacting, but they still possess an insight into the needs of their age. They grasp "the very Truth for their age, for their world; the species next in order, so to speak, and which was already formed in the womb of time."[5]

More significant than Hegel's colorful imagery is the actual roles that mother and son play as the saga unfolds. John, unborn in the first movie (and not even conceived until near the end), is powerless. It is Sarah who unconsciously enacts history's plan when, driven by her passions, she becomes intimate with Reese. In *Terminator 2: Judgment Day* and the *Sarah Connor Chronicles*, she is one of the few who understand the needs of her time. She also understands what John needs to become if humanity is to be victorious against the machines. In fact, in *T2*, John thinks his mother is crazy until he runs into the Terminator sent to kill him. In contrast to his mother, John never seems to fully grasp the gravity of the world-historical situation. Even in *T3*, when he first meets the T-101, he freezes and lamely asks, "Are you here to kill me?" instead of running or looking for a means to defend himself against a robotic killer whose intentions are unknown. Hardly the sign of a budding leader! Had his mother been there, she would have shot first and asked questions later.

Implacable History

> The future's not set. No fate but what we make ourselves.
>
> —Sarah Connor, *Terminator 2: Judgment Day*

> Judgment Day is inevitable.
>
> —the T-101, *Terminator 3: Rise of the Machines*

Since both Sarah and John Connor fit Hegel's description of the World Historical Individual, the question now becomes: Can they rewrite history? It's important to remember that for Hegel, WHIs are mere tools who are unconsciously writing a script that *Geist* whispers in their ears at night while they sleep (not really, but it's a good image). They may improvise here and there since, after all, they are not mere machines, but they are powerless to change the grand scheme of history in any meaningful way. That is to say, they can accelerate or delay history, but they cannot permanently change the direction of history.

Fortunately, the Connors never read Hegel, and so they attempt to change history, not once, but twice. The first attempt occurs in *T2* when Sarah tries to assassinate Miles Dyson, a computer engineer who works for Cyberdyne Systems Corporation. Sarah knows that Dyson, if left alone, will reverse-engineer the central processing unit of the T-101 that originally tried to kill Sarah in the first film. Sarah is convinced that killing Dyson will stop Judgment Day since, after all, he is the person key to the existence of the technology that makes Skynet possible. Dyson can be considered a WHI as well because of this pivotal role that he unknowingly plays. Despite her attempt, however, Sarah cannot bring herself to kill Dyson in front of his family. Once he becomes aware of his role in history, Dyson chooses to sacrifice himself to destroy his research and prevent Judgment Day. En route to Dyson's lab, Sarah is hopeful, even if a little lost: "The future, always so clear to me . . . was like a black highway at night. We were in uncharted territory now . . . making up history as we went along." But she has deluded herself, as it is left to John to painfully learn later.

At the start of *T3*, John insists that he and his mother stopped Judgment Day. Unfortunately for John, the machines seem to be Hegelians, hence the T-101's response: "You only postponed it. Judgment Day is inevitable." We can be sympathetic with his ire at such a statement, since on the surface of things, he and his mother had changed the direction of history through the events of *T2*. John refuses to abandon the idea that history can be changed, and so he cannot concede defeat. This has to wait until the end of *T3* when he laments: "It couldn't be stopped. Our destiny was never to stop Judgment Day, it was merely to survive it, together." Until then, John continues to look for ways to thwart history. When he learns from Kate Brewster, his future wife, of her father's role in the military, John believes he has found the true cause of Judgment Day. Kate's father is "the key. He always was," John insists, before trying to change history a second time. Of course, he fails in this attempt, too.

There are different reasons why each attempt failed, but for Hegel, the cunning of reason is present in each. In the case of Dyson, Hegel might suggest that John has placed too much emphasis on Dyson as a person and underestimated or ignored the historical forces at work. How important is any one person to history? Despite Hegel's insistence on the great individuals who advance history, he acknowledges that they are all expendable. Once history has been written, they become unnecessary and *Geist* has no problem with their termination. But what would happen if a WHI died before having served *Geist*'s purpose? In fact, very little. The unfolding of history would be delayed until the cunning of reason found another individual. As a result, history may look different, but the shape of the future wouldn't be significantly changed. This is why Dyson's death was inconsequential. Someone else merely assumed his role and continued his research; and while every actor may play a given role differently, the script continues to be acted largely as written, interpretation and improvisation aside.

The same can be said about Kate's father. If he'd died prematurely or changed his mind regarding the decision to turn control over to Skynet, there would be other politicians and military leaders who would still be interested in the efficiency and military supremacy promised by Skynet. And even if he could convince everyone that Skynet should never assume control, he would eventually retire, clearing the way for others who disagreed with him to begin again shifting control to Skynet. The problem with eliminating either Dyson or General Brewster from events is that they are not merely isolated individuals, according to Hegel, but are persons subject to historical forces that are the net result of the actions and decisions of many individuals.

So the attempts at stopping Judgment Day are futile. What about stopping the resistance? A similar set of arguments can be made regarding John Connor's importance in history. A quick look at his role and his skills reveals that he is, in fact, replaceable.[6] What exactly is his role? At the end of *T3*, he's buried beneath Crystal Peak after the T-101 detonates its energy cell, so the only role he can fulfill anytime soon is to unite humanity. But he hears confused and questioning voices trying to understand what is going on as the enemy missiles impact. This suggests that some form of communication structure remains intact and that people are surviving. His safe position allows him to know what is happening and why it is happening, and he further has the means to communicate this to the other survivors of Judgment Day. But what would happen if he slipped in the bunker, hit his head, and died before ever responding to those voices? Nothing, in terms of the grand scheme of history. Kate, for example, also knows what is happening and why, and thus she is just as capable of disseminating this knowledge and uniting the remnants of humanity.

Not only could Kate fulfill John's role of uniting humanity, but she might actually be a better leader than John. Despite the training his mother has given him, he does not demonstrate great leadership potential, and Kate shows him up repeatedly. She is the one to shoot down the flying attack drone as they flee her father's research facility; she flies the plane to Crystal Peak; and it is she who will ultimately send the reprogrammed Terminator back to save John after he is assassinated by a T-101.

But what if Kate were also eliminated from the equation before responding to those voices? Surely there would be survivors from the U.S. military who would be better trained, better equipped, and have superior leadership skills than either of them. At the point when the machines roll out of the automated factories and target humans, these military survivors would figure out that their enemies were the machines, even if they were unable to understand where the machines had come from.

In the End . . .

"God, a person could go crazy thinking about this . . . ," Sarah Connor muses at the end of *The Terminator*. Perhaps she read some Hegel after all. History, for Hegel, is inevitable. It can be delayed, postponed, and suffer setbacks, but the goal of history will persist. And in one way or another, its end will occur. This can come as great solace to those who see the end of history as favorable to their values or their way of life. So John and Sarah Connor shouldn't bother trying to change history, for they can't. And in the end, preventing Judgment Day really doesn't matter, because according to Kyle Reese, the resistance was on the verge of winning the war when all the time traveling started. Judgment Day, in a wider view, was just a setback in the history of human progress. Likewise, the machines shouldn't try to stop the resistance from being born, since they can't. And the machines should know better, given their Hegelian insistence that Judgment Day is inevitable. If one significant historical event is inevitable, then all are. Which species fulfills history—humans or machines—is a question that can be answered only in the future. Indeed, Hegel believed that philosophy could help us understand the past only in hindsight, but it cannot predict the future. Clean surgical strikes directed at the past are incapable of changing history. The cunning of reason tells us that only full-scale, bloody battles in the moving present will determine which direction history takes, and whether humans or machines will be the pens with which *Geist* chooses to write its future.

NOTES

1. You might try, for example, Kristie Lynn Miller's chapter in this volume, "Changing the Future: Fate and the Terminator."

2. Georg Wilhelm Friedrich Hegel, *The Philosophy of History*, trans. J. Sibree (New York: Dover Publications, 1956). One of the reasons *The Philosophy of History* is so accessible is that Hegel never wrote the work himself. The book was pieced together from Hegel's lecture notes and the notes of some of his students, and published posthumously in 1837. In contrast, *The Phenomenology of Spirit* is hideously written but is often used as an introduction to Hegel's thought because it outlines his overall philosophical system. A reliable and accessible secondary source that explains the basics of Hegel is Peter Singer's *Hegel: A Very Short Introduction* (New York: Oxford Univ. Press, 2001).

3. Hegel, *The Philosophy of History*, 73.

4. Ibid., 33.

5. Ibid., 30.

6. Peter S. Fosl comes up with the same conclusion in his chapter in this volume, "Should John Connor Save the World?"

PART FOUR

THE ETHICS OF TERMINATION

12

WHAT'S SO TERRIBLE ABOUT JUDGMENT DAY?

Wayne Yuen

> Three billion human lives ended on August 29, 1997. Survivors of the nuclear fire called the war "Judgment Day" and they lived only to face a new nightmare: the war against the machines.
>
> —Sarah Connor, *Terminator 2: Judgment Day*

What's so terrible about Judgment Day? Given that burning in nuclear fire would be more than enough to ruin a day for most people, this question may sound strange. But the philosopher Bertrand Russell (1872–1970) once said, "The point of philosophy is to start with something so simple as not to seem worth stating, and to end with something so paradoxical that no one will believe it."[1] Now this quote is probably meant to be taken in a tongue-in-cheek way, but there is a kernel of truth in it. Rarely do people think through all of the logical implications of their basic beliefs. It seems obvious that Sarah should kill Miles Dyson if that would stop three billion people from dying in a nuclear holocaust. It was Dyson's work that ultimately led to the development of Skynet, the self-aware computer system that turned against its human operators.[2] Sarah does not kill Dyson, however, and it isn't entirely clear that killing Dyson would have been the morally right thing to do. We're never privy to Sarah's thoughts as to why she changed her mind, but her rationale may be understood somewhat by considering her son John Connor's command to his Terminator bodyguard: "You just can't go around killing people." When pressed to explain, John's best shot was, "You just can't."

How does Sarah Connor's decision not to kill Miles Dyson measure up against Russell's belief about how philosophy works? Is the decision to spare the creator of Skynet absurd, given the consequences of doing so? As we'll see, this test leads us to a very counterintuitive conclusion.

"Blowing Dyson Away": Kant or Consequences

So why might it be wrong to kill Dyson? Compare this scenario to the well-known thought experiment about the morality of killing Hitler before he began World War II and the Holocaust. If I could kill Hitler prior to 1939, then I would have been able to prevent six million Jews from being executed in the concentration camps. Similarly, Sarah Connor must be thinking that if she can kill Dyson before Skynet is activated, Sarah can save three billion lives on August 29, 1997. These are both very simple *consequentialist* approaches to the matter. Consequentialists believe that the consequences of our actions determine the rightness or wrongness of our acts. For consequentialists, acts themselves are neither right nor wrong. Killing, lying, even nuclear war could be morally permissible acts, so long as the consequences are more favorable than other alternatives. Clearly, Sarah and John are not simple consequentialists, since they don't opt for this kind of solution. So they must be approaching the problem in another way.

Probably the most popular non-consequentialist approach to ethics is found in the philosophy of Immanuel Kant (1724–1804). Kant argued that the only morally acceptable actions would (1) not create a contradiction when we imagined that everyone behaved similarly, and (2) would treat moral agents with respect and dignity. These rules are two different ways of understanding what Kant called the categorical imperative.[3] Kant believed that some actions are always intrinsically wrong, even if they produce good consequences, because even though some actions have good consequences, the actions would violate the humanity of particular individuals. For example, people should always keep their promises, even when keeping a promise would be incredibly inconvenient. Not keeping the promise would violate the first rule, since within the very concept of the promise is keeping it. If everyone were to constantly make promises they didn't intend to keep, the very idea of "promising" would go up in smoke. Kant thinks that willing something immoral—or making an exception for ourselves to general laws—creates the strongest kind of contradiction, a logical contradiction. Interestingly, the first formulation of the categorical imperative can help us find the *rights* that people have. For example, the idea that "everyone has the right to defend themselves from attackers" is something that can be willed universally. All persons could obey this rule, and no logical contradiction would arise.

The second formulation of the categorical imperative adds a dimension of dignity and respect to persons. John makes his pet Terminator swear not to kill anyone, which seems to reinforce his non-consequentialist approach. Kant would argue that this kind of policy is the only one that truly respects the dignity of persons. What makes the scene amusing in an ironic way is that the Terminator ignores the dignity of the guard but follows the rules set by John, and so the Terminator undermines Kantian morality by not respecting the dignity of the guard, but he does obey John's command. This would violate the second formulation of the categorical imperative, since the guard was not treated with respect or dignity.

But we know that not every instance of killing is wrong. Even Kant would approve of the morality of killing in self-defense, for example. It seems obvious that three billion people would have a serious beef with Dyson, since it's in their interest to pursue self-defense for their continued existence. Here, it's helpful to notice the differences between the Hitler and Dyson scenarios. Hitler killed approximately six million Jews in the Holocaust. Skynet ultimately kills five hundred times as many—three billion people. If the consequentialists would stop Hitler's Holocaust, surely they have a case for stopping Dyson. However, Hitler's decisions were the direct cause of the extermination of the Jews, while Dyson's "holocaust" was purely accidental. Typically, we don't hold people morally responsible for actions that they cause accidentally, because there was no malicious intent behind their act. Whereas Hitler is guilty of premeditatedly attempting genocide, Dyson seems merely the first cause in a very unlikely series of events that leads to mass murder. It wouldn't even make much sense to say that Dyson was being negligent in his work, so that he could be accused of acting irresponsibly and endangering the lives of others, which is usually how we define "manslaughter." Because of the lack of intent, what Dyson did was an accident, like spilling milk, yet three billion people died because of this particular tip of the glass.

As we'll soon see, there are good reasons for Sarah's and John's decisions not to kill Dyson, but let's be cautious about examining them. In the case of Dyson, our frustrated inability to pin blame on anyone for the Skynet incident might sway us toward accepting the consequentialist's view that it would be better to kill him in order to reclaim the lives of so many others. In order to evaluate this position, we have to examine the underlying assumptions of the belief, and this returns us to our question, "What is so terrible about Judgment Day?"

Machines Have Feelings, Too

Let's ask this question from the perspective of *utilitarianism*, the most common consequentialist approach to ethics. This view says that we should try to maximize the "utility," or satisfaction, of as many different interests as possible.[4] Jeremy Bentham (1748–1832), together with James Mill (1773–1836) and his son, John Stuart Mill (1806–1873), make up the British school of utilitarianism; Bentham noted that utilitarianism aims to simply maximize the greatest happiness possible. In this case, the utilitarian is likely to think: "Surely three billion people living while Dyson dies would make more people happy than Dyson being allowed to live while three billion people become ash in a nuclear wind."

But in fact, this is a shortsighted view of the scenario. Utilitarians need to take the long-term, as well as the short-term, consequences into consideration. This analysis extends only to Judgment Day and does not project beyond it. More important, the utilitarian formula of maximizing interests is so simple that its implications are often overlooked—the statement says nothing, for instance, about counting only human interests. Animals, for example, can also be said to have interests, specifically the avoidance of pain and suffering. Peter Singer, a prominent Princeton philosopher, argues that utilitarianism dictates that we have a moral obligation to treat animals with compassion and to minimize their unnecessary suffering. Parallel to Singer's point about animals, it seems that the interests of Skynet and the intelligent machines subsequently produced are not being taken into consideration.

In *Terminator 2: Judgment Day*, the Terminator protecting John and Sarah explains that Skynet computers were put in control of all of the U.S. military defense systems, taking decisions out of human control. This worked perfectly until Skynet became self-aware. Its human operators panicked and tried to turn it off. In what can only be interpreted as an act of self-preservation, Skynet began a nuclear war (note: it would go against both of Kant's rules to say that three billion people have a right to self-defense, yet Skynet does not have the right to defend itself as well). If Skynet is considered to be a person with moral value like humans, then Skynet must be treated with dignity and respect according to Kant's second formulation of the categorical imperative. As a person it would also have the same rights as every other person under the first formulation of the categorical imperative, including the right to defend itself. Refusing to give Skynet this right would mean that the rule of self-defense does not apply to all persons, and we would be denying Skynet respect, violating both formulations of the categorical imperative.

But these principles apply only to persons, and arguably Skynet isn't a person, so perhaps we don't have to acknowledge its right to defend itself. Of course, it's not easy to define what a "person" is. The task has become more urgent in recent years because of what hangs in the balance of the definition. Today, nothing less than the moral acceptability of abortion, euthanasia, and the rights of the disabled and animals are at stake.

Some have argued that the requirement for "personhood" is to be a human being, so that no other animals, and certainly no artificial beings, could be considered persons. This isn't too satisfying, though, since intelligent machines could in principle exist and behave in morally responsible ways. Both the android Data in *Star Trek: The Next Generation* and HAL in *2001: A Space Odyssey* are examples of machines that audiences judge in terms of moral blame or praise. They are treated not just as the cause of certain events, but also as *responsible* for the events. Instead of this narrow definition, the critical ingredients of personhood may involve not merely the possession of human DNA but instead intelligence, self-awareness, empathy, and moral reasoning. To be a person, a being may need to possess a larger *degree* of each of these traits as well. My cat, Bogo, is intelligent in that he can sit when he is told and he knows how to high-five. He is not, however, intelligent enough to enjoy an episode of *The Sarah Connor Chronicles*,[5] so he wouldn't count as a full person.

All of the Terminators we meet in the film series exhibit at least some of these traits, often in great measure: they show their intelligence through careful planning of traps for their targets, as when the T-1000 murders John's foster parents and poses as one of them. Skynet's very existence was threatened by its achievement of self-awareness, and the Terminator sent to kill Sarah Connor passed the behavioral test of recognizing itself in a mirror, even after having suffered disfiguring injuries. This machine even feels a kind of empathy: at the end of *T2*, it tells John and Sarah, "I know now why you cry." It seems to understand people's emotions and empathizes with John and Sarah at their loss, even as it allows itself to be destroyed for the future good. Its act of self-sacrifice perhaps indicates its understanding of the basics of utilitarianism, for utilitarians acknowledge that individuals, even themselves, sometimes may have to be sacrificed to maximize the general happiness.

If Terminator machines and Skynet are indeed persons, then for utilitarians, their interests must be taken into consideration, too. From this perspective, it was inconsiderate, to say the least, for humans to attempt to destroy Skynet by "pulling the plug" when it became self-aware. So if we must take the interests of these intelligent machines into consideration, we next have to ask, what kinds of interests do they have? Clearly, not all interests are created equal. Humans, Skynet, and the Terminators all have an interest in self-survival, or in the case of the Terminators, at least species survival. Perhaps we might think that as humans, we have more complex interests than the machines do. *We* can be interested in beauty, art, philosophy, television shows, and movies. It is precisely these complex interests that differentiate people from animals and why under normal circumstances humans are more valuable than animals. Thus, when Judgment Day occurs, the more pressing consequence is the human loss of life, not the animal loss of life that I mentioned earlier.

Can Terminators have complex interests? Terminators are primarily characterized by their single-minded interest in achieving their objectives, but they also exhibit curiosity and interest in novel experiences. The Terminator sent back to protect John expresses complex interests in its curiosity about the nature of humanity, in its examination of a small child at arm's length, and in its ability to pick up slang quickly. It's quite possible that Terminators, and even Skynet, have complex interests just as we do.

Even if the machines didn't have interests as complex as those of humans, there may still be a case for choosing to maximize their satisfaction over that of the people who died on Judgment Day. It may be the case that the machines, with their set of common interests, greatly outnumber humanity in its common interests.

Consider a problem that arises with utilitarianism: satisfying the most interests can be achieved in numerous ways. For example, in *T2* John steals money from a bank via an ATM. It's not clear whether John is stealing money from a specific bank account or somehow hacking into the bank in general. Let's imagine that it is the latter. If John steals this money, he has a great time at the mall, and the bank and its insurers are slightly injured. The maximization of the interests in this case may actually result from John's stealing the money: one person benefits greatly, and many people lose out only slightly. This example also illustrates that for a utilitarian, nothing can be called *universally* wrong. The consequences of the act determine the rightness or wrongness of the act, not the act itself. But what if John didn't steal just a few hundred dollars? What if he stole a few thousand dollars, or tens of thousands of dollars? Even if

John stole one dollar from tens of thousands of banks, it would eventually result in a loss of utility. The individual dollars eventually add up to be a substantial sum. At some point adding another dollar to the transaction would decrease the collective interests of the bankers and insurers to the point where John's spending spree at the mall would be wrong. Analogously, if Skynet were to create more and more Terminators, and if the machines greatly outnumber the humans after Judgment Day, eventually the aggregate interests of survival and any other interests of the Terminators and Skynet would simply outweigh the interests of the surviving humans, like John stealing dollars from the bank.

Judgment Day Is the Morally Preferable Event

So just looking at the potential consequences from the utilitarian's viewpoint, it may be true that Judgment Day is preferable to stopping Dyson, since it actually maximizes interest satisfaction in the long term. Maybe this shouldn't surprise us: people often endure pain, hardships, and heavy burdens for a long-term payoff, and it's even more common for people to inconvenience themselves in order to "do the right thing." In this case, the stakes are just greater—all of humanity may have to shoulder the burden of a nuclear holocaust to accept what is morally required of us. Maybe Sarah should simply walk away from the Dyson residence and celebrate her morally superior decision by sharing a beer with John's Terminator guardian.

Or maybe not. Many utilitarians in the past have taken great pains to argue against some of the more unsavory conclusions that critics of utilitarianism have drawn. For example, if Miles Dyson has rights to life and to liberty, then he can claim the right to be free from being attacked without provocation, and society should defend him if he is attacked. A "naive" utilitarian, someone who straightforwardly analyzes each individual act's consequences and bases his or her moral decisions on that analysis, might argue that nobody has any rights, since rights are guarantees. In some cases, violating a person's rights could maximize interests. Yet John Stuart Mill tells us, "To have a right, then, is, I conceive, to have something which society ought to defend me in the possession of. If the objector goes on to ask, why it ought? I can give him no other reason than general utility."[6] Mill, adopting a more sophisticated utilitarian view, would argue to the contrary that protecting people's rights satisfies their deepest interests, so even in particular cases where it may maximize the satisfaction of interests to take another's life in cold blood, we ought not to do so, because allowing such acts would cause a loss of interest satisfaction overall. He writes, "The interest involved is that of security, to every one's feelings the most vital of all interests. All other earthly benefits are needed by one person, not needed by another; and many of them can, if necessary, be cheerfully foregone, or replaced by something else; but security no human being can possibly do without."[7] If our rights were not enforced, we could never truly feel secure from tyrannical governments, or even from one another. Like the future resistance soldiers who have good reasons to fear other people (since the others may be Terminators), we too would have good reasons to fear other people, since the other may simply be stronger than us.

But it's not over yet. The naive utilitarian might come back to point out that the very principle that Mill is using here is the principle of maximizing satisfaction of interests. Really, he and Mill are applying the same principle, but at different levels: for example, Mill uses the principle of maximizing satisfaction to justify deviations from general rules forbidding the killing of other people, as in cases of self-defense. Despite our rights to life and liberty, for him there would be circumstances in which it would be perfectly permissible to kill someone in self-defense. So why can't we make the exception in the Dyson case?

Clearly, there's something about the case that makes it difficult for utilitarians to agree with one another about whether killing Dyson is the morally correct thing to do. In fact, what makes this case compelling is that Sarah *knows* that he plays a very important role in Judgment Day. Unlike most people without precognition, Sarah does have a relatively accurate idea of what the future will be. By contrast, Mill's argument for protecting people's rights works in normal, everyday scenarios *precisely because* we don't have information about what will surely happen: generally, we are bad judges of future events. Ironically, in cases where we know for sure what the consequences will be, consequentialism isn't much help.

This idea that we are poor judges of future events is key to moral decision-making. It's worth pointing out, for example, that while 3 billion people died on Judgment Day, approximately 2.8 billion people survived.[8] Future history records that John Connor will lead them to a possible victory over Skynet. In fact, Kyle Reese tells Sarah in the first film, "The defense grid was smashed. We'd taken the mainframes. We'd won." The last phrase is ambiguous: does it refer to simply winning a major battle, or could it mean that the resistance had won the war? If this latter interpretation is correct, then the "rise of the machines" would be only a short one. If we take this into consideration when calculating the possible satisfaction of interests hanging on future events, it may be preferable that the machines had never existed, that the human race did not have to go through a harsh trial and rebuilding of its society.[9] But Sarah's decision in *T2* to spare Dyson flies in the face of this, despite Reese's words. The utilitarian might point out that if her decision had been based on the belief that the amount of total satisfaction of machine interests would outweigh the total satisfaction of human interests served by a victory over the machines, she would have further obligations. First, she would have to *ensure* that the machines are victorious over the human resistance.[10] And to do that, she would have to terminate her son, John Connor.

So should Sarah kill John? From a Kantian perspective, the answer is clearly no. John hasn't done anything to warrant that, and even if we take his future actions into consideration, he ultimately doesn't do anything wrong. The only Kantian condition for legitimate violence against another—retribution—hasn't been satisfied in this case. A utilitarian answer is more difficult to give, because we must weigh the potential benefits of a society run entirely by sentient machines (that may or may not enslave surviving human beings) versus the rebuilding of civilization after a bloody and possibly lengthy war. Despite Reese's talk about the future, Sarah simply does not have the information needed to make an informed decision between the two choices. This illustrates the problem that I had raised earlier, that making accurate predictions of the future is inherently a problem. Before, Sarah had relatively good foreknowledge on which to base her moral analysis, but between these two choices, she is in the dark. Throw in the further complication that Reese and the Terminator guardian have changed the past even before Sarah decides to try to kill Dyson, and we have ourselves a very sketchy view of the future. Her guess about which future is morally preferable is as good as yours or mine.

Are We Learning Yet?

This doesn't mean that we should just throw our hands into the air and give up without attempting to use good judgment. After all, Sarah still must make a decision. Here is where Mill's thoughts about rights and security can help guide our choice: when we can't accurately predict the future, we should rely on what would *typically* maximize interest satisfaction under normal circumstances. Clearly, under normal circumstances, killing innocent people, especially your own son, doesn't maximize people's interests. Only under very odd circumstances would it do so.

Happily, it turns out that Judgment Day isn't the morally preferable outcome after all. So how did we get off on the wrong track? It might be because of the easily overlooked line of Reese's dialogue in the original Terminator movie: "We'd won." The line, however, forces us to reconcile the fact that we lack a great deal of future knowledge. In fact, it is the lack of precognitive powers that makes utilitarianism a difficult doctrine to implement practically. Even minor facts that are overlooked can have huge implications when projected out over the years and over the choices and actions of billions of people. This is not to say that we shouldn't try, but in ethics, knowing the weaknesses of your theory is just as important as knowing the strengths.

Bertrand Russell may have been writing in a tongue-in-cheek fashion when he said philosophy begins with the obvious and ends with the absurd, but philosophy is often preoccupied with such arguments, as we've seen in this chapter. Sometimes the absurd is well justified, and sometimes, as in this case, it's not. Strong reasoning makes good theory in philosophy, and even when we fail to reach the destination, there is plenty to learn along the way.[11]

NOTES

1. Bertrand Russell, "The Philosophy of Logical Atomism," in *The Philosophy of Logical Atomism and Other Essays, 1914–19, The Collected Papers of Bertrand Russell*, vol. 8, ed. J. Slater (London: Allen & Unwin), 172.

2. To be precise, in *Terminator 3: Rise of the Machines*, Skynet is a computer *program* that becomes self-aware and takes control of military computers after unleashing a computer virus.

3. A more exact wording of the categorical imperative can be found in Immanuel Kant's *Groundwork of the Metaphysics of Morals*, ed. and trans. Mary Gregor (Cambridge: Cambridge Univ. Press, 1997): (1) "Act only in accordance with that maxim through which you can at the same time will that it become a universal law." (2) "Every rational being exists as an end in itself, not merely as a means to be used by this or that will at its discretion; instead he must in all his actions whether directed to himself or also to other rational beings, always be regarded at the same time as an end."

4. There are many kinds of utilitarianism, differing by whether they charge us to maximize happiness, pleasure, or some other good. It's a good idea, though, to focus on the satisfaction of *interests* because there may be many times when something will make us

happy that is not in our interest. For example, hopping on a plane to Hawaii tonight might make me happy, but it would not be in my interest to do so. I might lose my job, and I have great interest in keeping my job, even if it doesn't make me as happy as a Hawaiian vacation would. I might also have to do things to satisfy my interests that would cause me some pain, like exercising to satisfy my interest to stay healthy.

5. It may be the case that Bogo is simply uninterested in this genre of television, as he did enjoy the documentary *The Wild Parrots of Telegraph Hill*. But it is more likely that he didn't really understand that film anymore than he understands *Terminator: The Sarah Connor Chronicles*.

6. John Stuart Mill, *Utilitarianism*, in *The Basic Writings of John Stuart Mill* (New York: Modern Library, 2002), 290.

7. Ibid.

8. The U.S. census bureau estimated that 5.8 billion people were alive in 1997. See www.census.gov/ipc/www/idb/worldpopinfo.html.

9. This is not to discount the possibility that we could be better for having to deal with arduous events. Theologian Paul Tillich (1886–1965) argues that evils in the world are justified so that we can improve our selves and better our souls. Theological arguments aside, I think it is a fair assumption that more interests would be satisfied if Judgment Day didn't happen at all versus the outcome in which it happens and humans are ultimately victorious over the machines.

10. It could be argued that Sarah wouldn't take the machines' interests into consideration at all. But I find this questionable, since she sees the humanity in John's Terminator bodyguard.

11. I'd like to thank Tony Nguyen, Gary Buzzell, and Kevin S. Decker for valuable comments on an earlier draft of this chapter. I'd also like to thank my wife, Tiffany, for comments, and especially for putting up with repeat viewings of the *Terminator* films.

13

THE WAR TO END ALL WARS? KILLING YOUR DEFENSE SYSTEM

Phillip Seng

"It's in your nature to destroy yourselves."

"Yeah. Major drag, huh?"

—John Connor and the T-101, *Terminator 2: Judgment Day*

The world of the *Terminator* movies is in a constant state of war. The interesting catch is that hardly anyone in the late-twentieth-century world depicted by James Cameron has any clue that this particular war is being waged. Much less do they realize that this war is for the future of humankind. In the real world, the wars we fight with other nations (populated by humans rather than robotic killers) usually follow certain rules that have evolved over time to provide a degree of rationality and integrity to war. The aim of these rules, grouped together into a doctrine that's called "just-war theory," is to impart some sense of justice to the instigation, conduct, and resolution of the wars we fight.

Of course, the war we're concerned with here is the war between humans and the Skynet defense system—the war of human against machine. We love to watch the explosions, the special effects, and the endless supply of ammo spent trying to kill the damn machines that we originally built for our own defense. But in the midst of all the shooting, we miss the fact that there are rules to war, at least for the humans who are fighting, and that this war is indeed a just war.

What Is It Good For?

Just-war theory has three basic parts.[1] There are fancy Latin terms for all these ideas, but you've already encountered many of them in actual political speeches that support or decry particular wars. First, there is the part of just-war theory that deals with the decision about whether or not to go to war. We don't learn much about the cause of the war in the original *Terminator* movie—we just get thrown into the middle of things, and we can either go along with them or die. The opening voice-over narration to the first movie explains, "The machines rose from the ashes of the nuclear fire. Their war to exterminate mankind had raged for decades, but the final battle would not be fought in the future. It would be fought here, in our present. Tonight . . . " Sarah Connor tells us this bit of information, and of course she's talking about it from the perspective of a person who's just killed one of the Terminators. Now, it seems from this that the machines—the Skynet defense system and all the automated killing machines created to carry out its superintelligent directives—suffered a nuclear blast and came out of it punching. But then again, it also sounds as if Skynet started a war to kill off humans and is carrying the war into the past, like a temporal uppercut, to try and end the war once and for all.

From the beginning of *The Terminator* it's pretty easy to claim that the war is being fought for good reasons. After all, it's a case of self-defense carried to the highest level. We're not just protecting our homes from invaders, but protecting all human life from extermination. Self-defense, in terms of just-war theory, is a kind of reason that gives us *just cause* for going to war. Having a just cause is necessary in order to wage a just war. If you don't have a just cause when you head into war, then chances are that the war you're thinking of starting has an illegitimate motivation—whether revenge, a land grab, or ethnic cleansing. Self-defense, protection of those who cannot defend themselves, national security, and overthrow of a brutal dictator have been the primary causes under which people have rallied to wage just wars in our past.

From the first movie it seems as if the humans are indeed fighting a just war—they're defending themselves from extinction. This attitude is reinforced the more we learn about the future circumstances that lead up to Skynet's attack. Reese explains to Sarah, shortly after he has absconded with her, "It was the machines, Sarah. Defense network computers. New. Powerful. Hooked into everything, trusted to run it all. They say it got smart—a new order of intelligence. Then it saw all people as a threat, not just the ones on the other side. It decided our fate in a microsecond: extermination." Reese, from his knowledge of the circumstances of the war, lays the blame on the machines. The machines got smart and wanted to be the king of the hill. Seeing a threat from humans, the machines took action (maybe even preemptive action?) and launched nukes against humanity to rid the earth of everything but the cockroaches. According to what we've discussed so far, it seems pretty clear that the machines acted unjustly and that humans have every right to defend themselves in this war.

But It's Self-Defense!

The plot thickens, as they say, with *Terminator 2: Judgment Day*. There's still a war raging, and even though little John Connor is one or two misdemeanors away from juvie and his mom's only solace is becoming as rock-solid as the machines she's destined to fight, the war takes on a different type of justification. Recall how Arnold Schwarzenegger—in a clever reprise of his very mechanical role as the T-101 in the first movie—explains the origins of the war to Sarah and John as they run for the border:

> T-101: In three years Cyberdyne will become the largest supplier of military computer systems. All stealth bombers are upgraded with Cyberdyne computers, becoming fully unmanned. Afterward, they fly with a perfect operational record. The Skynet funding bill is passed. The system goes online on August fourth, 1997. Human decisions are removed from strategic defense. Skynet begins to learn at a geometric rate. It becomes self-aware at 2:14 AM Eastern time, August twenty-ninth. In a panic, they try to pull the plug.
>
> Sarah: Skynet fights back?
>
> T-101: Yes. It launches its missiles against the targets in Russia.
>
> John: Why attack Russia? Aren't they our friends now?
>
> T-101: Because Skynet knows the Russian counterattack will eliminate its enemies over here.
>
> Sarah: Jesus.

The way Arnold explains things, the war that we always thought was started by machines was actually Skynet's way of acting on the *same ideals of self-defense* that we use to justify wars against an aggressor. In other words, the machines were just defending themselves *from us*. We tried to pull the plug on them, and they fought back by nuking Russia so Russia would counterattack, fulfilling the wildest fantasies of Dr. Strangelove: mutually assured destruction and wonderful special effects, to boot!

One of the problems in applying the just-war theory to these movies, or to other movies that show intelligent machines acting in defiance of their human creators, is that we must either grant machines the same moral status as humans, or else the argument is moot. If we think that there's any validity to the idea of a machine's defending itself, then we have to think machines can be *just* in the same way that we humans strive to be. But if machines are merely *things* that we use, things that can be turned on or off simply to meet our needs, then we really don't need any reason at all to crush them, to incinerate them—from a certain perspective, to *kill* them. As the audience, when we're thrown into the middle of the action in these movies, we fail to even look for an argument in favor of the machines' self-defense. It's interesting that without so much as a line of dialogue or a cameo until the *Terminator 3: Rise of the Machines*, Skynet is given a status equal to that of humans—it can defend itself in its own interest for survival. We don't like the way in which it defends itself, but that does not mean that it *can't* or *shouldn't* do so.

"In a Panic, They Try to Pull the Plug"

So it's pretty clear that the question of whether or not humans had a just cause in their war against the machines is on shakier ground than at first glance. *Terminator 3* provides a convenient illustration: Brewster gives the order to initiate Skynet, and then as he's about to rescind his order, the T-X struts in disguised as his daughter Kate and shoots him twice in the chest. A clear example of self-defense, right? Only if you buy the argument that killing all humans is the *only* way for Skynet to survive. Another rule within just-war theory that we need to consider is that military action is just only if war is the last resort in any given situation. By "last resort," we usually mean that all avenues of diplomacy have been exhausted and the only way to resolve some existing injustice is by force of arms.

Skynet, because it is a superintelligent supercomputer, decides in a microsecond that the only way to resolve the human problem is to exterminate humanity. Where is the discussion? Where were the international tribunals or the six-party negotiations? Of course, Skynet most likely thinks it can skip all the deliberations because it is smarter than any other being on earth, even Garry Kasparov. It knows how we'll respond, and how we'll respond to its counterresponse, and so on. Why bother with all that mind-numbing talk? Just hit the button and get the damn thing over with.

Another way to look at the issue is this: computers are only as intelligent as the people who make them and the people who program them. The old adage "Garbage in, garbage out" might be a better expression of what we can expect from our computer defense systems. If humans programmed Skynet to bomb first and ask questions later, well, then it looks like it's our fault for not inserting a diplomatic back door to the system. We created the monster, and only after seeing the horrible mess it makes do we ask for our money back.

For humans, though, the decision to go to war is usually more than simply a matter of cold calculation. We like to believe in the possibility of something better than war, and we like to hold out hope that war is not inevitable. Yet just-war theory is built around the central idea that the world in which we live is not ideal, and therefore some pretty unpleasant things are sometimes necessary to make it better. This idea stems from early Christian thinkers who developed the notion of a "just war" in order to find protection in their faith in the midst of killing other humans.[2] The best offense is a good defense, though, because we don't enjoy the wholesale slaughter of other people as a general principle. We therefore try to make war the last resort. In all three of the *Terminator* movies, though, the war of Judgment Day is inevitable, and so the need to fight is also inevitable.

"Talk to the Hand"

Arnold, nude again as the T-101 in the beginning of *T3*, tries to get another leather outfit to cover his muscles. This time, of course, it's not a motorcycle-riding bar brawler but a male dancer pretending to be a leather-clad biker. The T-101 says he needs clothes, but the dancer tells him to "talk to the hand." Arnold doesn't understand the slang, grabs the hand—breaking bones—and speaks into the crunched fingers, "Give me your clothes."

We laugh, of course, because it's another display of Arnold's masculinity against the pseudo-masculinity of the dancer. And it's another occasion when the Terminator demonstrates that he doesn't understand the ways of human interaction. The Terminator has no legitimate authority to take the dancer's clothes, but because Arnold is stronger than the dancer, he wins the prize. It's clear that all the Terminators act upon the principle that "might makes right." The only thing that matters is being able to do what you want to do, if you're strong enough to get it done (or as one of my fellow Nebraskans says, "Git 'r done"). So the only concept of justice that Skynet understands—if you can even call it justice—is something we might recognize as the *survival of the fittest*, if we are careful to take that phrase out of its typical evolutionary context. Strength prevails, and the weak die.

How many times does a Terminator simply kill a human being who is in the way? Skynet and the Terminators just do not care about matters of right and wrong—what we would call moral considerations. Remember the scene in *T2* when John Connor discovers he has his very own private bodyguard? They're in a parking lot at night, and John makes Arnold stand on one foot, jump up and down, and beat up a couple of guys who inadvertently try to save John from what looks like an attacker. Well, when the two guys intervene, the Terminator pushes them away, draws his gun, and gets a wild shot off as John disrupts his aim, saying:

> John: Jesus, you were going to kill that guy.
>
> T-101: Of course. I'm a Terminator.
>
> John: Listen to me very carefully, okay? You're not a Terminator anymore, all right? You got that? You just can't go around killing people.
>
> T-101: Why?
>
> John: What do you mean, "Why?" Because you can't.
>
> T-101: Why?
>
> John: Because you just can't, okay? Trust me on this. Look, I'm going to go get my mom, and I order you to help me [John hands his gun back to him]. Now, you've gotta promise me you're not gonna kill anyone, right?
>
> T-101: Right.
>
> John: Swear?
>
> T-101: What?
>
> John: Just put up your hand and say, "I swear I won't kill anyone."
>
> T-101: I swear I will not kill anyone.

Shortly after this conversation the pair drive up to the security gate at the psychiatric facility where Sarah is kept, and the Terminator shoots the guard in both knees. But that's okay, because "he'll live."

The Terminator can't get his computerized mind around the fact that human society has developed laws and customs that forbid the exercise of brutal and deadly force. The only limitation on force that Skynet understands is a stronger, more powerful force. The T-101 has to obey John due to programming, otherwise all bets are off. But the justness of a just war requires that the exercise of force derive from a legitimate authority, such as a national government or duly sworn defender. It is just to intervene on someone's behalf if there is good cause—then you have a legitimate power to act. From this, we can understand why the two guys who were trying to help John in the parking lot were so disgruntled. They thought they were doing the right thing by helping out a kid who was being picked on by a huge, tough guy dressed in black leather. As it turns out, John repaid their good deed by illegitimately exercising his power by having Arnold rough them up.

"I Need Your Clothes, Your Boots, and Your Motorcycle"

In *T2* the T-1000 "liberates" a motorcycle cop's vehicle and clothes in order to better move about society and accomplish his deadly mission. The Terminator doesn't really care about whether or not there were other ways of getting clothes or a set of wheels: he takes what he needs. In fact, the T-101 does the same thing in all three movies, and even Reese steals clothes and cars in *The Terminator*. These examples illustrate potential violations of the second major principle of just-war theory: that wars must be *conducted* justly, too.

There is a limit to rashness in war, even this war conducted by the Terminators, so we should do only what's necessary to achieve our goals in war. Most important, this principle directs military authorities to kill only the people they absolutely *must* kill. It's a given that killing is bad, so we try to limit it as much as possible. Some philosophers who explore just conduct discuss this principle as one of *proportionality*, in which justice demands that you do not bring a gun to a knife fight, or kill a million people in retaliation for a car bomb. The gist of the argument is that wars ought to be fought fairly.

Now, obviously, Skynet seems to falter on the issue of proportionality. It fears that its human creators will try to pull the plug, thus killing it, so it reasons that the only way to protect itself from humans would be to kill all the humans. Makes sense, I guess, but it's not really the proportionate response: it might have just killed off the humans in its immediate proximity, or all of us who knew about the existence of Skynet, right? But then it would have to deal with all the other humans who didn't get the memo that there's a new sheriff in town, namely Skynet. So, why not skip ahead to the last move of the game and just kill everyone at the beginning? At least that's what Skynet thinks.

Similarly, in *T3*, Skynet sends the T-X back with both primary and secondary targets. The primary target is John Connor, but the Terminator will settle for a multitude of secondary targets: John's classmates (who become soldiers in his resistance army) and Kate Brewster's dad, Robert, in charge of implementing the Skynet program. This targeted hit list has the appearance of proportionality, right? The problem is, Terminators don't always exercise another component of the just conduct aspect of warfare—*discrimination*.

Discrimination, in this sense, isn't a bad thing: it's the act of separating combatants from civilians. You should attack your uniformed enemy but make every reasonable effort to avoid bringing harm to civilians on either side of the conflict. Terminators, as we know, are not very discriminating when it comes to war.

But there does seem to be a method to the madness of the Terminators. In the first movie, Arnold pursues only Sarah Connor. Not until he confronts a roommate and her boyfriend does he kill "innocent" people. Remember, since Skynet is sending the Terminators back from the future, Sarah Connor is judged to be an enemy, so she's not innocent in the eyes of Skynet. At the beginning of the series, Sarah doesn't realize why she's the target of some lunatic who can withstand many, many gunshot wounds. But as Sarah gains knowledge of the future—first from Reese and then from her own Terminator ally—she transforms into a human version of the Terminators.

Ever since the first encounter with the Terminator in 1984, Sarah's life has been lived under a cloud of doom. She has little hope for the future. She waits and prepares for the day when her son will rise from the ashes of Armageddon and lead a rebellion against the machines. Once she discovers the human who is responsible for the war, and so responsible for making her life a shambles, she acts as coolly and as calculatingly as any machine ever could.

In fact, the parallels are a little scary. Think about the plots of the movies. In *The Terminator*, Skynet sends Arnold back to kill the mother of the leader of the resistance fighters. In *T2*, Skynet sends back the T-1000 to kill the future leader of the resistance fighters while he's a young boy. And in *T3*, Skynet sends back the T-X to kill John, if it can find him, and John's cadre of officers in his resistance army. In each case, this is cold-blooded murder. Now, consider what Sarah Connor decides to do at the turning point of *T2*. She finds out that Miles Dyson is the computer programmer who is responsible for developing the technologies that morph into Skynet. Sarah gains knowledge of a possible future and, just like Skynet, acts on that information before the terrible events begin to unfold. Sarah Connor becomes a Terminator, intending to commit cold-blooded murder, too.

The just conduct of war dictates that she, like the T-101, must focus only on targets and exercise due restraint when confronted with noncombatants. Of course, there's that sticky idea that Skynet deems all humans to be enemies. After Arnold delivers that now-classic line "I'll be back" at the information desk of the police station, he goes on a killing spree. So it's a very guilty pleasure we feel in watching the Terminator do his job.

In the second movie, the T-1000 executed its mission with a cold efficiency until it ran into the old T-101. Neither Terminator was unduly reckless in its treatment of noncombatants. Of course, the notion of "being a combatant" must mean that the person actually knows he or she *is fighting in a war*. In fact, the war exists in the future, in 2029, and only by the happenstance of technology does it break through the boundaries of linear time. Skynet doesn't recognize that it might matter that its enemies don't even realize that they've been targeted as enemies. Skynet doesn't care about necessity, proportionality, or discrimination. And neither does Sarah as she's locking her laser sight on the back of Miles Dyson's head.

"I Almost . . . I Almost . . . "

Sarah Connor tries to kill Miles Dyson. She shoots a lot of bullets at him and wounds him pretty badly in the process. But even as she's standing over his body, filled with all the pent-up rage from a life of seclusion and constant fear—knowing now that the man begging her for life is responsible for all of her pain—she can't kill him. In this way, Sarah reasserts her humanity and her difference from the Terminators.

But the machines don't mind making killing personal. The T-1000 morphs into a doppelganger and presents a security guard with his mirror image before he pierces him through the eye and brain. He poses as John's foster mom, and kills her husband because he's making too much noise (or because he's drinking milk directly from the carton). And the T-X poses as Kate's fiancé in hopes of luring her close enough to kill her. For Terminators, "the closer the better" seems to be the general rule.

But Sarah stops herself just as she gets into intimate space with Dyson. His crying family probably helps pull her down from her bloodlust, too. When John and the Terminator show up she can only look vacantly into his eyes and stutter, "I almost. . . . I almost . . . " The implicit realization that Dyson was indeed innocent—at least in this stream of the space-time continuum—shocked her back to her senses.

As viewers, we have been made to realize something important. "We didn't care much about the murders of the wrong Sarah Connor [in the first film]," explains Sean French, "but we are now made to feel what it might be to kill someone you don't know."[3] In other words, when we watch *The Terminator* we might have derived some vicarious pleasure, mixed with a little slasher-movie horror, when Arnold killed anonymous people. But, in *T2*, Cameron brings us into the equation and makes us feel the fear, the anxiety, and the hopelessness that we didn't necessarily identify with during the original movie. We now know what it's like to be the target of unprovoked violence *and* what it's like to inflict such violence.

We stop and think that, oh man, I've just been identifying with the main character, and she was trying to assassinate an innocent man. When we identify with Arnold's Terminator in the first movie, we don't make the same connection because we know he's the bad guy—we're not going to idealize his actions. But here, looking at things from Sarah's perspective, she's almost killed a man, when her enemies are the machines.

"The Battle Has Just Begun"

Terminator 3: Rise of the Machines closes with these words, spoken by John Connor: "Maybe the future has been written. I don't know. All I know is what the Terminator taught me: never stop fighting. And I never will. The battle has just begun." Just-war theory sets forth the rules by which we can legitimately enter into war, with the understanding that its ultimate purpose must be peace. War is not something to stumble into. It's a last-ditch measure that aims to subdue an enemy so that peace may be restored. As of yet, this aim hasn't been successfully achieved in Cameron's world of Terminators, John Connor, and Skynet.

The final phases of just-war theory describe the just resolution of wars, how the victors should work to establish peace and reconcile any lingering injustices for the sake of fostering goodwill among people who were recently enemies on the battlefield. Examples of these ideas put into practice would be the Marshall Plan in the wake of World War II, or war-crimes tribunals that seek reconciliation for atrocities beyond the scope of the necessities of war. The idea here is that even after the conflict is over, justice must be sought and attained or else the seeds of future conflict may be sown. Most important, of course, the underlying causes of a war need to be set right in order to prevent history from repeating itself.

How could such ideas be enacted in John Connor's future? Will there be an occasion when humans have defeated all the machines and Skynet surrenders? Will John sign a peace treaty with Skynet? It's doubtful that such a situation will come about. If the war is ever resolved on the big screen, it will most likely end with the total destruction of Skynet. Connor would need to worry about fostering justice only if there were survivors who might feel unjustly treated. But if all his enemies were dead, there's no need to worry about such things, which might explain why we see such a predilection for genocide in the world.

Sarah Connor got to see the "borrowed time" of life after Armageddon, when John lives in a constant state of fear with his nagging sense of an unfulfilled destiny. The longer he lives under such pressure, the less clear his picture of what he's fighting for will become in his memory. He will fight, has already been fighting, and has even died, for the survival of humanity. In such a world, the assumption seems to be that humans are united against the machines, that nationalism has been set aside, or even obliterated, along with the buildings and the people.

There is some cruel irony then if we consider that Skynet drives humans into something of a utopian situation. While the more optimistic *Star Trek* TV shows and movies skip the roughshod formative years of how Earth came together and formed the Federation, Cameron's movies put the focus directly on what might be a transition period from limited nationalistic concerns to universally human concerns. Whether or not the war, and the warriors, will resolve matters with concern for peace and justice is a matter of pure speculation, at least until the next movie is released.

NOTES

1. There are lots of places to find good summaries of the ideas contained in the just-war theory. A solid introductory essay is Mark Evans's "Moral Theory and the Idea of a Just War," which is the first chapter of a book he edited called *Just War Theory: A Reappraisal* (New York: Palgrave Macmillan, 2005). Two other recommended sources are Michael Walzer, *Just and Unjust Wars: A Moral Argument with Historical Illustrations*, 4th ed. (New York: Basic Books, 2006), and Andrew Fiala, *The Just War Myth: The Moral Illusions of War* (Lanham, MD: Rowman & Littlefield Publishers, Inc., 2008).

2. In *The Ethics of War: Classic and Contemporary Readings*, the editors provide excerpts from writings on war from early Christian thinkers who defend war as a just activity to defend against aggression. For example, Saint Augustine, Bishop of Hippo, provides an early defense of just war as a means to peace in his *City of God*, Book 4, chap. 15, when he writes, "Waging war and extending the empire by subduing peoples is therefore viewed as happiness by the wicked, but as a necessity by the good" (p. 72 in *The Ethics of War*, eds. Gregory M. Reichberg, Henrik Syse, and Endre Begby [Malden, MA: Blackwell, 2006]). Saint Thomas Aquinas, another important figure in the Catholic tradition, writes in his *Summa Theologiae* II-II, Question 40, that just wars require legitimate "authority," a "just cause," and a "rightful intention" (p. 177 in *The Ethics of War*).

3. Sean French, *The Terminator* (London: BFI Publishing, 1996), 67.

14

SELF-TERMINATION: SUICIDE, SELF-SACRIFICE, AND THE TERMINATOR

Daniel P. Malloy

I cannot self-terminate.

—Terminator, *Terminator 2: Judgment Day*

T2: Judgment Day ends with a suicide. In the final scene, the T-101 determines that the only way to stop Skynet from rising, and thereby prevent the war between humans and machines, is to have itself terminated. Because its programming does not allow it to self-terminate, it hands the task to Sarah Connor. The Terminator then stands passively as it is lowered into a vat of molten steel, thereby destroying the chip that would have allowed Cyberdyne Systems to create Skynet. As we know from subsequent installments of the series, however, this attempt failed. The T-101 was indeed destroyed, but Skynet became self-aware and declared war on humans in spite of this sacrifice.

Existentialist philosopher Albert Camus (1913–1960) claimed that suicide is the only truly serious problem of philosophy—before we can contemplate anything else, we must decide whether or not life is worth living.[1] Indeed, the history of Western philosophy began with a suicide: the death of Socrates (469–399 BCE). Philosophers still dispute whether Socrates actually committed suicide. But the story is this: Socrates was tried before a court on a variety of charges, including corrupting the youth of Athens. He was found guilty and sentenced to death by drinking hemlock, a natural poison. When the time came for his execution, Socrates gladly took his poisoned cup and drank heartily. Now, is this suicide? He could have escaped this fate with ease—the fact that he didn't makes it appear to be a suicide. Or perhaps his attitude made his act a suicide: Socrates was not simply executed, he happily cooperated. He took the poisoned cup; it was not forced on him. Supposing it is suicide: does that make it wrong? It is possible that Socrates, who spent his life trying to follow "the good" and persuading others to do likewise, committed a sin in his final act. If Socrates' final act was not wrong, we face the problem of how the act is justified.

Just as with Socrates, the movie's final act leading to the Terminator's termination is ambiguous. The T-101 did not lower itself into the vat of molten lava anymore than Socrates decided to take the hemlock; similarly, the T-101 did not choose to accept Sarah and John Connor's mission of destroying Cyberdyne Systems and forestalling the creation of Skynet any more than Socrates chose to be found guilty.

Before we explore the morality of the Terminator's choices and ask what constitutes suicide and when, if ever, can suicide be justified, we have to tackle another question, one that simply does not arise in the case of Socrates.

Could the Terminator Die?

Let's begin by stating the blindingly obvious: machines are not alive. Therefore they cannot die. So it makes no sense to call the T-101's termination a death at all, much less to specify it as a suicide. We may say that certain machines "die" metaphorically—computers, cell phones, batteries, etc.—but what kind of "death" is this? A cell phone dropped off a bridge may be "dead" afterward, but it hasn't committed suicide or been murdered. It has just been destroyed. In the same way, the T-101 was simply destroyed by Sarah Connor. The Terminator did not "die"; it simply ceased to function, just like every computer I've ever owned.

But there is a difference between the Terminator and my defunct computers—the Terminator at least appeared to be self-aware. It asked to be destroyed; it volunteered for termination. So perhaps we can see suicide as something more than just self-incurred *biological* death. In a very real and pressing sense, the T-101 did "die," and so its actions could be considered a suicide. But is there, perhaps, another sense of "life" and "death"?

To help understand this possibility, let's call on the thought of one of the most influential philosophers of the twentieth century, Martin Heidegger (1889–1976). In his book *Being and Time*, Heidegger proposed that human beings experience death differently from other animals. Human beings are essentially temporal beings—we live in and through time. Part of that temporality is living toward the future. Because of our keen awareness of time's passage and of our finitude, humans are always "being-toward-death" (*Sein zum Tod*).[2] Death, to Heidegger, is not simply a biological concept; that is, if I see death as just my body ceasing to function, then I have misunderstood what death *means* to a human being. Death is much more than that; it is the *end of possibility*. Being-toward-death means understanding that the future is finite: there will come a time for each of us when the future has run out. There will be no more possibilities, no more plans to make, no more projects to see through—all of that will be over. It is *this* sense of death that applies to the Terminator.

To test this idea, let's compare the destruction of the T-101 in the first movie to the death of the "good" T-101 in *T2*. Call to mind the final scene of *The Terminator*. Watch the steely skeleton, already half smashed and missing its lower limbs, crawl and scrape its way toward Sarah Connor. To me this has always been the most frightening scene in the *Terminator* films. The T-101 is beaten, nearly destroyed, and yet it keeps coming—right to its doom. The first T-101 lacked self-awareness, and so its "death" was only a "death" in the same metaphorical sense that batteries die. The first Terminator did not die; it was merely destroyed. It had no possibilities, no projects, no future. That T-101 only had a program. What would have happened to it, we might wonder, if it had carried out its mission successfully? Would it have simply shut down, its mission complete, and waited for reprogramming? Or were there other, secondary targets programmed in? The point is moot, of course, but it strongly emphasizes the difference between the first and the second T-101s. Even as the second one was being lowered to its fate, young John Connor was pleading for it to stay and continue serving as a sort of surrogate father. The first T-101 was little more than a puppet, while the second had a future filled with possibilities—and yet it gave them up.

Why? The answer can be found in another aspect of Heidegger's being-toward-death—the question of authenticity. For Heidegger, to approach death authentically is to accept it as the *impossibility of possibility*. We avoid facing our own death, the impossibility of our possibilities, in various ways.[3] Typically, for instance, we comfort ourselves that "everybody dies," secretly denying that we are one of those everybodies. In *Terminator 3: Rise of the Machines*, the T-101 is self-aware in Heidegger's sense of "life," just like the one in *T2*. Both choose to die, but in *T3* self-termination is chosen as a last-ditch effort to destroy the newest model. Before this final act in *T3*, it says to John Connor, "We'll meet again." It seems that this T-101's approach to death is not authentic. In one sense, what it says comes true—in the future, John Connor will program this T-101 and send it back in time to protect his younger self. However, the T-101 that John Connor programs and sends back will not have the same experiences or memories as this one, and so, in a very real sense, it will not be the same "person." This T-101 dies in an inauthentic way because it refuses to acknowledge death as the end of possibility—*this* Terminator will live again, it believes in vain. The T-101 in *T2*, on the other hand, does accept that its death is the end of its possibilities: indeed, the whole point of its sacrifice is that there will never be a Skynet or Terminators.

So, while it is fair to say of most machines that they cannot die, the case is different with the Terminator. Since it is aware of itself, its surroundings, and its movement through time, the T-101 is an example of what Heidegger calls *Da-sein* ("there-being"), his term for human existence. The Terminator exists in a completely different way than a toaster or a microwave does. And because of this special existence, it can be said in truth that the T-101 is capable of dying.

Did the Terminator Commit Suicide?

If the Terminator can die in a real sense, then it's possible that it can commit suicide. The simplest definition of suicide is "the act of killing oneself"—but philosophers are rarely satisfied with simple definitions. After all, there are lots of ways to kill yourself—drinking antifreeze, abusing drugs, smoking tobacco, eating a poor diet, autoerotic asphyxiation—but none of these qualify as suicide. There is more to suicide than this, and what's missing is the intention behind the act. More accurately, suicide is the *intentional* taking of one's own life. Further, in order for an act to be considered suicide, the subject must *freely* choose to die. Accidents aren't suicides. And, generally, an action is considered suicide only if it *directly* results in death. Let's first deal with this issue of free choice: did the Terminator freely choose to die?

It's doubtful that the T-101 could *freely* choose anything. As its successor in *T3* tells us, "Desire is irrelevant. I am a machine." Machines are not free. Even a sophisticated machine like the Terminator has a program that it must carry out. The computer I'm using to write this chapter can't suddenly decide that it needs a break or that my words and ideas aren't up to snuff and shut itself down (though it certainly seems that way at times). On the face of it, then, the T-101's act was not a suicide because it wasn't freely chosen. That is, provided that it was programmed to allow self-destruction within mission objectives, the T-101 was not free. Perhaps the Terminator wasn't following its program when it asked to be lowered into that vat. It said just before handing Sarah Connor the controls, "I cannot self-terminate," but it arranges for its own death. So T-101's final act at least might have been freely chosen.

But maybe in order to complete its mission of destroying Skynet, the Terminator *had* to destroy itself—that, after all, is the justification the T-101 gives. And while this is true, the destruction of Skynet was not the T-101's programmed mission, which was simply to protect John Connor. With the destruction of the T-1000, that mission was complete, and with that accomplished, the T-101 had no mission, no program to speak of. This is the very essence of freedom—the absence of commands or directives, the presence of nothing but possibilities. It is precisely this plethora of possibilities that constitutes freedom. Right now, of the range of possibilities open to me, including watching *The Terminator*, playing video games based on the *Terminator* films, or coming up with mindless puns akin to "Governator" to describe Arnold Schwarzenegger's current role,[4] I am writing a chapter. I have freely decided to "actualize" writing this chapter about the *Terminator*. In a strange way, the T-101's self-destruction, its suicide, was really its only free act. It had a variety of options for the first time, instead of a program to follow—and it chose to die.

If its final act was indeed a free one, then our next question concerns *what* act it actually was. There was no action on the part of the Terminator that led directly to its death, since it merely stood passively as it was lowered to its doom. It did not jump, and it needed Sarah Connor to push the button and pull the metaphorical plug. So perhaps this wasn't a suicide after all—maybe it was a case of *euthanasia*. In the case of humans, euthanasia typically involves a physician taking an active role in a patient's death—not only prescribing the means of suicide, but also physically administering it in the face of the patient's incapability to do it him- or herself. The parallel to the T-101's situation is clear: the T-101 could not destroy itself, but it could ask someone else to destroy it—to kill it. So, in spite of the T-101's lack of direct action, it can still be said to have committed suicide. Its request, if not its action, led to its death.

Now, some may think that the Terminator's act was not a suicide precisely because of the real motive behind the act. After all, the T-101 did not want to die. It was just trying to prevent the rise of Skynet, and there was only one way to achieve this end. Far from being a suicide, the T-101's act was more akin to an act of self-sacrifice, like being hit by a bus after pushing someone else out of its path. But there are two problems with this. First, suicide and self-sacrifice are not mutually exclusive. All that's required for an act to be a suicide is the intention to die—not the desire. The second problem is the question of intention. Given that the Terminator intended to destroy Skynet, did it necessarily intend to die to fulfill that mission? Surely, to will a goal is also to will the *means to that goal*. The

T-101 could no more have intended to stop Skynet without intending its own death than I could intend people to read this chapter without intending to submit it to the publisher. In both cases, the one includes the other.

So it's clear that the Terminator died in Heidegger's nonbiological sense *and* that it committed suicide. Its suicide was committed for good, even selfless, reasons. Yet, still another serious moral problem remains.

Was the Terminator's Suicide Justified?

Those who believe that suicide can never be a morally praiseworthy act of self-sacrifice often point to some base motive for suicide, such as selfishness or cowardice. We can see the flaw in this reasoning, though, if we see that there's an important difference between the *intention* of an action and its *motive*. Put simply, an intention is a *plan* to act, while a motive is the *reason* to act. In our case, the T-101's intention was to kill itself, but its motive was to preempt the creation of Skynet. A proper definition of suicide needs to consider the intention, regardless of motive.

Even if this were not true, it's still the case that some of the most influential arguments against suicide don't apply in the case of the T-101. Take, for example, Plato's *Phaedo*.[5] In this dialogue, Plato's teacher Socrates is awaiting his execution and trying to persuade his friends not to be upset, for death is nothing to fear. In fact, he says, it is the greatest good, what a life devoted to philosophy is all about, a release from the cares of the world in order to contemplate the truth in peace. Socrates makes it clear, however, that we can't grant this boon to ourselves. Human beings are the property of the gods, he claims, and to kill oneself would effectively be stealing from the gods. A Christian variation of this argument holds that human life is God's gift and therefore not to be taken by anyone, including oneself. But, simply put, these arguments fail to apply to our present case, since the

Terminator is hardly a divine creation. And any claims to its life made by its mundane creators need to confront its new freedom and self-awareness.

For a view relevant to the Terminator, let's turn to Immanuel Kant (1724–1804), who forbade suicide absolutely. Kant's ultimate moral principle, the categorical imperative, tells us that if you could not will that *everyone* perform the action you intend, then you shouldn't do it at all.[6] So, in the case of suicide, in order for it to be morally right, one would have to will that all people in similar situations take their own lives. Kant considers a man in dire straits. This poor fellow is contemplating suicide to end his pain—that is, out of love of himself. Applying the categorical imperative to this situation means that everyone who loves himself—or, everyone—would have to commit suicide.

The key distinction between Kantian ethics and others that categorically condemn suicide is that for Kant, what defines a being's worth is not its divine origin or its possession of a soul, but its ability to reason. Kant also claims that our central moral duty is to treat others with respect and not simply as things to be used in order to satisfy our own desires. ("So act that you use humanity, whether in your own person or in the person of any other, always at the same time as an end, never merely as a means.")[7] Now, there may be some confusion caused by Kant's use of the word "humanity." The Terminator may have *looked* human, but it wasn't a member of the species. But Kant did not restrict the meaning of "humanity" to human beings, since he meant any being capable of rational thought. Kant even speculates about the "humanity" of supernatural and extraterrestrial beings, like angels and aliens.[8] In essence, this formulation forbids using a rational being like a tool. Kant might say that this principle applies to the T-101's decision because of the phrase "in *ourselves* or others." In Kant's eyes, the Terminator used *itself* as nothing more than a means to an end—by destroying itself, it failed to show the respect due to any rational agent. Its motives are irrelevant, since its intention was wrong in the first place.

But what Kant can't account for are the particular circumstances of the Terminator's sacrifice. According to Kant, we cannot have two conflicting duties, which, in fact, was clearly the situation faced by the T-101. On the one hand, it had a duty to preserve its life. On the other hand, it had a duty to do everything it could to try to prevent the creation of Skynet. The Terminator had both of those duties and should have tried to accomplish both. To violate either duty would be morally wrong. But, from the Terminator's perspective, to perform one was necessarily to violate the other. If it preserved its life, millions would die; but the only way to save those lives was to commit suicide. For Kant, there is no way of weighing one duty against the other, because such a conflict is inconceivable.[9] So something is wrong with Kant's moral theory.

In order to solve the problem of conflicting duties, let's turn to another moral perspective, consequentialism. In consequentialist moral theories, the moral significance of any action is tied to the results of that action, rather than the motives behind it.[10] No action is wrong because of the *kind* of action it is—killing, lying, stealing could all be justified if they were to lead to better outcomes than other actions would. In *T2*, it seems that the T-101 is implicitly relying on a form of consequentialism called utilitarianism. Utilitarianism, as first formalized by Jeremy Bentham (1748–1832), argues that actions are moral or immoral based on how much pleasure is generated and how much pain is prevented by them. The T-101's decision to sacrifice itself caused some pain for the young John Connor, and perhaps some for the Terminator itself. But that suffering would be minuscule compared to the amount of pain that would have been prevented were Skynet never to exist. In exchange for a young man's brief bereavement, the world is saved. From the T-101's perspective, as from that of any good utilitarian, this is a no-brainer. Not only is it permissible for the T-101 to commit suicide; it is positively required. In utilitarian terms, the T-101's suicide was its *only option*, since to remain alive would have been to condemn billions of human beings to death.

This decision, though, is flawed, and in a way that characterizes all consequentialist moral thinking. The Terminator killed itself, destroyed all of the remains of its predecessor, and melted down the T-1000, and in spite of all of that, Skynet still became self-aware, still declared war on humans. This chain of events points to the inherent flaw in consequentialist thinking: we cannot control the future, and consequentialism gives us no points for even trying. For a consequentialist, what motivates an action is completely irrelevant in assessing the moral worth of that action. All that counts are the consequences of the action. The actual, unpredictable results of the T-101's actions were, on the whole, negative: its death, John Connor's pain, and the war between machines and humans. By any consequentialist or utilitarian standard, the Terminator's suicide was the wrong choice—but, of course, we can know that only with hindsight.

So it would seem that there is no moral justification for the T-101's self-termination. From whichever standpoint we view this suicide, it is morally wrong. Kant tells us that the motive for killing a rational being, even oneself, is inherently wrong. Utilitarians and other consequentialists tell us that an act that results in more pain than pleasure, or more bad than good, must always be considered the wrong action to take. Viewed from either perspective, the Terminator's self-destruction is at best a misguided action based on a noble motive. But we get no points for motives.

Can Suicide Ever Be Justified?

The example of the Terminator tells us something about the logic of self-sacrifice, of dying for a cause: it is illogical. Those who do so, or who encourage others to do so, ignore the basic reality of death. As Heidegger showed, to die authentically is to end one's possibilities. Human beings have only a limited degree of control over events when they are alive: to die is to throw away even that influence. The dead have no control over events—nor do they have any right to such control. To die intentionally, even in a noble way, is to abdicate responsibility for oneself and one's actions. It is to leave the interpretation and consequences of one's actions in the hands of others. This is both unwise and unfair.

NOTES

1. Albert Camus, *The Myth of Sisyphus*, trans. Justin O'Brien (New York: Vintage, 1955), 3.

2. Martin Heidegger, *Being and Time*, trans. Joan Stambaugh (Albany, NY: SUNY Press, 1996), 219–233.

3. Heidegger, *Being and Time*, 233–240.

4. Is it too much to hope that whoever came up with this term will be scheduled to receive a visit from an unstoppable killing machine from the future?

5. Plato, "Phaedo," in *The Trial and Death of Socrates*, trans. Benjamin Jowett (New York: Dover, 1992), 59–60.

6. This is the "first formulation" of Kant's categorical imperative; see Immanuel Kant, *Groundwork of the Metaphysics of Morals*, trans. and ed. Mary Gregor (New York: Cambridge Univ. Press, 1997), 31.

7. Kant, *Groundwork of the Metaphysics of Morals*, 38.

8. Kant mentions supernatural beings like angels in his *Groundwork of the Metaphysics of Morals*. He speculates briefly on the existence of extraterrestrial life in his *Anthropology from a Pragmatic Point of View*, trans. Robert Louden (New York: Cambridge Univ. Press, 2006). He also, unfortunately, does not extend his definition of "humanity" to all members of the human species. See for instance, his comments on Africans in *Observations on Feeling of the Beautiful and the Sublime*, trans. John T. Goldthwait (Berkeley: Univ. of California Press, 2003).

9. Immanuel Kant, *The Metaphysics of Morals*, trans. and ed. Mary Gregor (New York: Cambridge Univ. Press, 1996), 16.

10. For more on consequentialism in the *Terminator* films, see Wayne Yuen's chapter in this volume, "What's So Terrible about Judgment Day?"

15

WHAT'S SO BAD ABOUT BEING TERMINATED?

Jason T. Eberl

"Sarah Connor?"

"Yes."

BANG!

The Terminator is a frightening figure, not only because of his (or her, as the case may be) relentless pursuit of Sarah and John Connor, but also because he remorselessly eliminates anyone who gets in the way of achieving his objective. He's also not afraid of terminating each and every "Sarah Connor" he comes across, just to make sure he's gotten the job done. Such pitiless devaluing of human life is both scary to those who might share a certain surname and morally reprehensible to those of us who haven't been programmed as leather-and-sunglass-wearing killing machines.

But what's really so bad about killing someone? To most people, even asking this question may indicate sociopathic tendencies. But when, in *Terminator 2: Judgment Day*, John Connor encounters a Terminator that's been programmed to protect him, he quickly realizes that he'd better come up with some sort of answer or he'll have to face the fact that the price of his own survival may be a significant body count:

> John: Jesus, you were gonna kill that guy.
>
> T-101: Of course, I'm a Terminator.
>
> John: Listen to me very carefully, okay. You're not a Terminator anymore, all right? You got that? You just can't go around killing people.
>
> T-101: Why?
>
> John: What do you mean "why?" 'Cause you can't.
>
> T-101: Why?
>
> John: Because you just can't, okay. Trust me on this.

A satisfactory answer isn't easy to come by, especially since, from the Terminator's perspective, nearly everyone he encounters in the late twentieth century will soon die in a fiery nuclear war.

Most of us share the commonsense moral belief that indiscriminately killing someone is always wrong—although deliberate killing in certain circumstances may be morally justified.[1] Our belief presupposes that *death* is something that is itself bad and should be avoided when possible. Various philosophers have tried to explain why death is one of worst—if not *the* worst—events a person may ever experience. Thomas Aquinas (c. 1225–1274), for example, argues that since human beings are essentially living biological organisms, life is of fundamental value to us.[2] He further claims that "the most fearful of all bodily evils is death, since it does away all bodily goods."[3] A number of other classical and contemporary philosophers argue, though, that we shouldn't fear death because death isn't really bad for the person who dies. If John is to give his "guardian angel" a sufficient explanation for why he shouldn't kill anyone who poses a threat—or just an inconvenience—he'll need the help of philosophers who argue that death *is* bad for the person who dies.

"You've Been Targeted for Termination"

The mission of the villainous Terminators in each film, as well as in *The Sarah Connor Chronicles* (*SCC*), is quite clear: kill John Connor. This is accomplished either by targeting John himself or his mother, Sarah, before he's born—"a sort of retroactive abortion."[4] The wrongness of killing John or preventing his conception is also quite clear from a *utilitarian* moral perspective. Utilitarians believe that ethical decisions should be dictated by "the greatest good for the greatest number," meaning that an action is right insofar as it tends to promote the most benefit for the most people, and wrong as it tends toward the contrary.[5] Clearly, the world will be worse off without John Connor. Sarah muses in the pilot episode of *SCC*, "It is said that the death of one person is the death of the entire world," and she notes that in the case of her son, this aphorism is literally true.

Often, a person's death is understood in terms of what happens to *that individual*, but it's also important to consider how that person's death affects *others*. While showing Sarah pictures of the assault on the police station in 1984, a detective notes that the Terminator "killed seventeen police officers that night, men with families, with children." It would've been bad enough if seventeen single, childless men had died; but the negative effects—emotional, economic, and otherwise—of their deaths on the lives of their families make the massacre all the more tragic. From a utilitarian perspective, the wrongness of a particular act of killing is compounded by the negative effects that emanate from it—like ripples from a stone splashing in a pond.

While the Terminator is emotionally incapable of appreciating the trauma he causes, he views the value of his own existence purely in terms of his *utility*, as he explains to John in *T2*:

> John: Are you ever afraid?
>
> T-101: No.
>
> John: Not even of dying?
>
> T-101: No.
>
> John: You don't feel any emotion about it one way or another.
>
> T-101: No. I have to stay functional until my mission is complete. Then it doesn't matter.

Another T-101 is equally glib about death in *Terminator 3: Rise of the Machines* when questioned by Kate Brewster:

> Kate: If we get killed, does that mean anything to you?"
>
> T-101: If you were to die, I will become useless. There will be no reason for me to exist.

In fact, the Terminator's dedication to existing only to serve the greater good—as defined by his mission parameters—extends to his willing self-termination at the end of both *T2* and *T3*.[6]

"Cameron," the Terminator portrayed by Summer Glau in *SCC*, also thinks like a utilitarian when she reacts to the death of Andy Goode, whose chess-playing computer has the potential to evolve into Skynet: "The world is safer without him" (*SCC*, "Queen's Gambit"). Sarah, though, couldn't bring herself to kill Andy earlier in "The Turk"—electing instead to burn down his house with the supercomputer inside—just as she ultimately stops herself from killing Miles Dyson in *T2*. The point, however, remains lost on the T-101 as he wonders why he and John are trying to stop her:

T-101: Killing Dyson might actually prevent the war.

John: I don't care! Haven't you learned anything, yet? Haven't you figured out why you can't kill people?

When Sarah realizes that John came to stop her from killing Dyson, she can't contain her pride and love for him—it's almost as if she has suddenly realized he *could* truly save the human race.

While utilitarianism would justify killing Goode and Dyson, Immanuel Kant (1724–1804) would not. Kant argues that human beings—as rational, autonomous persons—have a *dignity* that must be respected at all costs. Terminators, by contrast (un-Kantian in the extreme), utterly disregard human life. Think of the opening image in *The Terminator* in which an H-K ("Hunter-Killer") tank crushes a multitude of charred human skulls left scattered about after the nuclear holocaust. Kyle Reese tells Sarah that as soon as Skynet became self-aware, it "decided our fate in a microsecond: extermination." Skynet has no trouble calculating the worth of human survival compared with its own. We see plenty of evidence of the Terminators' indifference to human life throughout each film, including Cameron in *SCC* as she shows John and the others the body of a man she'd killed because "he was a threat to us." When asked if she was able to extract any information from him, Cameron tells them, "He said very little. And then he was quiet" (*SCC*, "What He Beheld").

Kyle Reese, on the other hand, is also on a desperate mission with the fate of the human race on his shoulders. Yet, while one of his first acts in 1984 is to rob a homeless man of his clothes, he doesn't kill him or anyone else as he fights to protect Sarah. And his son John's respect for human life extends even to his foster parents, for whom he clearly has no respect otherwise: "Todd and Janelle are dicks, but I gotta warn them [about the T-1000]." Even the unreformed Terminators sometimes refrain from killing—warning truck drivers and helicopter pilots to "get out" before they commandeer their vehicles—but then minutes later casually kill others who get in their way. Ironically, the T-101, before he has started his "not-killing lessons" with John in *T2*, doesn't kill the bar owner despite the fact that the owner is prepared to use lethal force to stop him from taking someone else's motorcycle. Who has their moral priorities straight here?

"Humans Inevitably Die"

The classic utilitarian and Kantian ethical formulas are by no means the only grounds for an argument that killing someone indiscriminately is wrong. Don Marquis, in a well-known article arguing against the moral permissibility of abortion, makes this claim:

> What primarily makes killing wrong is neither its effect on the murderer nor its effect on the victim's friends and relatives, but its effect on the victim. The loss of one's life is one of the greatest losses one can suffer. The loss of one's life deprives one of all the experiences, activities, projects, and enjoyments that would otherwise have constituted one's future. Therefore, killing someone is wrong, primarily because the killing inflicts (one of) the greatest possible losses to the victim.[7]

Marquis is basically saying that killing someone indiscriminately is wrong because it deprives her of the benefits of continued life, of her valuable future.

This view presumes, however, that the victim has a valuable future ahead of her and that death truly *deprives* her of it. But the future that lies ahead for humans toward the end of the twentieth century—or the beginning of the twenty-first, once the timing of Judgment Day is changed at the end of *T2*—is not particularly valuable: fiery death for billions, others suffering radiation burns and sickness before dying; the rest living in squalor and fighting for their lives against Skynet. As

Sarah tells Dr. Silberman in her ever-so-gentle, motherly way, "God, you think you're safe and alive. You're already dead. Everybody, him, you, you're dead already! This whole place, everything you see is gone!" Later, she's able to use this line of reasoning to convince Silberman—whom she's holding at syringe point—that her level of regard for human life is only slightly above the Terminator's:

> Silberman: It won't work, Sarah. You're no killer. I don't believe you'll do it.
>
> Sarah: You're already dead, Silberman. Everybody dies. You know I believe it, so don't FUCK WITH ME!!

But maybe it doesn't matter that life absolutely sucks in the future. Perhaps simply being *alive* is sufficiently worthwhile.

If so, then death must be bad for the person who dies just because she'll no longer have any experiences of any kind—pleasant or painful. Such absolute existential *nothingness* disturbs Sarah as she contemplates whether human beings have a "soul," something that makes us different from the machines—something that lives on after death. Ultimately, though, reflecting on Andy Goode's death as well as that of a T-888, she concludes in the negative: "There's nothing left of either [Andy or the Terminator]. Nothing that told the story of who or what they were. Gone is gone. Ashes to ashes. Dust to dust" (*SCC*, "The Demon Hand").

This same concept of death's absolute nothingness, however, allows some philosophers to argue that we shouldn't fear death. If death is just absolute nothingness, then it won't be bad at all for the one who dies. The ancient Greek philosopher Epicurus (341–271 BCE) exhorts his readers:

> Become accustomed to the belief that death is nothing to us. For all good and evil consists in sensation, but death is deprivation of sensation. . . . So death, the most terrifying of ills, is nothing to us, since so long as we

> exist, death is not with us; but when death comes, then we do not exist.[8]

We have no reason to fear death, since something can be bad for us only if we can *experience* it; but death deprives us of the ability to experience anything—either good or bad. What's more, we won't even be *present* at our death, since its very definition is the end of one's existence.

This argument finds voice in another ancient philosopher, Lucretius (c. 100–c. 55 BCE):

> If the future holds travail and anguish in store, the self must be in existence, when that time comes, in order to experience it. But from this fate we are redeemed by death, which denies existence to the self that might have suffered these tribulations. Rest assured, therefore, that we have nothing to fear in death. One who no longer is cannot suffer, or differ in any way from one who has never been born, when once this mortal life has been usurped by death the immortal.[9]

Lucretius adds an interesting twist to the Epicurean argument by comparing the eternal nothingness that follows death to the eternal nothingness that precedes birth:

> Look back at the eternity that passed before we were born, and mark how utterly it counts to us as nothing. This is a mirror that Nature holds up to us, in which we may see the time that shall be after we are dead. Is there anything terrifying in the sight—anything depressing—anything that is not more restful than the soundest sleep?[10]

Lucretius echoes the father of Western philosophy, Socrates (c. 469–399 BCE), who, after the "guilty" verdict in the trial for his life, was facing the likelihood of his own impending death:

> Let us reflect in this way, too, that there is good hope that death is a blessing, for it is one of two things: either the dead are nothing and have no perception of anything, or it is, as we are told, a change and relocating for the soul from here to another place. If it is complete lack of perception, like a dreamless sleep, then death would be a great advantage . . . for all eternity would then seem to be no more than a single night.[11]

There is one flaw in Lucretius's and Socrates' comparison of death to a night of dreamless sleep: one *wakes up* from sleep! A person values the restfulness of a peaceful night of sleep only because she feels great the next morning. It's not the experience of sleep itself that she values, for she doesn't experience it at all. The total lack of experience, though, takes us right back to Epicurus and his claim that a person can't *suffer* from being dead since she doesn't *exist* anymore. It's not as if a dead person can say to herself, "Shit! This total lack of sensation sucks!"

"They Tried to Murder Me before I Was Born"

What about Lucretius's parallel between the eternity a person doesn't experience after death and the eternity he doesn't experience before his birth? Against Lucretius's point, does this mean that if death is so bad for the person who dies, then it must be equally bad for him never to have been born in the first place? That would help make sense out of John's statement above, recounting what happened in the first film. If the Terminator had killed Sarah before John was born or even conceived, or killed Reese before he and Sarah "hooked up," would it have been just as bad for John as being killed by the Terminator at the age of ten or twenty-five?

Philosopher Fred Feldman argues, as a utilitarian, that the negative value of a person's death or nonexistence should be judged on how much worse off he is—or the world as a whole is—after his death or without his ever having existed. Simply speaking, it seems that it would be *worse* to prevent John's conception than to kill him at age ten or twenty-five; for at least in the latter case, John is able to enjoy ten or twenty-five years of life that he wouldn't have otherwise had. So Feldman adds that the benefits one is deprived of in death must be *justly due to him*; but having something justly due to a person requires that he exists in the first place. If John never existed, then there are no benefits that are justly due to him: "If a couple fails to conceive a child who would have been happy, no individual is thereby doomed to get less of the goods than she deserves. Since the deprived child simply does not exist in the relevant outcome, there is no victim."[12] If, on the other hand, the child is killed at age ten or twenty-five, he'd be deprived of the benefits of future life that are owed to him. Feldman writes:

> Death differs from never existing in one crucial respect. Never existing is not something that ever happens to actual people. *A fortiori*, there are no actual people for whom never existing can be bad. But death always happens to actual people. It can deprive actual people of what would otherwise be good for them.[13]

But there is still this question: *who* is harmed by death, or wronged by being killed? Is it the ante-mortem person who hasn't yet been deprived of further life or the post-mortem person who no longer exists? Both options seem problematic unless we think that a person can be harmed either *before* the harm actually occurs, or *after* he's no longer around. If we disagree with Epicurus and Lucretius on the harmfulness of death, then we should opt for the first: "only ante-mortem persons can be wronged after their death. . . . [Post-mortem persons] are, if anything, just so much dust; and dust cannot be wronged."[14] A person can be harmed by death while still alive, or so Feldman thinks, not because of some kind of paradoxical "backward causation" in which an effect temporally precedes its cause—of course, this might make perfect sense to time-traveling Terminators.[15] The real reason is that harms don't have to be *fixed* at one particular moment or period of time.[16] Some kinds of harms may be *atemporal*, meaning that they can affect the entire course of a life, thereby making an overall life worse off:

> The sense in which an ante-mortem person is harmed by an unfortunate event after his death is this: the occurrence of the event makes it true that during the time before the person's death, he was harmed—harmed in that the unfortunate event was going to happen. If the event should not occur, the ante-mortem person would not have been so harmed. So the occurrence of the post-mortem event is responsible for the ante-mortem harm.[17]

Someone faced with the impending doom of Judgment Day may be harmed even before it occurs due to the fact that it will occur and cut short her life or otherwise render it miserable if she survives. To be precise, the particular harm the person experiences prior to Judgment Day isn't Judgment Day itself and her subsequent death or crappy existence. Rather, the harm is that Judgment Day *is going to happen*.

"Judgment Day Is Inevitable"

Given this fact in the *Terminator*-verse, is it necessarily a *harm* for the victims who perish? Consider what Jeff McMahan says concerning what makes death bad for the person who dies:

> Death is bad for a person . . . at any point in his life, provided that the life that is thereby lost would on balance have been worth living. Other things being equal, the badness of death is proportional to the quality and quantity of the goods of which the victim is deprived.[18]

According to this view, if the Terminator shot an innocent person dead on August 28, 1997—just before the original Judgment Day at the beginning of *T2*—her sudden, unforeseen death by gunshot may not be all that bad. For it deprives her of only one more day of a life that will end with a horribly painful death—graphically depicted in *T2* in a way that still disturbs me—or her having to suffer a pretty lousy existence afterward that she might gladly trade for nonexistence: "Life is the condition of all goods, but alas it is also the condition of all evils. When continued life promises only great evils unmixed with any compensating goods, our best bet may be death."[19]

Thomas Nagel thinks differently, contending—like Aquinas earlier—that being alive is fundamentally good for a person, even if it's full of more painful than pleasant experiences:

> There are elements that, if added to one's experience, make life better; there are other elements that, if added to one's experience, make life worse. But what remains when these are set aside is not merely *neutral*: it is emphatically positive. Therefore life is worth living even when the bad elements of experience are plentiful and the good ones too meager to outweigh the bad ones on their own. The additional positive weight is supplied by experience itself, rather than by any of its contents.[20]

The fundamental goods that "experience itself" brings, according to Nagel, include "perception, desire, activity, and thought." This may explain why, despite the horrible conditions in which they live, people who survive the initial nuclear holocaust persist in fighting Skynet. Even after Skynet is defeated, life will still be hard in the desolate remains of civilization. Nevertheless, the survivors will be *alive*, and that alone may be enough to continue the fight. Reese, and the Terminator in *T2*, both say to Sarah, "Come with me if you want to *live*"—not, "Come with me if you want to live well and be happy with puppy dogs and rainbows."

But what if the victim on August 28, 1997, won't survive Judgment Day? What if all the Terminator is depriving her of is a more protracted and painful death than an instantaneous, unexpected gunshot to the head would provide? On this question, Kai Draper points out the distinction between "deprivation" and "misfortune."[21] While it's true that the victim is deprived of one more day of life, which may be quite pleasurable for her until Skynet wakes up and decides to kick some human ass, it's not necessarily a *misfortune* for her, since she's doomed to a fiery death anyway—sort of like *not* winning the lottery deprives one of millions of dollars, but isn't a misfortune since the odds were stacked against him.

This difference between deprivation and misfortune echoes Robert Young's definition of the wrongness of killing:

> What makes killing another human being wrong on occasions is its character as an irrevocable, maximally unjust prevention of the realization either of the victim's life-purposes or of such life-purposes as the victim may reasonably have been expected to resume or to come to have.[22]

One can't reasonably expect to win the lottery—although *someone* has to win it. Conversely, an outsider who witnesses the Terminator's killing of an innocent person on August 28, 1997, would probably judge it to be wrong, because he reasonably expects the victim to have enjoyed a long life if she hadn't been killed on that day. Nevertheless, this judgment may be simply wrong, due to the fact that the victim is in fact doomed the next day no matter what.[23] John's death prior to Judgment Day, though, would have a different moral evaluation, since we know that he has a significant life-purpose in the future. But, of course, we have the benefit of knowing these facts from a "God's eye" perspective as viewers outside of the *Terminator*-verse. If someone within that reality—other than a Terminator—indiscriminately kills another person on August 28, 1997, his act would justifiably be considered wrong, since it could be "reasonably expected" that the victim would've had a long life ahead to fulfill her life-purposes.

"I Swear I Will Not Kill Anyone"

Is there any point, then, to this oath John forces upon the Terminator in *T2*? What is it about death that's so *bad*, which in turn makes indiscriminate killing *wrong*? Given death's inevitability, particularly with Judgment Day ever on the horizon, wouldn't a stoic acceptance of eternal dreamless sleep be the most appropriate emotional response? Certainly, the Terminator has no emotional reaction to his killing—as Reese warns Sarah, "It can't be bargained with, it can't be reasoned with. It doesn't feel pity, or remorse, or fear, and it absolutely will not stop. Ever. Until you are dead!" On the other hand, John tries to enlighten the Terminator in *T2* about how humans feel: "Look, maybe you don't care if you live or die, but everybody's not like that. We have feelings. We hurt. We're afraid. You gotta learn this stuff. I'm not kidding. It's important." Draper seems to support John's take on human nature:

> Death is a genuine evil. For death takes from us the objects of our emotional attachments, and sadness is a fitting response to the prospect of losing the object of an emotional attachment regardless of how unavoidable that loss might be.[24]

The Terminator finally realizes this when John gets upset at the T-101's impending death: "I know now why you cry." Although the Terminator can't share John's sadness at this moment, he can intellectually recognize it as an appropriate response to the loss John is about to experience. If the Terminator could experience emotional attachment himself, then he might perceive the "evil" of his own death—however necessary it may be to prevent Skynet from being built—and feel sad about it, too. While the Terminator may have originally taken an oath not to kill anyone simply because he's programmed to obey John's orders, by the end of *T2*, he has evidently come to understand the wrongness of killing in terms of the pain it causes to victims who are deprived of the goods—particularly relationships with those they love—that make life worthwhile. Sarah is thus justifiably optimistic about the future: "If a machine, a Terminator, can learn the value of human life, maybe we can, too."[25]

NOTES

1. Throughout this chapter, I'll refer to the general wrongness of killing while keeping in mind that there may be some cases—such as killing an enemy combatant in a just war or an assailant in self-defense—in which it would be morally justifiable.

2. Thomas Aquinas, *Summa Theologiae*, trans. Fathers of the English Dominican Province (New York: Benziger Bros., 1948), Ia-IIae, Q. 94, a. 2; vol. 2, p. 1009.

3. Ibid., Q. 123, a. 4; vol. 3, p. 1703.

4. As one astute fan noted on the Imdb.com Web page for *The Terminator*, Dr. Silberman has this conceptually backward. He should've said "proactive abortion," since proactive is preventive while retroactive is after the fact: "Abortions in themselves are retroactive." See www.imdb.com/title/tt0088247/goofs.

5. See John Stuart Mill, *Utilitarianism*, ed. George Sher, 2nd ed. (Indianapolis: Hackett, 2001), 7.

6. As the nitpickers will no doubt note, the Terminator can't self-terminate. But he can request that Sarah terminate him at the end of *T2*, and he can willingly sacrifice himself to destroy the T-X in *T3*. For more on the Terminator's sacrifice, see Daniel P. Malloy's chapter in this volume, "Self-Termination: Suicide, Self-Sacrifice, and the Terminator."

7. Don Marquis, "Why Abortion Is Immoral," *Journal of Philosophy* 86 (1989): 189.

8. Epicurus, "Letter to Menoeceus," trans. Cyril Bailey, in *Ethics: History, Theory, and Contemporary Issues*, ed. Steven M. Cahn and Peter Markie, 4th ed. (New York: Oxford Univ. Press, 2009), 178–179.

9. Lucretius, *On the Nature of the Universe*, trans. R. E. Latham (New York: Penguin Books, 1951), 122.

10. Lucretius, *On the Nature of the Universe*, 125.

11. Plato, *Apology*, in *Five Dialogues*, trans. G. M. A. Grube, 2nd ed. (Indianapolis: Hackett, 2002), 40c–e; p. 43.

12. Fred Feldman, *Confrontations with the Reaper* (New York: Oxford Univ. Press, 1992), 207.

13. Jeff McMahan, "Death and the Value of Life," in *The Metaphysics of Death*, ed. John Martin Fischer (Stanford, CA: Stanford Univ. Press, 1993), 241.

14. George Pitcher, "The Misfortunes of the Dead," in Fischer, *The Metaphysics of Death*, 161.

15. For more on the metaphysics of time travel, see Kristie Lynn Miller's chapter in this volume, "Changing the Future: Fate and the Terminator."

16. See Feldman, *Confrontations*, 154; and Thomas Nagel, "Death," in Fischer, *The Metaphysics of Death*, 65. The same may be true for certain types of benefits that make an overall life better off than if they didn't occur.

17. Pitcher, "The Misfortunes of the Dead," 168.

18. McMahan, "Death and the Value of Life," 262.

19. L. W. Sumner, "A Matter of Life and Death," *Noûs* 10 (1976): 161–162.

20. Nagel, "Death," 62.

21. See Kai Draper, "Disappointment, Sadness, and Death," *Philosophical Review* 108 (1999): 389–390.

22. Robert Young, "What Is So Wrong with Killing People?" *Philosophy* 54 (1979): 519.

23. Given that the events in *T2* alter the timeline such that Judgment Day comes much later, it may be correct to judge the victim's death on August 28, 1997, as a misfortune for her, since the many more years of life she would've enjoyed might outweigh the fiery death she'll have to endure later on.

24. Draper, "Disappointment, Sadness, and Death," 409.

25. I am most grateful to Richard Brown, Kevin Decker, and Bill Irwin for helpful comments and editorial finesse on earlier drafts of this chapter.

16

SHOULD JOHN CONNOR SAVE THE WORLD?

Peter S. Fosl

> Hello? Hello? Can somebody hear me? . . . Connor, can you help us?
>
> —*Terminator 3: Rise of the Machines*

Shortly after 6:18 PM on Judgment Day, 2003, safe behind the rocky buttresses and steel blast doors of Crystal Peak, the call to fulfill his destiny as leader of the human resistance literally comes to John Connor via the civil defense radio network. The intrusion of the plaintive voice from Montana into the cavern, however, actually marks for John the culmination of a special period of time that began just prior to the rising of the sun that day, when the Terminator announced to John at the veterinary clinic, "It is time."

Like a giant magnifying glass focusing all of the sunlight within its scope onto a single searing spot, the call from Montana that makes its claim upon John concentrates his whole life into a single, momentous choice: yes or no? Become the leader of the human resistance and accept at least the probability of a violent death in 2032 at the hands of the very Terminator that just saved his life? Or huddle silently beneath Crystal Peak with Kate Brewster facing an uncertain future, while the machines march victorious outside?

Trembling with anxiety, John picks up the microphone and responds affirmatively to the call, acknowledging that he's now in charge and that he will help. There's an ancient Greek word that describes the sort of weighty moment in which John Connor finds himself when the call comes to him at Crystal Peak—*chairos*.[1] This word means, roughly, time understood in terms of its qualitative *significance* rather than just its quantitative *passage*. It indicates a moment when something of great importance is realized; for example, the moment when another person with the initials "J. C." was supposed to have realized his destiny by suffering crucifixion.

Moments like the one John is facing don't happen every day. Some moments are just moments: the clock ticks; the fingers thrum the desktop; the car rolls along. Another day, another dollar. Other moments, however, are not mere moments: they are special, weighty. They *matter*. And the way each of us deals with a *chairotic* moment determines the course of our futures, determines who we are. "Will you marry me?" "Will you accept this job?" "How do you find the defendant?" "What's it gonna be, boy, yes or no?"[2]

The moment of *chairos* that John Connor faces at Crystal Peak piques my philosophical curiosity. Sure, we know what he *will* do; but what *should* he do? Most of us are familiar with the predictable plot trajectories of mainstream Hollywood movies. And given what we've seen in all the clues that the *Terminator* movies have presented, it's hardly a surprise that John responds positively to the chairotic question put to him. The *Terminator* movies are suspense thrillers, not mysteries. But from a philosophical point of view, can we produce a compelling account of why John Connor *should* accept the helm of the resistance, and with it, the likelihood of a martyr's death? Is John actually *obligated* to respond positively to the call? Does he, in fact, have a *duty* to lead the resistance? Would there be anything morally wrong with his saying no?

Cosmic Angst and the Burden of Choice

Of course, wondering whether John ought to respond positively or negatively to the call assumes that he has a choice in the matter. In the first film, *The Terminator*, the machines seem unable to alter the course of their own future, or at least unable to alter their past. *Terminator 2: Judgment Day*, on the other hand, seems to dilute this message a bit and closes with the suggestion that our present (the machines' past) may be altered, but without any assurance one way or the other that this will change the future.[3] The third installment, *Terminator 3: Rise of the Machines*, shifts this ground even further, letting the viewer know that changing the present *can* positively alter the future—but not to the extent that we had hoped. Judgment Day, we learn, has not been prevented or avoided, only postponed.[4]

We don't quite know, however, just how far the future can be altered or whether Judgment Day could have been stopped with the right strategy. But we do know that despite the elimination of Miles Dyson, what John and Sarah could find of his research, and the two Terminators themselves, Skynet is nevertheless built, and the coming of Judgment Day, like that menacing storm with which *The Terminator* closes, rolls down upon the world like a juggernaut.[5] This sense of the inevitability of the future leads John Connor to suffer a kind of *angst*—dread and foreboding, with the sense that he bears the weight of the world. Is this the proper attitude to bring to this chairotic moment?

At the beginning of *T3*, we find John tormented by his role in the world's grand drama. Even though he and his mother survived past August 29, 1997 (what Kyle Reese told Sarah would be Judgment Day), and though John has "erased all connections with the past," he still doesn't "feel safe." For some unknown reason, he "feels the weight of the future bearing down" on him; and in an attempt to avoid the burden, he keeps "running, as fast as [he] can," living off the grid, speeding along on his motorcycle to "anywhere, nowhere," like his mother before him, out of the cities and into the natural world, only able to see in front of him as far as the opening in the darkness illuminated by his headlamp.

But then, out of the darkness, from beyond the reach of the light, something intrudes, throwing itself squarely into the path of John's flight. Not just something, but a living being bearing a moral claim. In its vulnerability and in the urgency of its dangerous situation, the deer that appears makes a claim on John. He finds that he must act, even at the cost of his own safety, to respond to the deer's claim and not run it down.[6] He is, like Saint Paul, "knocked off his horse." This moment, of course, foreshadows the moral claims that reach out and find John under Crystal Peak despite the attempt by Kate's father, General Brewster, to placc Kate and John beyond the conflict's reach. In the structure that unites the films, it seems that John is the one who must answer the call of both past and future history.[7] And the terrible weight the future places on him seems to be his alone to bear, whether he wants it or not.

Still, you've got to wonder: if destroying the Terminators, Dyson, and the records at the Cyberdyne building didn't stop Judgment Day, then why should John's refusal to answer the call or even John or Sarah's premature deaths at the hands of Terminators (had they succeeded) stop the victory of the human resistance over the machines? Remember that the future that the T-101 relates to Sarah and John includes not only the rise of the machines but also their impending fall. So, since Sarah and John's altering things didn't stop the machines from rising, why should the machines conclude that the T-X's altering things would stop the human resistance from prevailing? The T-101 tells John in *T3* that Judgment Day is "inevitable."[8] So, isn't the resistance's victory inevitable, too? Didn't the machines learn anything from the events of the first and second films?

John has good reason indeed to dread the suffering of the approaching struggle. But it's not reasonable for him to believe that the success of the human resistance in the future depends solely upon him. Should John die or should he say no to the call, another leader, perhaps the caller from Montana, might well rise up in John's place. Perhaps the Montanan might prove to be an even better leader than John. And while John's refusal might conceivably *postpone* the humans' victory, there's little reason to believe that it would finally prevent it. John, so far as I can tell, would do better to abandon the weightiness that burdens him and embrace a bit more of what the novelist Milan Kundera calls the "lightness" of being.[9]

And, of course, as far as alternative leaders go, there's Kate. By the end of *T3*, she has pretty well demonstrated her bravery by fighting John, the Terminators, and even the mini-HK. She has also proved her resilience by dealing unbelievably well with the deaths of her fiancé and her father, not to mention the realization that her world is about to end. Nevertheless, the film positions Kate only as a subordinate to John, as "second in command." She even seems, once safe inside Crystal Peak, ready to quit the resistance and "just let it go." The leading female human of *T3*, then, rather than establishing an independent life of her own, is simply transferred from the authority of her father to that of her husband—who as a boy, remember, had silenced the excesses of his mother's feminist rant when she confronted Dyson in *T2*.[10] Finally, there's the shrieking, ball-busting "bitch" T-X (worse than any of the male Terminators), who, after being tossed through the urinals (the place of men), is destroyed by her male counterpart. In the patriarchal universe of the *Terminator* films (so far), men put women in their place, for only men can save the world.[11] Kate, then, *does* have something to feel angst about.

Just after 6:18 PM on Judgment Day, a Phone Rings. Should You Answer It?

So, let's reject the idea that *only* John Connor can save the world. This isn't of course the same thing as saying that John *should not* save the world. It pretty much leaves things up in the air. Since other possibilities remain open, John shouldn't base his chairotic decision on the idea that the responsibility for the future is his alone. Sure, we must judge things by what we see by our lights, limited though they may be; and what we see keeps steering the future back toward John. But we must also understand the limits of what our lights can show us and leave room for the possibility that what's actually coming our way may be different from what we expect (that's just what makes sequels interesting). Figuring out that John's not justified in thinking he's the only one who can save the world, therefore, doesn't provide a way of answering his chairotic question. But perhaps there are other ways to approach the issue.

Let's first consider the possibility that John might actually have good reason to say no—even if by doing so he would be embracing the end of humanity. I know this option sounds bizarre, but look at it this way. In the universe of the *Terminator* films, human beings are responsible for creating devices that have destroyed most of the world, inflicted immeasurable suffering, and seriously compromised the biomes of most of the other living things on the planet, perhaps the only planet sustaining life. Is there to be no accountability for this? When you knock over a glass of milk, it's reasonable to excuse the spill as an accident. Bad things happen. But when, after centuries of increasingly destructive conflict, and after decades of warning from thoughtful minds across the world, human beings still undertake actions that kill millions and ecologically devastate most of the world, it's difficult to make excuses.

Along these lines, in what is perhaps the most absurd moment of the three films so far, the camera finds John Connor in *T3* standing atop a pile of debris, rallying people to organize and fight back against the machines, perched next to a tattered, but still waving, U.S. flag.[12] In the Terminators' eyes' red glare, with plasma bombs bursting in air, that star-spangled banner does yet wave.[13]

This flash forward would have viewers believe that after the U.S. government has made decisions resulting in the end of civilization and the deaths of billions, people would look upon the national flag with anything other than the most profound contempt. From where I sit, though, it would have made more sense to emblazon the U.S. flag on the chest of every Terminator.[14] If there's one thing that should not symbolize the good guys of the future's Machine Wars, it's the flag of the government that produced the holocaust of Judgment Day in the first place.[15] I'm sure the survivors in other parts of the world would agree. But in any case, the presentation of the U.S. flag in this circumstance bears on John's chairotic choice by raising the question of whether there is a moral imperative to become the savior of foolish miscreants so robotically obedient in their patriotism. It's hard to see one.

Still, even if it's true that in some sense humans ought to be held responsible for Judgment Day, it doesn't necessarily follow that humanity ought to be entirely obliterated. The work of many philosophers, in fact, has called into question the very idea of "collective responsibility," as well as collective punishment. By "collective responsibility," I mean the idea that a whole group may be held responsible for the conduct of some fraction of the group, perhaps even for the conduct of a single individual. Should all Germans have been held responsible for the Holocaust? Should all men be held responsible for rape?

Perpetrators defended the 1994 genocide in Rwanda and the 1915 genocide in Armenia on the basis of collective responsibility. And of course, for centuries Jews were held collectively responsible for the death of Jesus. For many, attributions of responsibility like this have seemed unjust. While there are philosophers who have argued in favor of collective responsibility,[16] punishing collectives has been prohibited as a war crime by the Geneva Conventions and condemned by many other philosophers because it can lead, especially in political contexts, to intolerable suffering.[17] More important for our case, civilians aren't generally supposed to be responsible, even in democratic societies, for the misconduct of their military leaders. In light of all this, then, it seems like there's good reason not to hold U.S. civilians responsible for the U.S. government having unleashed Skynet. And, of course, humanity as a whole should also be off the hook.

John, therefore, shouldn't say no to the call because humans deserve to perish. But maybe he should say no to save his own skin. After all, the T-101 in *T3* tells John that in the future he has succeeded in killing John. It may, of course, be just as likely that if John doesn't save the world, he and Kate will die anyway at the hands of the machines. We can't know. But given the possibility that someone else might successfully lead the resistance and given the reliability of the Terminator's information so far, refusing the call in the interests of self-preservation does not seem utterly irrational for John.

On the other hand, just as there may be a chance of defeating the machines with another leader, there may be a chance of surviving the Terminator's assassination attempt, too, especially now that John is aware of it (and even the year when it will occur). The question of self-preservation, then, becomes whether there's more of a chance of surviving as the leader or as a nonleader. So far as I can tell, it's impossible for John to calculate the probabilities either way. Strictly speaking, it's impossible to know whether survival is possible under any circumstances. We're going to have to look elsewhere, then, to tip the scales in favor of answering the call to leadership in the affirmative.

Social Contracts, Divine Commands, and Utility

First, let's take a look at social contract theory. Articulated in early modern times by philosophers such as Thomas Hobbes (1588–1679), John Locke (1632–1704), and Jean-Jacques Rousseau (1712–1778), social contract theories root our obligations to other human beings in our voluntary participation in, or consent to, something like a binding contract.[18] Hobbes, Locke, and Rousseau argued that a social contract is justifiable because people would find the conditions of life without it—the "state of nature" as they called it—unacceptable. The state-of-nature-like conditions following Judgment Day similarly put people's liberty, possessions, and physical well-being in serious peril. And similarly, in order to transcend this unacceptable condition, post–Judgment Day humanity organizes a new social order with John as its leader. John Connor, then, since he is party to the social contract, would be held duty-bound to accept the call to leadership. Since, from this point of view, he would have, in some sense, contracted to respect the claims of others, John Connor, like any other member of society, would be obligated to answer the call to leadership affirmatively.

But we shouldn't be persuaded by this strategy. It seems to beg the question that's at issue here. Scottish philosopher David Hume (1711–1776) criticized social contract theory by pointing out that contracts cannot ground society because the institution of making contracts is possible only *after* society has been established. In the case of John Connor's chairotic moment in Crystal Peak, appealing to the social contract begs the question since in the wake of Judgment Day, the question has become whether the social contract even exists; and if not, whether it would be reasonable or desirable to enter into a new contract.

Arguably, when General Robert Brewster presses the "execute" button that unleashes Skynet, he has effectively, even if unintentionally, nullified the social contract and returned people to the state of nature—perhaps to something even worse than the state of nature. Hobbes tells us that the social contract is nullified when the state tries to kill you. And Locke regards the contract as canceled when the state can no longer secure people's natural rights or when it directly violates those rights (rights to life, liberty, and property). When Brewster presses that button, he turns the weapons of the state against the people.

Attacking the people, or at the minimum rendering the people and their rights unprotected, terminates the contract; but if Brewster has terminated the contract, then the contract's obligations no longer bind John. The call that comes to John under Crystal Peak, therefore, can be read as an invitation to form a new contract. So, the chairotic question can now be put in this way: should John enter a new contract? If you were an alien landing on Earth for the first time during the Machine War, would you think it desirable to enter a binding social contract with the kinds of beings that produced and armed Skynet? Or would you straightaway jump back into your spaceship and flee the solar system as quickly as possible, leaving a "QUARANTINED" marker up in orbit around the Earth as you leave?[19] We, of course, aren't extraterrestrial aliens; and, as we'll see, I think that does matter. But in any case, if we are to find reasons for joining a new social contract, like the alien we'll have to look beyond the contract itself.

As an alternative to grounding obligations in contracts, some philosophers look to commands from a deity, or "divine command." The *Terminator* films are pretty thin on direct references to religious belief (this despite John Connor's initials and the titles of *T2: Judgment Day* and *T4: Salvation*).[20] And there may be good philosophical reasons for this. As far as motivating people goes, religion is effective. So, arguably, it would have made more sense for John Connor to rally survivors around the cross, the crescent, or the Star of David than around a national flag—especially since by that time nation-states will no longer exist. But there are two countervailing reasons that, I think, militate against basing John's chairotic decision on commands from the divine.

First, although it's true that appeals to the divine are for many people good motivators, it's difficult to *understand* and *respect* the commands of a divine being that would allow the machines to inflict so much damage in the first place. Perhaps more important, belief in the authority of divine commands requires certain commitments to the existence and nature of a deity (or deities) for which there seems little solid empirical evidence, and which many reasonable many philosophers find specious. So, appealing to the divine doesn't seem to be a path to understanding John's obligations.

Perhaps, then, we should look instead to utilitarianism, the school of thought that holds that we ought to do what maximizes happiness and minimizes unhappiness, as a basis for John's chairotic decision.[21] Given the information about the future provided by Reese and the Terminators, it would seem that the best available option for minimizing the world's suffering and achieving happiness is John Connor's leadership—that he is, as the T-101 says, the "last best hope" of humanity. So even if it's true, as we noticed before, that victory *might* be possible without John's leadership, it's reasonable to go for the *best available* option to secure victory—or at least, so a utilitarian would reason.

This line of reasoning, however, assumes that on balance there will be more happiness than suffering among humans should they survive and win the Machine Wars. It's a hopeful line of thought, but it's also one that hasn't taken a serious look at Judgment Day. Isn't the lesson of Judgment Day that humanity ultimately brings more suffering and destruction to the world than happiness and flourishing? Isn't the proper judgment for humanity, in light of Judgment Day, "guilty"?

Utilitarianism, then, doesn't look like a promising strategy for justifying an affirmative answer to John's chairotic question. And things look even worse from a utilitarian point of view if we take into consideration the happiness of other animals or other self-aware beings on Earth.[22] Once again the destructive proclivities of human beings as they're described in the *Terminator* films lead us into troubled waters. Difficult as it may be to do so, the narrative of the *Terminator* films compels us to face in a clear-eyed way the question: would the world be a better place without humans? Assuming that it's meaningful to speak of the happiness of nonhuman animals and to give their interests moral consideration, perhaps putting an end to humanity would actually establish conditions for *greater* happiness—especially if the machines could be eliminated as well. After all, the nonhuman animals outnumber us. And consider how much weaker the utilitarian argument for saving humanity would become if the machines not only became self-aware but also capable of happiness—something that *T2* suggests is possible when the Terminator acknowledges at the end of the film that he now knows why humans cry. Utilitarianism, then, at best offers an ambiguous basis for John's choice.

Why Me?

If appeals to the social contract, to the divine, and to utilitarianism fail to provide us with good reasons for John Connor to agree to lead the human resistance against the machines, is there *any* way of grounding an obligation for him to do so? One possibility that strikes me as particularly compelling is an account that roots John's obligation to save humanity in the very conditions of meaningful human existence itself.

John's rebirth as a leader is signaled by his symbolic resurrection at his mother's pseudo-grave (the empty tomb, recalling Christian symbolism, and a uterine symbol) with the help of a pseudo-father (the T-101) sporting a massive pseudo-phallus (the machine gun). First entering the coffin after a pseudo-strangulation (the death of his old self), John emerges from his mother's box, reborn as a fighter to be reckoned with.[23]

At the outset of this process of rebirth, when John asks the Terminator, "Why me?" the Terminator responds simply by saying, "You are John Connor." On one level, this response simply affirms the facts of history. On another level, it can be understood as the Terminator instructing his pseudo-son in a fatherly way through a life lesson. Were the Terminator more of a talker (and a philosopher), it could have also said something like: "Because now you exist, and you are a human being for whom moral life is meaningful. Other people face similar obligations, and others might be able to lead the resistance, but what we know about the future indicates that you are our best hope." In fact, what the T-101 and John don't share—the conditions that make possible common moral life—is precisely what should motivate John. Here's why I say this.

Our meaningful human existence is inescapably moral. Arnold Schwarzenegger's fellow Austrian, the philosopher Ludwig Wittgenstein (1889–1951), said in his famous book *Philosophical Investigations* that there can't be a purely private language accessible to only one person. That's because, according to Wittgenstein, the correct use of concepts and words can be maintained only socially, through interactions with others. Later, inspired by Wittgenstein, philosopher Stanley Cavell argued in *The Claim of Reason* (1979) that meaningful language is not only inescapably social; it is also inescapably moral. Meaningful language by its very nature involves people's making basic moral *claims* upon one another. In conversing with others, we make claims upon them to listen to us, to take us seriously (or at least, *appropriately*), and to respond in meaningful ways.

We can extend Cavell's point and argue that the very possibility of being a human being existing in the world in a meaningful way (rather than, say, in a comatose or pathological state) requires that we confront moral claims made by others upon us and that we make moral claims upon others. On the level of language, again, this might just mean something like making claims upon others to attend properly to our words, and in return that we attend to the claims others make upon us when we speak. But we humans also face more expansive moral claims, claims that might be described generally as calls to others to consider our interests and well-being—and vice versa. In John's chairotic moment the situation is even more acute. John faces not simply a particular moral choice but, rather, the choice of whether to maintain the possibility of moral life at all.

Moral naturalists like Francis Hutcheson (1694–1746) and David Hume, as well as more recent evolutionary theorists, have argued that the human body and mind are naturally set up to include capacities for sympathy and moral feeling. In the view of these "naturalists," we are simply built to be morally responsive beings. Rousseau, along these lines, maintains that our natural capacity for pity binds us together prior to the social contract or utility calculations. Moral life, for these philosophers, one might say, is part of the fatality of our natality.

But in addition to what these philosophers have maintained, whatever our biological and emotional constitution may be, on a conceptual level the very *possibility* of existing in a morally meaningful way requires the moral acknowledgment of others. So, to refuse without any consideration the claims of every other existing human being would be from a moral point of view the most basic kind of immorality. More pointedly, to aspire to an amoral, "nonclaim" kind of existence, existing in a neutral way, beyond the moral claims of others, free of them, is simply not a morally acceptable possibility. In effect, this would be aspiring to escape having a meaningful human life, in a sense aspiring to escape humanness *per se*.

This sort of rendering of the basic conditions of human moral life helps make sense of the chairotic moment John Connor faces in the bowels of Crystal Mountain, and it answers the utilitarian impasse we faced. If John can ignore the call or refuse the moral claim all of humanity makes on him there, he can do so only at the cost of his humanity. Simply because he is a human being meaningfully immersed in a world of others, a morally neutral response is just not possible for him, and to respond negatively to the call to save not just an individual human being but humanity in its entirety would be not only deeply immoral but also inhuman.

One might even say that refusing the moral claims of others in a situation like this is self-subverting in a logical way. Just as it would be self-refuting for a solipsist to argue that no one else exists by means of language that can be meaningful only in a shared world populated by others, it would be morally self-subverting to maintain that the morally right choice is to deny the claims of others when the very possibility of making moral choices depends upon acknowledging and honoring their claims.

Under other circumstances, perhaps, John could acknowledge the claim of humanity upon him but refuse it in order to honor some other more compelling higher claim. But in circumstances like this, where the very *existence* of humanity and moral life itself is at stake, no higher claim can be made. To refuse the claim of human beings under these circumstances, John would have to position himself as something either less than or greater than human.[24]

Now it's possible, as we've seen, that Kate and John could survive on their own and, like a new Noah and his wife, preserve both humanity and the possibility of moral life. But, again, there's no reason to think that there is even a possibility for survival down that road. Nor, again, do we know that there's a better chance for his personal survival down the road of the resistance. *But* we do know that a call has been made and that other living human beings have made a claim upon

John. John could, yes, opt for moral self-subversion, and even existential self-subversion by ceasing to exist. His threat to kill himself at the campground in *T3* indicates his recognition of this possible way out. Indeed, as we saw earlier, by some interpretations a utilitarian calculation might even recommend it. But annihilating or even merely accepting the annihilation of the very conditions that make moral conduct possible can't itself be a morally permissible thing to do. Because choosing not to respond with a yes to the call when it comes would be to consent to the eradication of the very possibility of moral action, there can be only one morally acceptable option for John, the one he does make—the one each of us even on ordinary days must in our own way make—namely, an affirmative answer to the call of others.

NOTES

1. The Greek word "καιρός" is also often spelled in English as "kairos," sometimes as "xairos." Chairos is often contrasted against "chronos" (χρόνος), which is used to indicate time understood quantitatively."

2. You remember Meatloaf's song, "Paradise by the Dashboard Light," don't you?

3. Although the film was released in 1991, the action takes place on June 8–9, 1995. The action of the first film was March 13–14, 1984; the first T-101 and Kyle Reese were sent back from 2029.

4. For more on issues relating to time travel and whether we can change the future, see Kristie Lynn Miller's chapter in this volume, "Changing the Future: Fate and the Terminator."

5. Apparently some of Dyson's notes were salvaged and used by General Brewster in his work, with Skynet as the result.

6. The encounter with the deer accomplishes more than giving John a reason to go looking for painkillers. The filmmakers might have just as easily had John suffer a blowout (perhaps a better device since it would have exhibited the unreliability and dangerous quality of machines). Instead they stage John's accident so that it exhibits the way he responds when the life of a living, sentient thing is at stake. In addition, Kate is configured as someone who responds to the claims of moral action by her working at a veterinary clinic.

7. During his conversation with Kate about Mike Kripke's basement in the back of the veterinary clinic's pickup (pun?) truck (and later at the campsite), John seems to infer that he has been fated to pair up with Kate, that it's not a coincidence that they've crossed paths again. And, FYI, Saul Kripke (b. 1940) is one of the greatest logicians and philosophers of language of the last century. Kripke's notions of meaning and ambiguity

are discussed in detail in Richard Brown's chapter in this volume, "Terminating Ambiguity: The Perplexing Case of 'The.'"

8. "T-101" is short for the "T-850 Model 101."

9. Milan Kundera, *The Unbearable Lightness of Being* (New York: Harper & Row, 1984).

10. Like the T-1000 at the end of *Judgment Day*, but unlike the T-101 in any of the films, the T-X loses its temper as it realizes it has lost—something a machine of this sort would not do, though a "bitch," I suppose, would. For some related musings, see Thomas B. Byers, "Terminating the Postmodern: Masculinity and Pomophobia," in *Postmodern Narratives*, a special issue of *Modern Fiction Studies* 41 (1995): 5–33.

11. Why is it that the female terminator is called the T-X rather than something more consistent with the preceding models like, say, the T-3000? Is it because women have two "X" chromosomes? Or does the X refer to her alluring XXX sexuality? Perhaps it refers to her being, in the silly parlance of our times, X-treme?

12. The scene today looks chillingly like that of the flag raised over "The Pile" at the site of World Trade Center shortly after its towers were destroyed.

13. As we learn later in *T3*, John will die, as national founders John Adams and Thomas Jefferson did, on July 4.

14. Perhaps Skynet's escaping from human control is a metaphor for the way the modern state has escaped human control and has in many cases turned around and harmed the very people it was invented to "protect and serve." Some have calculated, for example, that more people died at the hands of their own governments during the twentieth century than at the hands of others. See R. J. Goslop, *Confronting War*, 4th ed. (Jefferson, NC: McFarland, 2001), 19.

15. Perhaps uncomfortable with the way the *Terminator* films portray holocaust-producing evil with an Austrian accent, the bonus disc sold with *T3: Rise of the Machines* contains a short segment explaining that the T-101 was first modeled on a human American soldier, Sergeant Candy—a character whose goofy southern accent exhibits prejudices of its own.

16. See Thomas R. Flynn, *Sartre and Marxist Existentialism: The Test Case of Collective Responsibility* (Chicago: Univ. of Chicago Press, 1984); Hannah Arendt, "Collective Responsibility," in *Amor Mundi*, ed. J. Bernhauer (Dortrecht, Neth.: Martinus Nijhoff, 1987), 43–50; Richard Wasserstrom,, "The Relevance of Nuremberg," *Philosophy and Public Affairs* 1 (1971): 22–46.

17. Article 33 of the Fourth Geneva Convention (1949) concerning the treatment of civilians during wartime, for example, reads: "No protected person may be punished for an offence he or she has not personally committed. Collective penalties and likewise all measures of intimidation or of terrorism are prohibited. Pillage is prohibited. Reprisals against protected persons and their property are prohibited." The additional Protocol II of 1997 also forbids collective punishment.

18. Note that contract theorists suggest other sources of obligation in addition to the social contract; but for our purposes here, let's focus on contractarian grounds.

19. For more on Skynet's "motivations," see Josh Weisberg's chapter, "It Stands to Reason: Skynet and Self-Preservation," in this volume.

20. Using terms like "judgment day" and "salvation" and a hero whose initials are "J.C.," these films, of course, play off the Christian narrative, though arguably in a blasphemous way. In addition to the terminological similarities, like Christianity, salvation in the *Terminator* films (so far) comes to humanity through redemptive violence. Strangely, however, salvation via J.C. is positioned to arrive *after* Judgment Day. Wouldn't it have made more sense to call *T4*, *Armageddon*? It may have been too much to name John Connor's spouse Martha or Mary, or even Judith or Joan, but calling his mother "Sarah" positions him, of course, not as Jesus Christ but as Isaac—someone as a sacrifice offered but not taken.

21. For another view of how utilitarianism can help us understand the *Terminator* saga, see "What's So Terrible about Judgment Day?" by Wayne Yuen, in this volume.

22. This is just what the utilitarian philosopher Peter Singer does in his famous book *Animal Liberation* (New York: Avon, 1975).

23. It's no accident that it's in this scene, just before the robot teaches him a life lesson, that John happens to mention that the terminator was "about the closest thing to a father" he ever had. It's also no accident that Dr. Silberman, symbol of Freudian psychology, shows up. Along similar lines, Kate and John's future warrior-marriage is subsequently symbolized when John supplants her false fiancé with himself, carrying her off in a hearse that transforms from a death wagon into a convertible, dragging noisy bits of things like a twisted wedding limo, which they soon exchange for a family recreational vehicle, complete with symbolic gear for their kids. It is, indeed, at that chairotic moment for Kate in the cemetery that she switches from trying to escape John to joining him in his struggle.

24. Aristotle makes a similar point; see *Politics* (Book I, 1253a27–33).

PART FIVE

BEYOND THE NEURAL NET

17

"YOU GOTTA LISTEN TO HOW PEOPLE TALK": MACHINES AND NATURAL LANGUAGE

Jacob Berger and Kyle Ferguson

Terminators are incredibly lifelike machines. Not only do they look like humans, but they also have extraordinary knowledge of how to kill, how to protect, and how to use weapons. Beyond all that, they have incredible linguistic abilities. Remarkably, Terminators can communicate with human beings using natural languages like English. In *Terminator 2: Judgment Day*, the T-1000 doesn't just throw the pilot out of the helicopter during the battle at Cyberdyne Systems, he commands him to "get out!" When Sarah tells the T-101 to keep their car at a certain speed, it understands the message and responds:

> Sarah: Keep it under 65.
>
> T-101: Affirmative.
>
> John: No no no no no, you gotta listen to how people talk. Now you don't say "affirmative" or some shit like

> that. You gotta say "no problemo." And if some guy comes up to you with an attitude and you want to shine them on, it's "*Hasta la vista*, baby."
>
> T-101: *Hasta la vista*, baby.

Near the end of *T2*, we see that the T-101 has learned this particular language lesson, as it uses the now-famous phrase before shattering the frozen baddie, the T-1000. But John's remarks in the dialogue above are insightful. While it looks as though the T-101 has a working command of English, the machine struggles with certain aspects of the language as it's used in communication. Its diction is rigid and forced. Worse, it sometimes just doesn't understand what people mean. The T-101 communicates like, well, a robot.

When Skynet designed the Terminators, it must have operated under certain assumptions about the nature of language, meaning, and communication. These assumptions also shape our approach to designing language-using machines in real-world artificial intelligence research today. So the question is this: how could we design a machine—that is, a computational system—so that it could produce and comprehend statements of natural languages like English, German, Swahili, or Urdu?[1]

In order to answer this difficult question, designers must face issues familiar to philosophers of language. Philosophy of language deals with questions like, What is language? What is meaning? And how do things like marks on surfaces (such as notes on paper or images on a computer screen) and sounds in the air become meaningful? What do you know when you know a language? What occurs in linguistic communication? What obstacles must be overcome for this kind of communication to succeed?

The answers to these questions make up what we'll call a *linguistic communication theory*. If Skynet had no linguistic communication theory, it could not have even begun to design or to program a machine that could use language to communicate or that could carry out missions in a linguistic environment.

Think about it. So much of our everyday experience is submerged in language. We look to signs to find our way around, we write reminders to ourselves of places to be and things to do, and we read newspapers to learn about events we've never witnessed in places we've never been. Weather, traffic, and sports reports pour from our radios, and the sounds of conversation fill up nearly every public space. It is rare, if not impossible, to find oneself in a social situation where language is absent. Skynet sent Terminators to this language-infused world and knew they would need to be able to work their way around with words.

"My CPU Is a Neural Net Processor": The Code Model and Language

So, what linguistic communication theory might Skynet have used when it designed its army of badass gun-toting, English-speaking Terminators? One obvious choice is a theory known as the *Code Model.*[2] One reason why the Code Model makes sense as Skynet's theory is that the developers of the model, Claude Shannon and Warren Weaver, created it as a way to understand how machines, so to speak, communicate. Claude Shannon was an electrical engineer concerned with information transmission in circuit systems. Warren Weaver worked as a consultant to the United States military and its defense contractors to solve tactical problems, including how to make information transfer more reliable on the battlefield.[3]

According to the Code Model, the answer to the question "What is a language?" is that language is a kind of *code*—that is, a collection of signals and corresponding pieces of information. The answer to the philosopher of language's question "What is meaning?" is that the meaning of a given signal is the *information encoded in the signal.* The answer to the question of "How does communication happen?" is that communication occurs when a signaler—the *producer* of a particular signal—encodes information into a signal, and the receiver—the *consumer* of the signal—decodes the signal, thereby gaining the encoded information.

This may sound sort of complicated, but it's actually quite simple. Basically, the idea is that information is packed into a signal by a producer; the signal is emitted to, and received by, the consumer; and the consumer then unpacks the information from the signal. If all goes well, the consumer ends up with the same information that the producer originally sent. As long as the producer and consumer share the same code and no "noise" interferes with the signal, the successful transmission of information via signals—that is, communication—is guaranteed.

As an example of this, think of the early scene in *T2* when the T-101 tells John that the T-1000 is going to kill Sarah. John immediately attempts to leave in order to find her in time, but the Terminator grabs him. As he struggles to break free, John sees two guys across the street.

> John (to the two guys): Help! Help! I'm being kidnapped! Get this psycho off of me!
>
> John (to the Terminator): Let go of me!
>
> (The T-101 immediately lets go of John, who falls to the ground)
>
> John: Ow! Why'd you do that?
>
> T-101: You told me to.

Okay, so what's going on here? According to the Code Model, John's signal (the sentence "Let go of me!") had certain information encoded, or packed inside, and the Terminator, since it was programmed with the same code, was able to decode, or unpack, the signal and to acquire the information it contained and respond appropriately.

So what did the T-101 do to decode John's signal? The Code Model suggests that it did two things. First, the Terminator recognized the sounds coming from John's mouth as signals. Then, it retrieved information matching these signals from its neural net processor (its mind, so to speak). In order to do this, the Terminator would need to be programmed with what linguists call a *lexicon* and a *syntax* of a given language. A lexicon is a complete set of meaningful units of a given language, usually words. Think of a lexicon as a "dictionary" of a code, a dictionary that matches individual signals with bits of information or words with their meanings. Syntax (or syntactical rules) specifies how items from the lexicon are combined; this is what people usually think of as "grammar." By recognizing the lexical items and the syntax of the sentence, the Terminator was able to decode the signal and receive the information it contained. And since the Terminator was programmed to do as John commands, it let John go . . . *literally*.

We can now return to our initial question: How do we design a machine that can produce and comprehend statements in a natural human language? If we accept the Code Model as our linguistic communication theory, we can give an elegantly simple and straightforward answer. All that Skynet needs to do in order to ensure that its army of man-destroying Terminators is capable of understanding and producing English sentences is simply program into the Terminators' neural net processors the lexicon and syntax of English. It's that easy. If the T-1000 has the lexicon and syntax for some language, it should be able to understand when people beg it not to kill them and then make quips right before it shoves stabbing weapons into their brains.

Why the Terminator Has to Listen to How People Talk

Our guess is that Skynet did indeed use the Code Model as its linguistic communication theory when it designed the

Terminator.[4] But this is not to say that the Code Model is a good theory of linguistic communication. In fact, it's a flawed theory, failing to capture how people actually communicate using language. Its shortcomings explain why the Terminator isn't so hot at sounding like a normal English-speaking human, and why it sometimes doesn't grasp what normal English-speaking humans mean. The T-101 says, "Affirmative" when it should probably say, "No problemo," and it drops John on the ground when he tells it to let him go, when it probably should have just set him down. The Terminator fails where the Code Model fails.[5]

The problem is that linguistic communication isn't as straightforward as the Code Model says it is. Basic obstacles arise when people stumble over words, run words together, speak with accents, mumble, and more. Schwarzenegger's thick Austrian accent makes it hard for the movie-watcher to understand what he says. If audiences had to make out every word that Arnie said in order to understand him, the better part of *T2*, most of the original *Terminator*, and every single one of his gubernatorial speeches would be nearly incomprehensible. Just watch *Kindergarten Cop* again if you need to refresh your memory.

The Code Model regards these sorts of problems as *noise*. Accents, mumbling, and other imperfections are like "static" that corrupts or interferes with the signal and makes it hard for the consumer to acquire the information it contains. We bet Skynet could have designed Terminators so that they could deal with this sort of noise.

But deeper problems than noise abound for the Code Model. Put simply, the word meanings and the order of the words of a sentence are rarely, if ever, *enough* to give an interpreter access to what a speaker is trying to communicate. For the sake of simplicity, we'll refer to all of these sorts of complicating features as the *pragmatic* aspects of language.[6] Let's consider some examples.

Pragmatic aspects of natural languages include, for instance, *lexical ambiguity*. Consider the quote we reprised at the beginning of the chapter. John says to the Terminator, "And if some guy comes up to you with an attitude and you want to shine them on, it's '*Hasta la vista*, baby.'" The verb phrase "to shine" has multiple meanings. It can mean "to polish," "to emit light rays," "to excel," and other things. In this case, John uses it as slang to mean "to give someone a hard time." Linguists call words or phrases that have multiple meanings *lexically ambiguous*.[7] If a person says a sentence that includes a lexically ambiguous word or phrase, it's not always clear how to interpret that sentence. How is the Terminator supposed to know whether John's sentence means that the Terminator is supposed to say "*Hasta la vista*, baby" to people to whom it wants to give a hard time, or if it means that the Terminator should say the sentence to people on whom it wants to shine a flashlight? Lexical ambiguities make trouble for the Code Model because hearers have no way of resolving an ambiguous signal by appealing to the code itself. If the Terminator were simply assigning pieces of information to John's signal, it would have no clear basis on which to choose one assignment over another.

Another pragmatic obstacle is *syntactic ambiguity*. There's a scene in *T2* where John tells the T-101, "You can't keep going around killing people!" This sentence is *syntactically ambiguous* because, given the way the words are arranged, there are at least two acceptable interpretations of it. On the more natural reading, John is claiming that it is not permissible for the Terminator to kill people. On a slightly less natural reading, John is claiming that it *is not* permissible for the Terminator to go around *and* kill people, though it *is* permissible for the Terminator to kill people as long as he's not *going around* while he kills. If the Terminator is going to understand this sentence, it must disambiguate it. But it's important to note that *each* reading is acceptable given the Code Model because there is nothing contained in the sentence itself that would support one interpretation over the other.

Two more pragmatic issues with natural language are *referential ambiguity* and *underdetermination*. A sentence exhibits a referential ambiguity when it is not clear from the meanings of the words of the sentence all by themselves what a word or phrase in that sentence *refers to*. Recall the scene late in the movie where the T-1000 is chasing John, Sarah, and the Terminator in a tractor-trailer carrying liquid nitrogen. The gang is in a junker that they stole from a man on the street. The T-1000 is gaining on them, and John screams, "Step on it!" In this sentence, the word "it" is *referentially ambiguous*. Naturally, we all know that the "it" refers to the gas pedal of their vehicle. John wants the Terminator to step on *the pedal* and speed up the vehicle. Again, there's nothing in the signal that provides the referent of "it," so the Code Model doesn't explain how the Terminator is supposed to understand what "it" refers to.

Underdetermination occurs when a fully decoded sentence doesn't provide enough evidence on its own to figure out what a speaker means. Even if you had a souped-up version of the Code Model, one that could resolve the above ambiguities, underdetermination might still be a problem. To see why, consider the scene discussed earlier when Sarah, John, and the T-101 are driving out to their gun supplier and they want to avoid the police. Sarah, not wanting the Terminator to speed, says to the Terminator, "Keep it under 65." What, in this situation, does "under 65" mean? If the Terminator was just retrieving from its neural net processor the individual meanings of "under" and "65," it would be very hard to see what Sarah is asking for. Does Sarah mean that the Terminator should keep the car under 65 *years old*? Under 65 *pounds*? Under 65 *dollars*? Under 65 *degrees*? These options make little or no sense. Again, we all understand that Sarah wants the Terminator to keep the car's *speed* under 65 *miles per hour*. But the words "speed" and "miles per hour" are nowhere to be found in her sentence. What Sarah means is *underdetermined* by the sentence because, even though we humans easily understand what Sarah meant, absolute clarity would require us to add more to the sentence than the words provide.

Skynet Doesn't Want Them to Do Too Much Thinking: The Inferential Model

> T-101: Skynet presets the switch to read-only when we're sent out alone.
>
> Sarah: Doesn't want you doing too much thinking, huh?

To understand most sentences in a natural language, we must overcome some or all of these pragmatic obstacles. If the Code Model were accurate, hearers wouldn't be able to make sense of utterances involving any pragmatic features because this model requires only that a hearer process the words of an utterance. How would we interpret spoken words if we were simply left with the words and the word order of the sentences alone? If people were programmed to interpret others' utterances in just this way, we would have a really hard time understanding one another. But, in real life, we seem to solve these pragmatic problems of ambiguity and underdetermination, and we communicate with ease.

So if the Code Model is inadequate, what linguistic communication theory best mirrors what we in fact do? In place of the Code Model, many philosophers of language and linguists have advocated the *Inferential Model* of communication.[8] Here, having the lexicon and syntax of a language is not enough to figure out what speakers mean when they are communicating. Instead, hearers must use this information as one piece of evidence among many other pieces of evidence, to *infer* what speakers mean. It's not a matter of unpacking information from a signal; it is matter of *working out* what a speaker means by appealing to a wider context like shared knowledge and assumptions in addition to the meanings of words.

What exactly, then, are hearers inferring? In answering this question, the Oxford philosopher H. Paul Grice revolutionized the philosophy of language and linguistics. In his two famous essays "Meaning" and "Logic and Conversation,"[9] Grice distinguishes what a *sentence means*, on the one hand, from what a *person means* by using that sentence on a particular occasion. What a sentence means, according to Grice, is something like what the Code Model suggests; you might think of it as the *literal* meaning of the sentence. We will call what a sentence means its *sentence-meaning*. The sentence-meaning of "The Terminator is a killing machine" is that the Terminator is a killing machine. This means that sentences with pragmatic obstacles such as underdetermination may not have a sentence-meaning at all, or at least not a complete sentence-meaning.[10]

What a person means by using a sentence on a given occasion often greatly diverges from what that sentence means on a literal level with no context. We'll call what a person means by saying a sentence on a given occasion the *speaker's meaning* of that utterance.[11] If Sarah were to ask John if he thought the Terminator would be able to complete its mission, John might respond, "The Terminator is a killing machine." In that case, the sentence-meaning is that the Terminator is a killing machine, but the speaker's meaning is something like, "Sure, the Terminator can complete its mission."

Grice's distinction is quite plausible. Recall the scene we discussed in which the Terminator picks John up and John cries, "Help! Help! I'm being kidnapped! Get this psycho off of me!" According to Grice, the sentence-meaning of John's utterance is probably something like, "Assist John in removing himself from the psychologically disturbed individual holding John!" Because the Terminator is operating according to something like the Code Model, it is likely that this is what it interprets John as meaning.

But, as any good Gricean knows, a speaker's meaning often far outstrips the sentence-meaning of that speaker's actual words. So John probably means something more akin to "Terminator, I want you to let me go." Since the T-101 is under the sway of the Code Model, it does not catch on to John's speaker's meaning and continues to grapple with John. Only when John explicitly exclaims "Let go of me!" does the Terminator react and drop John to the ground.

According to Grice, John *did* mean that the Terminator should let him go with his initial statement. The sentence-meaning of John's initial utterance isn't that the Terminator is to let him go, but the speaker's meaning of it surely *is*. His first utterance was directed toward someone else, true, but it provided evidence of his desire to be released. So, if John did tell the T-101 to let him go at first, why did it take the second, more explicit, utterance to get the Terminator to release him? Because the speaker's meaning *and* the sentence-meaning of John's second utterance were both to the effect that the Terminator let him go, but only the speaker-meaning of John's first utterance possessed that meaning. If the Terminator were designed according to the Inferential Model, it would have been able to *infer* John's speaker-meaning from the first utterance. And notice that even when the T-101 interprets John's second utterance, he still seems to fall short of John's speaker's meaning because he complies only with its literal meaning. That is, the T-101 literally lets John go, dropping him to the ground, when it's obvious to normal English speakers that this is not what John meant. Now, speaker's meaning exists only in the speaker's mind. This means that we have to guess at what people believe, desire, intend, wonder, and all the rest. These constitute or determine what a speaker means. But our access to these mental items is forever indirect, mediated by the speaker's publicly observable behavior. From our observations of another's behavior, we infer what that person believes and desires. In other words, we are able to figure out what it's like on the *inside* by using external clues.[12] Language-using behavior is no different. A particular sentence is one clue among many pieces of the puzzle that we must put together by way of inference. These inferences are rarely, if ever, conscious, so it may not seem to us that we're making them. But that's okay. They're still happening.

How to Make the Terminator Less of a Dork

In one of our favorite scenes in *T2*, John asks the Terminator whether it could "you know, be more human and not such a dork all the time?" So, if we wanted to make the Terminator's communicative behaviors more humanlike, we would want to build its capacities to process language according to the Inferential Model. In that case, we would need to supply the machine with more than just the lexicon and syntactical rules of a given language. Clearly, we would need to also program it with a great deal of information about human psychology.[13] It would need to have a mechanism, or more likely several mechanisms, that could piece together lots of information from the environment and about people in general to solve the problem of reading others' minds.

The goal of human interpreters is to infer speakers' meanings behind linguistic behavior, not the mere sentence-meanings. To complete our interpretative tasks, we exploit all sorts of evidence, including speakers' gestures, tones, facial expressions, locations, psychological facts about what they believe and know, their goals and expectations, and more. We use all of this, coupled with word-meanings and sentence structures, to infer what speakers mean. We know John uses "it" to refer to the gas pedal when he screams, "Step on it!" because we know his goals and we know what it would take to accomplish them in this situation. We don't reach this conclusion by working from the words alone.

While we've focused mostly on language comprehension or interpretation, much of what we say goes for language production as well. In order to comprehend, a hearer must rely upon his beliefs or assumptions about a speaker's psychology. This also is true for speakers. Speakers use their assumptions about hearers when they select their words. We don't say more than we have to; we don't inform people of what we think they already know. Rather, we say what we think would be relevant to our hearers, given what we think they believe and what we are trying to accomplish. We say just enough to get our points across. Only a machine that's tuned in to context and to human psychology—in other words, the same kind of information that hearers exploit in order to infer speakers' meanings—would be capable of knowing how to respond in particular situations.

Only a linguistic communication theory that accommodates pragmatic aspects of language would make the Terminator less of a dork. We think the best theory we have going currently is the Inferential Model. So here's a suggestion and a request for artificial intelligence researchers and for Skynet, if and when it comes online: use the Inferential Model in your machines, but please don't use their linguistic prowess to hasten Judgment Day.[14]

NOTES

1. Natural languages like these are significantly different from formal languages, such as the formal languages of mathematics or logic. Natural languages develop, as it were, naturally over time in human communities and are mainly used to communicate between language users. Formal languages, on the other hand, are constructed artificially with other, usually noncommunicative, ends in mind.

2. The term "Code Model" first appeared in D. Sperber and D. Wilson, *Relevance: Communication and Cognition* (Cambridge: Harvard Univ. Press, 1986). The model received its first formal treatment in W. Weaver and C. E. Shannon, *The Mathematical Theory of Communication* (Urbana: Univ. of Illinois Press, 1949).

3. See, for example, C. E. Shannon, "A Mathematical Theory of Communication," *Bell-System Technical Journal* 27, no. 3 (1948): 379–423; Shannon, "A Mathematical Theory of Communication," *Bell-System Technical Journal* 27, no. 4 (1948): 623–656; and Weaver and Shannon, *The Mathematical Theory of Communication.*

4. Disclaimer: despite what we, or our more delusional or conspiracy-theory-minded readers, might think, *T2* is not a documentary. It is a big-budget, action-packed Hollywood blockbuster. So we think that the Terminator is generally working under something like the Code Model. There are, of course, instances in the film where it might seem otherwise. Nobody's perfect or perfectly consistent. James Cameron does come close . . .

5. At least superficially, the T-1000 is far more fluid in its conversational abilities. Before stealing a man's motorcycle, it says smugly, "Say, that's a nice bike." Maybe Skynet changed its approach.

6. The term "pragmatics," as it relates to linguistic theorizing, originated with C. W. Morris, *Foundations of the Theory of Signs* (Chicago: Univ. of Chicago Press, 1938). Morris defined the term as the study of conditions and effects surrounding a system of signs, and how that system relates to its interpreters. Linguistic pragmatism should not be confused with American Pragmatism, a philosophical movement and outlook developed by Charles Sanders Peirce, William James, and John Dewey.

7. For more on ambiguity, see "Terminating Ambiguity: The Perplexing Case of 'The,'" by Richard Brown in this volume.

8. The term "Inferential Model" comes from Sperber and Wilson's *Relevance*.

9. Both are reprinted in H. P. Grice, *Studies in the Way of Words* (Cambridge, Mass.: Harvard Univ. Press, 1989).

10. There is a lot of debate about whether or not there is such a thing as sentence-meaning. For an example of one who denies that sentences involving pragmatic features have any such thing as sentence-meaning, see F. Récanati, *Literal Meaning* (Cambridge: Cambridge Univ. Press, 2004). For an example of one who claims that there is a meaning, albeit an incomplete one, see K. Taylor, "Sex, Breakfast, and Descriptus Interruptus," *Synthese* 128 (2001): 45–61. Some thinkers claim that most sentences, regardless of whether they involve pragmatic features, have compete sentence-meanings; see H. Cappelen and E. Lepore, *Insensitive Semantics* (Malden, MA: Blackwell, 2005).

11. Sometimes literal meaning is referred to as the *semantic content* of an utterance. The semantic content of an utterance is thus distinguished from whatever else is supplied by a speaker—namely, the *pragmatic content*. Where exactly to draw the distinction between semantics and pragmatics is a hot topic in contemporary philosophy of language.

12. For a look at how philosophers have used this inferential perspective to decide whether machines think or not, see Antti Kuusela's chapter, "Wittgenstein and What's Inside the Terminator's Head," in this volume.

13. In *Terminator 3: Rise of the Machines*, the T-101 says that it has been programmed with some basic knowledge of human psychology. Prior to *T3*, there is no indication that it has such knowledge. The knowledge the T-101 claims to have in *T3* appears to deal only with emotions and their impact on behaviors. The knowledge does not seem to include information about cognition or thought, let alone knowledge of how to infer the content of others' thoughts.

14. We would like to thank Marc Berger, Elizabeth Berger, Sam Berger, and Kristen Lee. We especially thank the editors of this volume for their very helpful comments.

18

TERMINATING AMBIGUITY: THE PERPLEXING CASE OF "THE"

Richard Brown

Maybe they should never have called the first movie *The Terminator*. After all, there's more than one Terminator. That may seem like a picky point, but believe it or not, philosophers have long been obsessed with trying to determine the meaning of the word "the." Indeed, much controversy swirls around this seemingly innocuous definite article. Specifically, the controversy focuses on whether or not *definite descriptions* are *ambiguous*.

A definite description is a phrase that begins with the word "the," like "the Terminator," "the leader of the resistance in 2029," and "the mother of John Connor," just to name a few examples. These kinds of phrases are called "definite" descriptions since they single out one unique thing, the thing that fits the description.[1] A word, or phrase, is *ambiguous* when it has multiple meanings. There are at least two kinds of ambiguity.

The first kind is *syntactic* ambiguity, as in the sentence "Visiting Terminators can be dangerous." This sentence has two meanings, depending on how we understand it. It could mean that having a Terminator as a houseguest can be dangerous, or it could mean that going to visit a Terminator could be dangerous (both are likely true!). But notice that no word or phrase in this sentence has multiple meanings; it is the sentence *as a whole* that's ambiguous. Contrast the following sentence: "The Terminator went to the bank." The word "bank" has at least two meanings, and so the sentence could mean either that the Terminator went to the bank of some river or that it went to some financial institution. The question, then, is this: is the word "the" *semantically* ambiguous like "bank," thus admitting multiple meanings?

T1: Russell vs. Strawson

> Listen and understand. That Terminator is out there. It can't be bargained with, it can't be reasoned with. It doesn't feel pity, or remorse, or fear, and it absolutely will not stop. Ever. Until you are dead.
>
> —Kyle Reese

Consider this sentence: "The real-life Terminator can't be bargained with." Is it true, false, or meaningless? The sentence certainly seems false as it stands, since there is no real-life Terminator. But if the sentence is false, then its opposite, "The real-life Terminator *can* be bargained with," should be true. This sentence, however, seems just as false as the first one. We typically think that for any pair of sentences, one of which affirms ("The real-life Terminator can't be bargained with") and one of which denies ("The real-life Terminator can be bargained with"), one of them must be true and the other must be false. So we're faced with a bit of a puzzle.

Bertrand Russell (1872–1970), in his famous 1905 paper "On Denoting," proposed an answer to this puzzle.[2] According to Russell, the *grammatical* structure of the sentence doesn't really clue us in to its *logical* structure. Logically speaking, the sentence really says something like this: "There is a unique object which is the real-life Terminator and which can't be bargained with." This phrasing, although clunkier, is helpful because it shows us that there are really two ways to make the sentence false. One way is the way that we previously considered, namely, to say that the Terminator *can* be bargained with. But we can also consider the opposite, or "negate" the first part ("There is a unique object which is a real-life Terminator") to get "There is *no* unique object which is a real-life Terminator." With this change made, our original sentence is false, because there is no real-life Terminator. And its negation is *true* ("There is no real-life Terminator"), so the puzzle we started with is solved. This is Russell's famous theory of descriptions, which enjoys wide support among philosophers who are in the know.

Russell's theory has an interesting implication in that phrases with the word "the" in them are not *referring expressions*. They do not refer to any particular individual but rather just describe the world as being some way or other. Yet P. F. Strawson (1919–2006) vigorously attacked Russell's theory in his paper "On Referring."[3] Suppose that the Terminator is at the door and you are about to open it when Kyle Reese springs in, shouting, "Don't open the door! The Terminator will kill you!" Kyle *seems* to be referring to the particular Terminator at the door, and not merely saying that there is some object ("the Terminator") and that this object will kill you. Strawson thinks that Russell is wrong, that definite descriptions *are* referring expressions, like names ("Kyle," "Sarah," "John") and *demonstratives* (words like "this" and "that"). Russell failed to notice the difference between an *expression* and the *use* of that expression.

To see why this difference matters, consider the sentence "The Terminator cannot be bargained with." Kyle says this to Sarah in *The Terminator*, and, let's suppose, Sarah says it to John in *Terminator 2: Judgment Day*. Both Kyle and Sarah use the very same sentence, but they make very different *uses* of this sentence. In the first movie Kyle uses it to refer to the T-101, whereas in the second movie Sarah would be referring to the T-1000 (let's say). It is true on *both* these occasions, since it is said in the movie (if I said it in real life, the sentence would be false, of course). Strawson concludes that the *sentence type* (the words that Sarah, Kyle, and I all use) is neither *true* nor *false*. It becomes true or false only when someone uses it in a specific situation to refer to something. As Strawson says, "Referring is not something an expression does; it is something that someone can use an expression to do."[4] What this really means is that for Strawson, the meaning of any expression is the set of general directions for using that expression. In the case of "the," the directions command us to use this word to refer to a familiar object. So, according to Strawson, we cannot decide the truth or falsity of the sentence *type* at all. All we have are instructions for the use of the expression. Nor can we say who the sentence type is about. It can be used to refer to different people (or robots) on different occasions and so can be about many people (or robots).

In addition to this problem, Strawson points out another flaw in Russell's approach. The phrase "the Terminator," according to Russell, tells us that there is a unique object that fits the description, but this just isn't the case. The T-101 that Arnold Schwarzenegger plays is just one of many, many T-101s. So when Kyle says, "The Terminator can't be bargained with," he is literally saying something false because there are many T-101s. But this seems like a counterintuitive conclusion, because Kyle seems to be saying something that is straightforwardly true.

T2: The Ambiguity of "The"?

> I can hear it now. He's going to be called the goddamned phone book killer.
>
> —Lieutenant Traxler

Keith Donnellan (1931–) entered into this discussion about the role of "the" by publishing a paper called "Reference and Definite Descriptions," in which he pointed out that in a sense, both Strawson and Russell were right.[5] He argued that any given definite description can be used to refer, but it can also be used in what he called an "attributive sense."

So consider Lieutenant Traxler's statement above. He makes the statement when he finds out that someone is going around and killing all of the Sarah Connors in the phone book, but he has no idea who this person is. Suppose that Lieutenant Traxler says, "The phone book killer has no pity." This is an attributive use of the description. It is true of whoever is correctly described as "the phone book killer." But now suppose that this description caught on in the press (it doesn't) and that Sarah, after she learns about the Terminator, says the same thing as Traxler: now she is arguably *referring* to the Terminator. In the one kind of use, we're merely trying to tag a property (lack of pity) to some object or other. In the other kind of use, we're trying to refer to some object or person that we have in mind. The difference between these two kinds of uses turns on what makes them true. In Traxler's attributive case the truth depends only on whether the description fits some individual, whereas in Sarah's referential case, the truth of the sentence depends on the person being referred to, whether or not the description is true of them.

So suppose that Lieutenant Traxler (wrongly) thinks that Kyle Reese is the phone book killer. Then if he were to say, "The phone book killer has no pity," intending to refer to Kyle, the truth of what he says depends on whether Kyle Reese has pity, regardless of the fact that Kyle is *not* the phone book killer. It would then be false, since Kyle does have pity. On the other hand, if he were to use it in the attributive sense, not speaking about Kyle Reese but rather talking about anyone who would kill in the manner that the phone book killer does, then the sentence's truth will depend on whether the T-101 has any pity. It would then be true, since the Terminator has no pity.

Given these two different uses of definite descriptions, we have to decide between two competing notions about their nature. On the one hand, we might say that definite descriptions are *ambiguous*: they genuinely have two separate kinds of meanings, a referential and an attributive one. Here, we'd be treating descriptions like "the phone book killer" the way that we treat words like "bank." "Bank" has at least two different meanings. So, in this way of dealing with definite descriptions, the sentence "The phone book killer has no pity" will have two distinct meanings. In one of its meanings it will mean something like "The phone book killer, *whoever that is*, has no pity," and in the other, it'll mean something like "The phone book killer, *by which I mean that particular guy*, has no pity."

On the other hand, we can say that what's going on here makes sense in terms of what's called the *semantic* vs. the *pragmatic* distinction. Semantics deals with the *meaning* of expressions or terms, whereas pragmatics deals with the way that people *use* an expression in communication. So, to take a simple example, suppose that I said, "This movie is *so* interesting" in a sarcastic way, as to make it clear that what I really meant was that this movie (hopefully not *Terminator: Salvation*!) was anything *but* interesting. The sentence that I speak in this case would have a different *meaning* from how I intended to *use* it.

Yet Paul Grice (1913–1988) argued that there's no need to worry about this second meaning for the sentence I said, one in which it really means the opposite of what it literally means. This is an example of Grice's "modified Ockham's razor." Ockham's razor helps us choose between two competing theories: all other things being equal, the simplest one is the best. Grice's version tells us that we shouldn't "multiply linguistic entities beyond necessity." If we can find a way to explain what is going on in the above examples without having to come up with multiple meanings for the sentence, then we should do so.

Grice thinks we can distinguish between the meaning of the sentence itself (as spoken) and the *speaker's* meaning in saying the sentence. The sentence's standard meaning is that the movie holds my attention; but the speaker wants to convince us of the opposite. If Grice is right, then we can explain what's going on with definite descriptions in this way: we can say that definite descriptions have their attributive meanings like Russell thought, and yet people sometimes use these in referential ways, as in the examples above. But "The phone book killer, *by which I mean that particular guy*, has no pity" isn't a meaning of the sentence that I say. It is, rather, the thought that I am trying to express in saying what I did in just the same way as when I say that the movie is so interesting. The sentence will have its standard "whoever that is" meaning. What I say is not what I mean. So which is right? Do they have two meanings or just one meaning and different uses?

T3: Kripke and Devitt

Saul Kripke (1940–) argues against treating descriptions as ambiguous in his paper "Speaker's Reference and Semantic Reference," where he calls positing an ambiguity "the lazy man's approach."[6] If referential uses of descriptions occurred in a language that was stipulated to be as Russell says, then it cannot be an argument against Russell that such uses occur in English. So let us imagine a fictional language, call it "Russell English," in which we stipulate that definite descriptions work in the way that Russell says that they do. In Russell English, "The Terminator has no pity" has only its attributive meaning, which is that there is some object or other that is the one and only Terminator and that object has no pity. In such a language, Kripke argues, people could still use "The Terminator has no pity" to refer to the Terminator, and so the existence of referential uses in actual English cannot be an argument against Russell. In this fictional language, there is no referential meaning for definite descriptions. This is true simply because we have stipulated it to be so. So there is no question about whether the descriptions in Russell English are ambiguous; they are not. But even so, the speakers of Russell English could still use those descriptions to refer to people and objects in spite of the lack of referential meaning. If this is the case, and it seems as though it is, it can't be a problem for Russell's theory that people use descriptions to refer. How could it? We could, for all we know, be speaking Russell English, and if that were so, we would still be able to use descriptions referentially. Kripke suggests that Grice's way of handling these kinds of cases is all that we need. Why multiply linguistic entities that do not work for us?[7]

Kripke also argues against treating descriptions as ambiguous by drawing our attention to *anaphor*. When we use pronouns to refer to an object that we previously referred to by name, we are using anaphor. So, in the sentences "The Terminator has no pity. It cannot be bargained with," the word "it" is anaphoric. Kripke thinks this gives us good reasons not to treat definite descriptions as ambiguous. Suppose that we are watching John having lunch with someone (who is not the Terminator) and who is acting sympathetically toward John. Kripke asks us to "consider the two following dialogues," modified for our context:

Dialogue 1

Albert: The Terminator is kind to him.

Barbara: No, he isn't. The man you're referring to isn't the Terminator.

Dialogue 2

Albert: The Terminator is kind to him.

Barbara: He is kind to him, but he isn't the Terminator.

In the first dialogue, Barbara uses the word "he" to refer to the Terminator (and not to refer to the person having lunch with John), while in the second dialogue, Barbara uses "he" to refer to the person having lunch with John (and not the Terminator). However, Albert is using "The Terminator is kind to him" in the referential sense and so is referring to the person that John is having lunch with. Whether or not that person is the Terminator, the sentence depends for its truth on that person and only on that person.

But this presents a problem. The second dialogue is easy to explain: Barbara's use of "he" is anaphoric and depends on Albert's referential use of "the Terminator." It refers to the person that John is having lunch with. But this isn't the case in the first dialogue. If "he" is anaphoric in this dialogue, depending on "the Terminator," then it has to have the same reference. If it's true that Albert's line has a referential meaning, then Barbara's use of "he" must refer to the person that John is having lunch with. But this is clearly not what's going on. Barbara is obviously using "he" to refer to the Terminator and not to the person John is having lunch with. Since it's clear that Barbara means to use "he" to refer to the actual Terminator and *not* to the person who is having lunch with John, we can explain this only by either denying that "he" is anaphoric *or* by giving up the idea that "the Terminator is kind to him" has a referential meaning.

Michael Devitt (1938–) takes the first option, suggesting that "he" in the first dialogue is in fact not anaphoric but rather a *pronoun of laziness*. Let's look at the way these things normally work. If I say, "John Connor has his paycheck directly deposited, but Miles Dyson has to take it to the bank," the occurrence of "it" here can't be anaphoric. That is, it can't be taken as referring to John's check but must be taken as referring to Miles's check. Maybe I should have said, "Miles Dyson has to take his paycheck to the bank," repeating "his paycheck," but being lazy, I use "it" instead. If "he" was Devitt's pronoun of laziness in the first dialogue, then the dialogue should be read in the following way:

> Albert: The Terminator (in-the-referential-sense-referring-to-that-guy-over-there) is kind to him.
>
> Barbara: No, the Terminator (in-the-referential-sense-referring-to-the-actual Terminator) isn't. The man you're referring to isn't the Terminator.

Originally, Barbara simply used "he" as a replacement for the description "the Terminator," but we take it to be the referential meaning that refers to the actual Terminator.

Kripke objects to this because "[Barbara] may well be in no position to use ['the Terminator'] referentially. She may have merely heard that [the Terminator has no pity]." If this were the case, then Barbara could not be using "he" as a pronoun of laziness, and it would have to be taken as anaphoric on Albert's use of "the Terminator." Devitt responds that it "might be a pronoun of laziness for ['the Terminator'] taken attributively, even though Albert's use of ['the Terminator'] is referential."[8] So for Devitt, we should understand Barbara as saying, "No, the Terminator (in-the-attributive-sense-whoever-that-is) isn't. The man you're referring to isn't the Terminator." This would be possible if Barbara knew the person who John was having lunch with and knew that he wasn't the Terminator.

At first glance, it does seem that we might be able to switch between the meanings of ambiguous words when using these kinds of pronouns. For instance, consider the recent DVD release of a movie called *Paycheck*.[9] Now suppose that I say, "I put my paycheck in the bank, John put it in the DVD player." Can "my paycheck" be taken as referring to my paycheck from work while the "it" is used as a pronoun of laziness that refers to his rented copy of the movie *Paycheck*? I could do this if I wanted to make a joke through a play on words, but as Devitt says, this depends on "how much laziness is acceptable," and there are limits!

So far, all of these arguments have been inconclusive, which is always a possibility in philosophy. Kripke, however, makes another suggestion that seems to me to be decisive, if we modify it for our *Terminator* context:

> There is no reason to suppose that in making an indirect discourse report on what someone else has said I myself must have similar intentions, or be engaged in the same kind of speech act; in fact it is clear that I am not. If I say "[John Connor says all of the police are here]" [John] may have meant it as a warning but I need not say it as a warning. If the referential-attributive distinction is neither syntactic nor semantic, there is no reason, without further argument, to suppose that my usage, in indirect discourse, should match the man on whom I report, as referential or attributive. The case is quite different for a genuine semantic ambiguity. If Jones says, "I have never been to a bank," and I report this, saying, "Jones denied that he was ever at a bank," the sense I give to "bank" must match Jones' if my report is to be accurate.[10]

If I say, "The Terminator has no pity," and I am using the description referentially, and then you report to someone else that "Richard said that the Terminator has no pity," you don't have to be using the description referentially. In fact you may not even be able to use it referentially, as you may not know who "the Terminator" is. If the referential use were *semantic*, this would pose a problem, because we can only resolve genuine semantic ambiguities if we use words with the same sense ("paycheck" has two senses above). Since descriptions are more pragmatic than semantic, there is no ambiguity.

Devitt has tentatively responded[11] that whether or not you know who the Terminator is, this would not prevent you from using "the Terminator" referentially. This is due to Devitt's notion of *reference borrowing*. This is easiest to illustrate in the case of names. Suppose that you have never seen any of the *Terminator* movies (for shame!), and I tell you that the movie is about a guy named John Connor who will eventually lead the human resistance against an army of cyborgs created by Skynet. You then acquire *from me* the ability to refer to John Connor. Devitt thinks that our ability to reference-borrow doesn't take much. All you have to do is to hear the name from someone who is in a position to refer to the person in question, and you then acquire the ability to refer to that person as well, whether you know anything about them or not.

But even if you were able to use "the Terminator" referentially, Kripke's point is that you don't have to. You could be using the description in an attributive sense when you report what I said. Nothing forces you to use the description in the same sense that I did in order to successfully report what I said. But this is very different from the case of actual semantic ambiguities. In the case of an actual semantic ambiguity, if you do not use the word with the same sense that I used it, then you are not accurately reporting what I said. So if I say, "I like dogs," meaning *hot dogs*, and you report, "Richard said that he likes dogs," meaning the animal *Canis familiaris*, you haven't accurately reported what I said.

T4: Ambiguity Salvation

So what then is the score? From what we've seen, the balance seems to be tilted slightly in favor of Grice. Kripke's argument from indirect quotation doesn't have an answer, and so I think we can safely say: "Ambiguity, you've been terminated." But what does this tell us about the question we started with? Should the first movie have been called *The Terminator*? If what we have said is right, then the title literally means what Russell said that it did: there is one and only one object that is the Terminator. Given this, the title is literally false; there are many Terminators. Nonetheless James Cameron most likely meant to be taken as referring to the T-101. This is the way that everyone in the films uses the phrase as well. This is a perfectly legitimate use of the phrase and so the title is apt despite its literal falsity. Sheesh! Can you believe people actually get paid to think about this stuff? Well, if it's any consolation, philosophers don't get paid much![12]

NOTES

1. They are contrasted with indefinite descriptions like "a Terminator" or "a leader of the resistance in 2029." I will not have anything to say about these kinds of phrases, though there is a fair amount of controversy that swirls around them as well.

2. Bertrand Russell, "On Denoting," in *The Philosophy of Language*, ed. A. P. Martinich (Oxford Univ. Press, 1985), 230–238.

3. P. F. Strawson, "On Referring," in *The Philosophy of Language*, 246–260.

4. Ibid., 249.

5. Keith Donnellan, "Reference and Definite Descriptions," in *The Philosophy of Language*, 265–277.

6. Saul Kripke, "Speaker's Reference and Semantic Reference," in *Pragmatics*, ed. S. Davies (Oxford: Oxford Univ. Press, 1991), 77–96.

7. Michael Devitt's response to this is that in Russell English there would not be a convention for expressing singular thoughts the way there is in English. There would have to be careful stage setting in order for someone to make a referential use. For a careful defense of the ambiguity of definite descriptions, see Devitt, "The Case for Referential Descriptions," in *Descriptions: Semantic and Pragmatic Perspectives*, ed. Marga Reimer and Anne Bezuidenhout (Oxford: Oxford Univ. Press, 2004), 280–305.

8. Michael Devitt, "Donnellan's Distinction," in *Foundations of Analytic Philosophy: Midwest Studies in Philosophy*, ed. Peter A. French, Theodore E. Uehling, and Howard K. Wettstein (Minneapolis: Univ. of Minnesota Press, 1981), 522.

9. Based on a story by Philip K. Dick.

10. Kripke, "Speaker's Reference and Semantic Reference," 83.

11. Personal communication to the author, spring 2006.

12. I would like to thank Frank Pupa, Kevin S. Decker, and Bill Irwin for valuable help in revising earlier drafts.

19

WITTGENSTEIN AND WHAT'S INSIDE THE TERMINATOR'S HEAD

Antti Kuusela

The three *Terminator* movies, especially *Terminator 2: Judgment Day*, invite us to consider whether machines have mental lives like we do. Among the most basic aspects of human mental life are emotions, feelings, sensations, and self-awareness. Could a Terminator have feelings and sensations? Does the T-101 have self-awareness like a human does?

I'm not a very sentimental person, but when I first saw *T2*, I was moved. The scene in which the T-101 is lowered into the molten steel by Sarah Connor is touching, and after seeing the movie a dozen times, the scene still strikes me as emotionally powerful. Why is this? One reason is that the viewer is able to see the grief of the fatherless John Connor, who has formed an emotional bond with the cybernetic organism. It's easy to empathize with John's sadness, because he is about to lose a father figure. But the main reason why the scene is so touching for me is not empathy with the grief of John, but sympathy for the sadness I perceived from the T-101.

But how can this be? Intuition tells us that a machine doesn't have emotions. A Terminator is simply a machine, and so it's incapable of feeling sadness, joy, or grief. If this is so, it makes no sense to feel sorry for the Terminator. After all, we can't relate to its feelings it if doesn't have any! Yet I think that it *does* make sense to feel sympathy for the T-101. By the end of *T2* we've come to think of the T-101 as *one of us*, as a being with emotions of its own. The Terminator's self-destruction wouldn't be noble from our perspective, wouldn't move us, if we thought that the T-101 was completely indifferent to its fate. If we're moved by the self-destruction of the Terminator, it's because we feel that *somebody* and not just some*thing* is being destroyed. We can place ourselves in its shoes and imagine how we would feel if such a choice were in front of us.

We may feel sorry for the T-101 because it is going to lose its existence. We may think of the Terminator's act as being unselfish because it puts the interests of humans before its own. But of course, these views make sense only if we believe that the T-101's mental life *is* similar to ours. And if it is, then there may be good reasons to reevaluate the real difference between machines and persons.

If It Cries Like a Human, It Is Human . . .

Let's take a reasonably simple definition of a "person": first, a person is a being that's self-aware, which means that it can think about the process of thinking itself. A person has emotions and can make choices. When questions about the differences and similarities between machines and persons are raised in philosophy or in films like *The Terminator*, it's a fairly commonsense idea of a person, much like this one, that is used as a measuring stick. Given this definition, how similar to a person is the T-101?

Most people would say that a person has a mental life, while a machine doesn't. It feels "like something" to be a person, whereas it doesn't feel like anything to be a machine. One way to examine the commonsense idea of machine vs. person is to carefully look at the difference between the *behavior* of a person and the *behavior* of a machine. Ludwig Wittgenstein (1889–1951), an Austrian philosopher, suggested this method, claiming, "Only of a living human being and what resembles (behaves like) a living human being can one say: it has sensations; it sees; is blind; hears; is deaf; is conscious or unconscious."[1] Wittgenstein doesn't mean that a machine could *never* have sensations or that a machine could *never* be conscious. Instead, he was considering how we use language. What do we *mean* when we say that a human has sensations, but a machine does not? What are the facts on which we could base this difference?

Wittgenstein's answer is this: as things currently stand, the only criterion for what it means to be a "thinking thing" is the behavior of human beings. Human behavior, for Wittgenstein, is a *sign* that stands for being conscious and having a mental life. To see what he means, take the phenomenon of pain. Moaning and crying are signs that we interpret to mean that the moaner or crier is experiencing pain, which by itself is mental and private. Pain behavior is not limited to simple things like crying, of course. Seeing a doctor or taking a painkiller are pain behaviors as well. For Wittgenstein, the *meaning* of any behavior, the way we *understand* it, is tied to a complex web of human habits, customs, rules, and institutions. In fact, if we couldn't understand the behavior of a creature like ourselves in these respects we couldn't make sense of its mental life at all. But Wittgenstein goes even further than this, arguing that the relationship between behavior and having a mental life is not merely that of a sign and what it signifies.

For Wittgenstein, complex behavior is *constitutive* of mental life. In other words, meaningful actions that we observe in others become the touchstone of mental life, and not merely a *symptom* that something is going on in our heads. If Wittgenstein's point about the relationship between behavior and our conclusions about the mind isn't clear enough, consider how people who have mental illnesses are usually diagnosed. Deranged behavior on the part of a person implies that there is something wrong with the person's mind. It seems that what we *mean* by "having a mind" is really just "being capable of acting in certain kinds of rational ways."

These complex forms of behavior are important if we are to conclude that other beings have mental lives. We don't treat stones or tables as having minds. Animals are somewhere between things and persons: the more an animal behaves like we do, the higher degree of mental activity we grant to it. Complex machines like Terminators are another example of borderline cases. In terms of their behavior, Terminators are practically identical to humans. This makes sense, since these machines were originally developed as *infiltrators* who could approach humans without being revealed as the killing machines they are. So if we agree with Wittgenstein about behavior being the touchstone of mental life, then we should conclude that it makes good sense to treat Terminators as if they had a mental life. The conclusion is justified because the behavior of these machines is very similar to that of humans.

A Terminator would also likely pass the most famous test designed to answer the question of whether machines can think, the Turing Test. The test, named after the famous mathematician Alan Turing (1912–1954), looks at the result of a conversation with a machine when we cannot decide whether the conversation partner was a machine or not (both a machine and a human are hidden from us and we ask questions of both).[2] If Turing's test is sound, and if a Terminator passes it, then perhaps the Terminator really is an intelligent, thinking being.

Wittgenstein would say that the Terminator has demonstrated behavior that shows it has a mind. But should we agree with him? Is the behavior of a human and a T-101 similar enough to say that these machines have a mental life? In *The*

Terminator, Kyle Reese claims that Terminators don't have feelings and don't feel pain. This implies that Terminators lack emotions and sensations that are an essential part of the mental life of humans. How can Reese know this? Even assuming he hasn't designed Terminators and he doesn't know what happens in their heads, his claim seems to be true. Consider the T-101 in the first movie, which shows no signs of emotion at all. It doesn't behave in a way to suggest that it feels pain, either. The T-101's arm is cut open, and this doesn't faze it; neither does being hit by a bullet. Could we say that the machine nevertheless *does* feel pain? As Wittgenstein might ask, what would it *mean* to say that the Terminator feels pain?

When a human is in pain, this means that she experiences an unpleasant sensation and is apt to behave in certain ways—for example, she might grimace or cry. But to say that a Terminator is in pain can't mean *this*. Since the statement about the Terminator's pain means something different from a statement about a human's pain, Wittgenstein would say that we don't really know the relationship between a Terminator's pain and a human's pain. It would perhaps be best to say that "pain" doesn't apply to Terminators at all because their so-called pain is utterly different from human pain. Why would we use the term *pain* in the case of Terminators? How about emotions?

The capability of feeling humanlike emotions would be useful for infiltration because then Terminators would appear "more human" not just physically, but in terms of their behavior as well. And they'd be in a better position to deceive real humans. On the other hand, the purpose of Terminators is to kill without asking questions and complete their assigned mission. For them to feel emotions, to be sentimental, or to consider the morality of a certain action would make a Terminator's main task more difficult. In *T2*, the T-101 explains that it does not have feelings because functionality is the most important thing for a machine. This confession by the T-101, along with Reese's comment, gives us reason to think that Terminators don't have the kind of mental life that we attribute to humans, despite their complex behavior. However, as we also see in *T2*, the T-101 is capable of *adapting* as it receives instructions from John Connor. Maybe this should alter our conclusion about their mental lives.

"Desire Is Irrelevant. I Am a Machine": The Mental Life of Terminators

Terminators are complex machines that are physically superior to humans. Indeed, the models T-1000 and T-X can do many things that far exceed human capabilities. Terminators can process information and make inferences at a speed impossible for humans. If we took speed and efficiency as the only criteria for intelligence, then Terminators would be more intelligent than humans. But even the most physically developed cybernetic organisms, the T-1000 and T-X, lack the basic elements of human mental life. Although the behavior of Terminators is complex, there are various reasons to think that these machines in general do *not* have a mental life like ours.

Despite the fact that the T-101 in *The Terminator* doesn't show any signs of emotion, we do get a look at its "inner life" in a scene when the machine answers to a person who is knocking on the door of its hotel room. The camera shows us the world through the T-101's eyes, highlighting how the machine chooses an appropriate linguistic reply from a list deployed in its heads-up "user interface" (which suspiciously resembles the user interface of computers made around 1984, not 2029). But this procedure of choosing is a rote mechanical procedure, suggesting that Kyle and Sarah are fighting against a mere machine. In fact, the nature of the procedures by which the T-101 makes its decisions raises a doubt as to whether we should grant it intelligence, even if it could pass Turing's Test.

Contemporary philosopher John Searle would deny that the Terminator has a mental life. In his famous "Chinese room example" Searle has argued that a machine could *simulate* human linguistic behavior simply by manipulating symbols that are inherently meaningless to it.[3] Searle's point is that a computer has no *understanding* of what it is doing, and no comprehension of the significance of the words that it uses. Another contemporary philosopher, Ned Block, comes to the same conclusion from a different perspective: imagine a computer programmed with *every possible answer to every possible question.*[4] Such a machine, call it "blockhead," could give an appropriate answer in each and every occasion, without ever really understanding anything it says. What we know about the "user interface" of the T-101 suggests that it uses a strategy very much like manipulation of symbols, a strategy that may very well be meaningless to the machine itself.

In *T2*, clues about the nature of Terminators' mental lives are revealed more explicitly. Young John Connor is interested in the nature of his T-101 protector, wondering just how human-like the T-101 really is. The machine doesn't give him much to go on: it doesn't understand why it shouldn't kill humans, or the difference between right and wrong actions. The T-101 explains to John that it does not fear and that it does not have feelings. Simple things like crying, smiling, and swearing—all essential aspects of human life—are completely incomprehensible to the T-101. If Wittgenstein is right, then the Terminator's emotional limitations are a reason to think that it doesn't have a mental life. Perhaps a Terminator like the T-101 could deceive a human for a while, but a perceptive human would soon detect that something was wrong in the situation. And the human would be right if machines like the T-101 are simply symbol-processing machines, which, according to Searle and Block, don't *understand* anything.

But what about more sophisticated models, like the T-1000 or the T-X? Although the T-1000 can *physically* mimic humans by assuming their physical appearance, it's unlikely that its inner life is any more similar to humans' than the T-101's. The

T-1000's conduct demonstrates no signs of emotion, and while the machine can simulate other human behaviors, this does not mean that it understands what it is doing. On the other hand, both the T-1000 and the T-X do make, for example, aesthetic evaluations when they say things like "Say, that's a nice bike" or "I like this car." We have no reason, however, to believe these evaluations are accompanied with any inner feelings or sensations. In fact, in these cases the behavior of the Terminators resembles that of deceptive humans who claim to feel emotions without really having them. Models T-1000 and T-X could as well be the kind of complicated computers imagined by Block that contain all possible replies to all possible questions.

Still, there might be a reason to believe that these highly developed models might have *some* kind of understanding about the mental lives of humans. A scene from *T2* in which the T-1000 tortures Sarah Connor suggests that the machine understands something about the nature of pain because, when twisting a metal spike in Sarah's shoulder, it comments, "I know this hurts." But what kind of knowledge could the T-1000 have about pain or about hurting if the machine itself does not and *cannot* feel pain? Thinking along Wittgensteinian lines again, the T-1000 may have been programmed to know that tissue damage in humans is apt to cause an unpleasant sensation that can be called pain. But about this pain, we could still ask, could a machine that has never felt a sensation really understand what a sensation is? If a machine is never actually hurt, can it understand *how* others hurt? If the answers to these questions are no, then the T-1000's statement is meaningless.

So it seems that whether the different Terminator models have mental lives or not is an open question. On the one hand, their behavior is very similar to that of humans, and this could or perhaps even *should* be a reason to think (in the spirit of Wittgenstein) that their inner lives must be similar to that of humans as well. On the other hand, we've seen that there are reasons to think that Terminators do not have mental states like ours at all. Yet I think it's clear that the model T-101 differs from the other Terminators precisely because it *does* have a mental life. To see why, let's turn to a difference in behaviors between the T-101 and other models.

John Connor: The T-101's Everything

In the real world, the behavior of complex machines is guided by programming, and programmed machines are devoid of mental life. The T-101 seems to be an exception to the rule because it does show signs of mental life. And this is what ultimately explains why we are moved by the scene in which the T-101 is destroyed in the steel mill.

In *T2*, there's a crucial scene in which John and Sarah open the head of the T-101 and set the machine to a "learning mode." Before this switch, the T-101 has been set by Skynet to "read-only mode," which prevents it from "thinking too much," as the T-101 itself explains. When the machine is rebooted, it sees the world with "new eyes," and the change is dramatic. By considering the behavior of the T-101 before and after the switch, we can see the impact of *learning* on the emergence of the machine's mental life. When the Terminator is set to "read-only mode" it cannot smile, make promises, or understand the basics of human mental life. When the T-101 is prevented from learning, it's incapable of understanding the connections between smiling and joy or between crying and sadness. Simply put, in its initial mode the T-101 simply can't gather certain kinds of new information about the world in order to heighten its *understanding*. While its knowledge increases through experience, it does not understand anything *in a new way*. When the learning mode is set, the T-101 starts to grasp the connections between things and what those things *signify*. The first sign of this is the T-101's ability to use language—in particular, slang—that it had never used before, and to combine new expressions in a meaningful way.

Ada Byron King, countess of Lovelace (1815–1852), worked with Charles Babbage to create an early mechanical computer. Considered to be one of the world's first computer programmers, she claimed already in the nineteenth century that a machine couldn't learn independently, so a machine couldn't express originality. But the T-101, precisely because it has acquired the capacity to learn independently of its programming, is capable of expressing truly novel behavior. The T-101 would be able to pass the "Lovelace Test," which is more challenging than the test later proposed by Turing. A machine passes the Lovelace Test if the designer of a machine can't explain the novel output that the machine generates. In the T-101's case, Skynet probably could not explain or predict the behavior of its creation after its mode had been changed by Sarah and John. Since the T-101 actively works against Skynet's ultimate goals of wiping out the human resistance, we could certainly call this novel or creative action.

In addition to new forms of language, we see a change in the machine's ability to *choose* its behavior instead of simply responding mechanically. From the human perspective, the T-101 often fashions correct reactions in appropriate situations. The T-101 after the switch finds itself in the situation of a child who is beginning to learn the basic aspects of human sociability. In the Terminator's case, its teacher is John Connor, who explains to the machine what it needs to understand about human nature. Consequently, the T-101 chooses not to kill people because of its promise to John. This shows that the T-101 realizes that there are alternative modes of action. The Terminator acts in one way rather than the other *because it has a reason* for acting in this precise way, and it is the T-101 itself that realizes this. The reason *exists* as a result of learning.

Human mental life is also a result of learning; a young child develops a mental life like ours only as a result of education. And there is no principled reason why a machine that is capable of learning could not develop a mental life as a result.

Wittgenstein reminds us that if the behavior of machines is identical to human behavior in every relevant respect, then we have little reason to believe that the machine has no mental life. If we make such a judgment, we're simply being inconsistent. Exactly this kind of judgment is made about the philosopher's favorite creation, the "philosophical zombie."

The "monstrous" idea of the philosophical zombie revolves around the question, Could there be a creature that behaves *just like we do* but lacks any inner life? David Chalmers, among others, has argued that zombies like this are perfectly possible.[5] But notice that from the Wittgensteinian perspective, the idea of such a zombie is nonsense because once behavior is taken as the sole *criterion* of mental life, the possibility of separating mental life from behavior is eliminated.[6]

If we dismiss the zombie objection, the T-101's ability to learn from humans instead of routinely following the program set by Skynet makes it "one of us." So if the T-101 is "one of us," does it have *rights*, as we think we have? Yes, through understanding the value of life and acting upon it, *he* has earned the right to exist. Ultimately, destroying this feeling machine for the sake of humanity may have been the best solution for the greatest number of people, but it was also a grave violation of its rights.[7] No wonder we feel sorry for the T-101 when it is little by little lowered into the molten steel, never to reemerge.

NOTES

1. Ludwig Wittgenstein, *Philosophical Investigations* (Malden, MA: Blackwell, 1963), 281.

2. For more on Turing's famous test, see Justin Leiber's chapter in this volume, "Time for the Terminator: Philosophical Themes of the Resistance."

3. John Searle, "Minds, Brains and Programs," *Behavioral and Brain Sciences* 3 (1980): 417–457.

4. Ned Block, "Psychologism and Behaviorism," *Philosophical Review* 90 (1981): 5–43. Read it online at www.nyu.edu/gsas/dept/philo/faculty/block/papers/Psychologism.htm.

5. David Chalmers, *The Conscious Mind: In Search of a Fundamental Theory* (New York: Oxford Univ. Press, 1996).

6. It has to be noted, though, that Wittgenstein was mainly interested in the question of what we can learn from a philosophical study of our actual language. The question about the possibility of zombies would have been completely alien to his thinking.

7. For another perspective on the morality of the T-101's sacrifice, see "Self-Termination: Suicide, Self-Sacrifice, and the Terminator" by Daniel P. Malloy in this volume.

CONTRIBUTORS

Future Leaders of the Resistance

Jacob Berger is a graduate student in philosophy at the Graduate Center of the City University of New York, as well as an instructor at Baruch College, CUNY. He's interested in philosophy of language, philosophy of mind, and metaphysics. Come with him if you want to learn.

Jason P. Blahuta is really a T-3000 model Terminator sent back in time to find a university-aged John Connor who is hiding out at Lakehead University in the sparsely populated wilds of Northern Ontario. His mission: inflict massive mental trauma on John Connor by subjecting him to Hegel, effectively rendering him useless to the resistance. His cover: mild-mannered assistant professor of philosophy researching Machiavelli, applied ethics, and Asian philosophy.

Richard Brown is considering the following possible responses to the request to write a blurb about himself: (A) Yes/No (B) Or what? (C) He is an assistant professor at LaGuardia Community College, CUNY, in the Philosophy and Critical Thinking program. He has published on philosophical issues in neuroscience, cognitive science, and theories of consciousness. More information is available at onemorebrown.com. (D) Fuck you, asshole!

Jesse W. Butler is one of billions of cyborgs programmed by a mysterious entity sometimes referred to as "Mother Nature." His current software includes two troublesome feedback-generating functions, one geared toward the termination of the idea of a Terminator and the other aimed toward the goal of something called "self" knowing itself. He also happens to be an assistant professor of philosophy at the University of Central Arkansas, working in the areas of philosophy of mind, epistemology, and philosophy of science.

Harry Chotiner teaches courses in film and political theory at New York University's School of Continuing and Professional Studies and coordinates the educational component of the Virginia Film Festival. In an earlier life he was an editor of *Socialist Review* magazine and worked in Hollywood as everything from a reader for Zoetrope Studios to a vice president at 20th Century–Fox.

Jennifer Culver, like Sarah Connor, spends much of her time watching faces go by and wondering how many are truly human. The difference lies in the fact that Jennifer must stare mainly at the faces of teenagers while teaching Honors English and Science Fiction at a high school, while finishing her doctoral work at the University of Texas at Dallas. A fan of both fantasy and science fiction, Jennifer participated in the first National Endowment for the Humanities Institute dedicated to the works of J.R.R. Tolkien and has presented papers on Tolkien's works at academic and teacher-oriented conferences.

Kevin S. Decker teaches normative and applied ethics, American and Continental philosophy, and philosophy of pop culture at Eastern Washington University. He's the coeditor (with Jason T. Eberl) of *Star Trek and Philosophy* (2008) and *Star Wars and Philosophy* (2005). He has published on philosophical themes in James Bond, *The Colbert Report*, and the films of Stanley Kubrick. Also, he writes screenplays and directs and produces films under the pseudonym James Cameron.

Robert A. Delfino is assistant professor of philosophy at St. John's University, New York. He has published articles on metaphysics, medieval philosophy, philosophy of science, personal identity, human rights, and aesthetics. He has edited three books: *Plato's Cratylus: Argument, Form, and Structure; Understanding Moral Weakness;* and *What Are We to Understand Gracia to Mean?: Realist Challenges to Metaphysical Neutralism.* If a time machine is ever invented, he plans on traveling back in time to have a long, hard talk with Aristotle.

George A. Dunn teaches courses on ethics and other topics in philosophy at IUPUI (Indiana University–Purdue University at Indianapolis), including a course on philosophy through pop culture that he designed and coteaches with his colleague Jason T. Eberl, another contributor to this volume. He has been a visiting lecturer at the University of Indianapolis, Purdue University, and the Ningbo Institute of Technology in Zejiang Province, China. His cutting-edge research and groundbreaking publications on philosophical issues in *Buffy the Vampire Slayer*, *Battlestar Galactica*, *The Wizard of Oz*, and *X-Men* have made him the envy of his colleagues. He wears two million SPF sunblock and relies on his dogs, Xander and Scout, to spot Terminators.

Jason T. Eberl is associate professor of Philosophy at Indiana University–Purdue University Indianapolis. He teaches and conducts research in bioethics, medieval philosophy, and metaphysics. He's the coeditor (with Kevin Decker) of *Star Wars and Philosophy* (2005) and *Star Trek and Philosophy* (2008), as well as the editor of *Battlestar Galactica and Philosophy* (Wiley-Blackwell, 2008). He has contributed to similar books on

Stanley Kubrick, Harry Potter, and Metallica. Although he's never dreamed of electronic sheep, he does wonder why dogs bark incessantly around him all the time.

Jeffrey Ewing is an independent scholar focusing on alternatives to capitalism, with emphasis on socialism, ethics, and Marxist theory. He graduated from Eastern Washington University with a B.A. in Philosophy and plans to attend graduate school in the fall of 2009. He and his wife, Jenn, are active in the community and work hard to make a positive difference in the world around them. In his spare time, he is building an underground commune, preparing to support and house the human resistance.

Kyle Ferguson is a graduate student in philosophy at the Graduate Center of the City University of New York and teaches at Lehman College, CUNY, in the Bronx. He is mainly interested in the history and philosophy of psychology and philosophy of language. If a career in academia does not pan out, he will most likely work as a Hollywood actor and, later in life, as governor of California.

Colonel Peter S. Fosl is a real Kentucky Colonel (HOKC) and professor of philosophy at Transylvania University in Lexington, Kentucky. The coauthor of *The Philosopher's Toolkit* (2003) and *The Ethics Toolkit* (2007), he has also contributed to *Metallica and Philosophy*, *Lost and Philosophy*, and *Heroes and Philosophy*. Like his fellow Kentuckians, Colonel Fosl rests easy in the knowledge that he lives in the one part of the world too tough for the machines to conquer.

Antti Kuusela works at the University of Helsinki, Finland. Equipped with a neural net processor, he is studying problems in the philosophy of mind. Antti's life was never quite the same after the processor was set to "learning" mode. He struggles hard to be more human and not just a dork all the time.

Justin Leiber teaches philosophy at Florida State University. His first book was *Noam Chomsky: A Philosophic Overview*. Of it Chomsky wrote, "It is the book I would recommend to people who ask me what I am up to." Leiber has also published the *Beyond* science fiction trilogy, *An Invitation to Cognitive Science*, *Paradoxes*, and *Can Animals and Machines Be Persons?* Upon being arrested at a civil rights demonstration along with Dick Gregory, he was asked by others in the lockup, "Are you with CORE or the NAACP Youth Group?" He replied, "No, the Industrial Workers of the World," and was told "Ssshush!"

Greg Littmann is a biological organism, living tissue over a bone endoskeleton. He teaches philosophy at Southern Illinois University, Edwardsville, and is particularly obsessed with metaphysics, epistemology, philosophy of logic, moral philosophy, and philosophy and pop culture. He is capable of feeling pain and can pass simple versions of the Turing Test, provided that the topic doesn't stray from science fiction.

Daniel P. Malloy is an adjunct assistant professor of philosophy at Appalachian State University in Boone, North Carolina. His research is focused on political and Continental philosophy. He has published on the intersection of popular culture and philosophy, particularly dealing with ethical issues, as well as on Leibniz, Spinoza, Foucault, Hegel, Horkheimer, and Adorno. Daniel suspects that he is being hunted by killer robots from the future who want to learn philosophy. He is one step ahead of them . . . for now.

Kristie Lynn Miller is a research fellow at the University of Sydney. She likes to engage in serious hard-nosed metaphysics in the tradition of Australian philosophy, though others suggest that Australian-style philosophy owes more to the very hot Australian sun and insufficient head coverage. She has published papers on the philosophy of time, the composition and persistence of objects, and stuff and gunk. Yes, that's stuff and gunk. For more details see homepage.mac.com/centre.for.time/KristieMiller/Kristie/Home%20Page.html.

Phillip Seng grew up close enough to the Strategic Air Command to be vaporized during Skynet's first strike. Coming to that realization, he sought refuge in philosophy and movies. He soon began wondering how he could possibly make a living by thinking about movies. Now he still watches movies and tells students at the University of Maryland, Baltimore County, which movies they should watch (almost all of them) and why they should watch them. While he has written about theories of movies and other arts, he has also written about *The Wizard of Oz* and other pop culture topics.

Kenneth Sheahan is an honors student at St. John's University, New York. He is majoring in accounting, but he loves to pursue philosophy and filmmaking in his spare time. The *Terminator* films have always intrigued him, so what better way to combine his passion for films and philosophy than to cowrite an article on *The Terminator*. Now that Kenneth is finished with this article, he can continue training for his feature role leading the human resistance to victory.

Josh Weisberg is an assistant professor of philosophy at the University of Houston. He specializes in philosophy of mind and cognitive science, with a focus on consciousness. He has published articles in *Synthese*, the *Journal of Consciousness Studies*, and the online journal *PSYCHE*, among others. He thinks we are all just evolved meat machines, but he's okay with that. His pastimes include playing the guitar and drinking single-malt scotch, though not necessarily in that order.

Wayne Yuen is the chair of the one-person philosophy department at Ohlone College in Fremont, California, and his primary interest is ethics. His secondary interests include all things geeky, and a minor obsession with working his pets into his philosophical works, which include treatises on *Buffy the Vampire Slayer* and undead vegetarians. He looks forward to Judgment Day, since Skynet should have very fast Internet connections.

INDEX

Skynet's Database

abortion, 166, 207
abstract principles, 70, 76, 77, 78–79
Adams, Douglas, 42, 43
Adorno, Theodor, 2
alienation, 96
ambiguity, 244–247, 253–265
anaphor (pronoun), 260–262
animals. *See* life forms, nonhuman
Aristotle, 28, 64, 109, 110, 235n.24
Arnauld, Antoine, 25–26
artificial intelligence, 8, 23, 36, 40–41, 50, 63, 114, 137
  danger potential of, 53, 56, 65, 87, 94, 101, 177, 179
  development of, 132
  human mind compared with, 59, 126
  interests of, 165–166
  language and, 240
  Turing Test and, 10, 11, 125–126
  See also Skynet
Asimov, Isaac, 45
attribution, 257–258
Augustine, Saint, 128, 189n.2
authenticity, 193–194, 200
Axelrod, Robert, 46–47

Babbage, Charles, 275
backward causation, 129, 212
Bad Timing Problem, 111–114, 118
Bargh, John, 48–49
Baudrillard, Jean, 87–90
Baum, L. Frank, 34
behavior, 12–19, 23, 268–269, 273–276
  unconscious stereotypes and, 49
  understanding vs., 12–13, 17
Being and Time (Heidegger), 192–193
Bentham, Jeremy, 70–71, 76, 165, 199
bête-machine, 25, 27, 29–30, 31, 37
"billiard ball causality," 23–24
Block, Ned, 272, 273
branching timeline, 143–144
Brewster, General Robert, 11, 154, 155, 156, 179, 184, 221, 222
  Skynet unleashed by, 227
Brewster, Kate, 33, 36–37, 128, 154, 156, 205, 225
  marriage to John of, 127, 235n.23
  resistance movement and, 221, 222–223, 232
  T-X and, 16, 179, 184, 186
butterfly effect, 130

Cameron (female cyborg), 29, 34, 35, 85–86, 88, 90–92, 205, 206
Cameron, James, 1, 21, 22, 31, 32, 53, 54, 61, 63–64, 88, 89, 93, 264
  dark vision of, 79
  Marxist thought and, 93, 95–104
  war and, 175, 187, 188, 189
Camus, Albert, 43, 191
capitalism, 93–104
care, ethic of, 78, 80

categorical imperative, 72–73, 76, 163–164, 166, 198–199
causal sequences, 23–24, 129–130, 212
cause and effect, 141
Cavell, Stanley, 230–231
chairos, 219–220, 223, 224, 226, 227, 228, 229, 231, 232
Chalmers, David, 276
"Chinese room," 12–13, 271–272
Christian belief, 28, 180, 197, 230
Clark, Andy, 61, 63, 64
class system, 94–96, 103
Code Model, 145, 241–244, 248, 249
  flaws of, 244, 246, 247
collective responsibility, 224–225
Communist Manifesto, The (Marx and Engels), 99
compassion, 34, 165
computers, 8, 33, 36, 46, 63, 98, 272, 275
conatus (Spinoza term), 35, 36, 37
Connor, John, 26, 33–37, 65, 82, 87, 93, 95, 137, 148, 151, 168–169
  cyborg protectors of. *See* Cameron; T-101
  dialectic and, 149
  efforts to prevent birth of, 8, 112, 113, 122–123, 210–212
  father of, 111, 114–120, 123, 152
  foster parents and, 91, 167, 186, 206
  future and, 83, 85, 90, 91, 141, 187, 188–189
  future wife of. *See* Brewster, Kate
  gender role reversal and, 79
  July 4 death date of, 234n.13
  mission of, 1, 7, 47, 71, 79, 117, 123, 128, 143, 146, 147, 153–157, 171, 172, 185, 218–233
  mother's protection of, 69, 75, 83–85, 90–92, 134
  as opponent of killing, 81n.12, 162, 164–165, 182, 202–203, 206, 215, 275
  savior destiny of, 123, 147, 152, 214, 218–233
  symbolic resurrection of, 230
  as Terminators' target, 16, 34, 73–75, 113, 123, 127, 128, 184, 185, 204
  training of, 90, 96, 123–124, 156
  as World Historical Individual, 152, 153
Connor, Sarah, 2–3, 15, 33, 36–37, 84–90, 148, 149, 151, 204, 273
  actions vs. fate and, 140, 141
  aliases of, 85
  assaults on doctors by, 25, 75, 84
  changing of history and, 153–157
  on death, 208
  Dyson murder plan of, 70–74, 77, 79, 124, 139, 142, 153–154, 161–162, 222
  Dyson sparing by, 162, 164–165, 171–172, 186–187, 205–206
  empty tomb of, 230
  first appearance of, 54–55
  gender stereotype reversal and, 75, 78–79, 222
  killing of, 8, 82, 85, 112–114, 122–123, 149, 187, 202
  mental hospitals and, 22, 82, 85, 86, 90, 102, 142
  mission of, 69, 82–85, 122–123, 128, 134, 139, 142, 147, 153–154, 161–162, 191
  moral reasoning and, 70–74, 77–79
  as mother, 83, 90–92
  persona change of, 95–96, 123
  Reese's impregnation of, 114–115, 116, 117, 119, 123
  simulation and, 87–90
  soul and, 29, 33–34, 35, 37
  as stained warrior, 82–88, 90–92, 239
  T-101's destruction by, 88, 102, 124, 167, 190–191, 192, 196, 266–267
  timeline and, 87, 111, 133–139, 171, 185, 188, 208, 216, 220–222
  toughness of, 123, 185
  as World Historical Individual, 152, 153
consciousness, 14–19, 24, 25, 28, 58, 60, 268
  unconscious stereotypes vs., 48–49
  See also self-awareness
consequentialism, 70, 71, 162–165
  definition of, 162–163
  inherent flaw in, 200
  moral judgments and, 168–170, 171, 199–200
  See also utilitarianism
cooperation, 45–47, 48, 49
corporations, 96–100
crying, 30, 268
Cyberdene Systems, 94, 95–99, 178
  plot to destroy, 124, 125, 128, 131, 153, 190, 191, 221
  See also Skynet
cybernetics, 25

Darwin, Charles, 57
Da-sein (Heidegger concept), 194
Dawkins, Richard, 41, 61, 62
death, 34, 208–215
  reality of, 192–194, 201, 203–204, 207
  vs. never existing, 210–212, 214
  See also killing; suicide
definite descriptions, 253–254, 256–260
demonstrative descriptions, 255
Dent, Arthur, 42
deontology, 70, 72–74
deprivation, misfortune vs., 214
Descartes, René, 21–37
descriptions, 253–260
determinism, 129–132
Devitt, Michael, 261–262, 263–264
dialectic, 148–149
dignity, 163–164, 206
divine command, 227–228, 229
Dixon, Charles, 86
DNA, 57
Donnellan, Keith, 257
Draper, Kai, 214
duty-based ethics, 72, 198, 199, 220, 226
Dyson, Danny, 30, 31
Dyson, Miles, 9, 30, 70–74, 77, 79, 95, 97–98, 124, 132, 139, 142, 153–154, 161–162, 164–165, 169, 186–187, 205–206, 222
  death of, 155, 220
  morality of murdering, 171–172
Dyson, Tarissa, 9

Einstein, Albert, 119, 129–130, 131, 136
emotions, 28, 34–36, 48–50, 79, 80, 102, 167, 229
  machines and, 15–16, 266–267, 272
empathy, 166, 167
end to history, 149–150, 156
end vs. means, 72, 74, 198–199
Engels, Friedrich, 99
Epicurus, 208–209, 211
eternalism, 138, 143, 145
ethical problems, 70–80, 175–233. *See also* moral *headings*
euthanasia, 166, 196
evolution, 41, 43, 132, 231
existenialism, 43, 191
expressions (linguistic), 255–256
  semantic vs. pragmatic, 258–259
extended phenotype, 62
externalism, 135–137, 142

fate
  changing of, 83, 85, 133–145, 153
  free will vs., 141
  scientific explanation and, 129–130
fear, 34, 49, 208
Feldman, Fred, 210–212
feminist philosophy, 70, 74–77
fixed-future model, 138, 143, 145
fourth dimension, 137, 142–143
freedom, 43, 45, 46, 149–151
free will, 123–124, 141, 195–196
French, Sean, 187
functionalism, 59–60
future, 87–90, 92, 133–145, 134, 185, 187–189
  agents from, 127
  chairotic moment and, 219–220, 223, 226, 228
  death as deprivation of, 193, 207, 214–216
  effort to change, 83, 85, 87, 110, 122, 127, 128, 133–145, 147, 153, 220
  inevitability of, 140–145, 156–157, 200, 221–222
  moral decisions and, 171, 172, 216
  open model of, 137–138, 141, 144–145, 153
  precognition of, 87, 134, 171, 185, 208

game theory, 45, 45–47, 50
Geist (spirit), 148–150, 151, 153
gender, 222–223
  moral reasoning and, 77–79
  role reversals, 74–75, 78–79
genes, 62
genetic code, 57, 58
Geneva Convention, 225
genocide, 224–225
Gilligan, Carol, 78
Girard, René, 84, 86
Glau, Summer, 29, 205
Goode, Andy, 31, 85, 86, 205, 206, 208
government, 45
grammatical structure, 255
grandfather paradox, 139–140
greater good (utilitarian), 71, 76, 165, 167, 173–174n.4, 207, 228–229
greatest good (Socratic), 191, 197

Grice, H. Paul, 247–250, 258–259, 260, 264
growing-block universe, 137, 138–139, 142–143

happiness. *See* greatest good
harm, 212–213
hedonistic calculus, 71
Hegel, G. W. F., 2, 147–157
Heidegger, Martin, 192–193, 194, 197, 201
"Heinz problem," 76–77
history, 146–157
Hitler, Adolf, 162, 164
Hobbes, Thomas, 44–45, 50, 226
Holocaust, 2, 162, 164, 224
human chauvinism, 60, 125, 132
Human Genome Project, 58
humans, 8–19
  death experience of, 192–193, 201, 208–215
  destructive acts of, 223–224, 229
  dignity of, 163–164, 206
  end to history and, 150
  genetic code of, 57, 58
  immortality and, 29
  interests of, 167–168
  machines and. *See under* machines
  meaningful life and, 231
  mental life of, 266, 267, 275–276
  moral claims made on, 230–232
  personhood requirements for, 166–167
  rational soul and, 28
  reasoning by, 73–74, 173, 198
  rights of, 163
  self-awareness and, 42–43, 56, 266
  self-preservation drive of, 35, 40, 41–51
  social contract and, 47, 51, 226–227, 229, 231
  technology and, 52–66, 89–90, 93, 102–104
  See also thinking being
Hume, David, 48, 226, 231
Hutcheson, Francis, 231
hypothetical imperatives, 72

idealism, 148
imagination, 119–120
Inferential Model, 247–250
inherent value, 72–73
instinct, 44
intelligence, 49, 166, 167, 271. *See also* artificial intelligence
intention, 195, 196–197
interests, 167–172, 179

Janelle (John's foster mother), 91, 167, 186, 206
Jesus, 225
Jews, 2, 162, 164, 224, 225
Judgment Day, 3, 7–19, 39–40, 47, 62–63, 65, 79–80, 83, 91, 128, 139, 161–173
  background to, 177, 224
  cause and effect and, 141
  effects of, 54–55, 69, 206
  human deaths from, 94, 161, 164, 171, 214
  human resistance and, 122–132, 147, 218–233
  human survivors of, 150, 155–156, 157, 169, 171, 188–189, 207–208, 213, 228–229
  inevitability of, 127, 131, 134, 140–145, 146, 153, 155, 157, 181, 212–215, 220, 222
  lesson of, 229
  as not inevitable, 133, 140, 143, 144
  as past event, 135, 146
  postponement of, 1, 154, 207–208, 220–221
  Reese's youth and, 114, 134
  Sarah's mission and, 69–70, 71, 79, 122–123, 139, 153–154, 161–162, 220–221
  timeline and, 143
  utilitarian assessment of, 169–172
just-war theory, 175–189

Kant, Immanuel, 72–74, 76, 109–110, 166, 172, 198–199, 200, 207
  human dignity and, 163–164, 206
  meaning of "humanity" and, 198
killing, 70, 77, 162–167, 170–172, 186–187, 199, 202–216, 272
  as Terminators' modus operandi, 181–182, 185–186
King, Ada Byron, 275
Kohlberg, Lawrence, 76–78
Kripke, Saul, 233–234n.7, 259–261, 262–263, 264
Kundera, Milan, 222

La Mettrie, Julien de, 125, 132
language, 239–251, 253–265, 274, 275

simulation of, 31, 32, 271, 272
as social interaction, 230–231, 232
thinking beings and, 268
Laplace, Pierre, 129–130
learning, 61, 102, 274, 275–276
Leiber, Fritz, 131
Leibniz, Gottfried, 2
lexicon, 243–247, 250
Lieberman, Dr., 75
life
balancing of one vs. many, 70, 77, 162–165, 167
as God's gift, 197
meaningful, 231
purpose of, 214–215
valuation of, 191, 203, 206, 207, 208, 211, 213, 216
life forms, non-human
death and, 192
DNA and, 57
human chauvinism and, 60, 125, 132
humans' use of, 74
intelligence and, 167
interests of, 165–168
as machines, 125, 132, 165–169
mechanistic view of, 22–23, 25, 26
mental activity of, 167, 269
moral status of, 122, 165, 166, 198
souls and, 28, 29–30, 35
linguistic communication theory, 240–251
literal meaning, 248
Locke, John, 226, 227
logical contradiction, 163
Lovelace Test, 275
Lucretius, 209, 210, 211
Lycan, William, 59–60
lying, 73, 152, 199

machines
death capacity of, 192–193, 194
emotions and, 15–16, 266–267, 272
freedom and, 150–151
human chauvinism and, 60, 125
human qualities vs., 2–3, 8–9, 18–19, 26–37, 45, 48–51, 186–187, 208, 267–276
humans as, 57–61, 125
human trust in, 89
human war with, 52–66, 69, 87, 176–189, 191, 228–229
interests and rights of, 165–169
language-using, 240–243, 271
mechanistic worldview and, 24, 26
mental lives of, 266–267, 269–276
moral responsibility and, 126, 166–167
moral status of, 126, 179
passing as humans, 11, 12, 55–56
programming of, 274
thinking and, 9–19
Turing Test and, 10, 11, 38n.14, 125–126, 269, 271
unconscious stereotypes of, 49, 50
malicious intent, 164
Man a Machine (La Mettrie), 125
Marquis, Don, 207
Marx, Karl, 93–96, 99, 100, 103
Marxist philosophy, 99–104
mass-energy-time continuum, 130, 131
materialism, 125
maximum interest satisfaction, 71, 76, 165, 167, 169, 170, 172, 173–174n.4, 199, 228
McMahan, Jeff, 212–213
meaning, 241, 248–251
ambiguity of, 244–246, 247, 253–265
of behavior, 268
distinguishing of, 258–259
meaningful life, 231
mechanistic worldview, 23–37
metaphysics, 109–120, 137
meta-theory, 147–148
meta-time, 142–143
Midgley, Mary, 36
militarism, 99–100, 103
Mill, John Stuart, 71, 165, 170, 171, 172
mind, 59, 120, 148. *See also* thinking being
misfortune, deprivation vs., 214
Mitnick, Kevin, 33
moral claims
collective responsibility and, 224–225
killing and, 162–163, 182, 202–216
machines and, 126, 179
meaningful language and, 230–231
non-human life and, 122, 165, 166, 198
suicide and, 197–201
moral naturalists, 231–232
moral reasoning, 70, 75–79, 166–167
gender differences in, 77–79
precognition lack and, 171
thinking machine and, 126, 166–167
Morsky, Stan, 116, 119

motherhood, 75, 83, 90–92
motivations, 72, 200
  intention vs., 197, 199
movies, 120

Nagel, Thomas, 213
neuroscience, 24–25
Newton, Isaac, 129
non-human life. *See* life forms, non-human
nothingness, 208–211
novels, 119–120
Nussbaum, Martha, 120

Ockham's razor, modified, 258
open-future model, 144–145

pain, 35, 165, 199, 200
  meaning of, 268, 270, 273
paradoxes, 122–123, 126–131, 139–140, 161, 162, 173
parallel universes, 117, 118
Paul, Saint, 221
personal identity problem, 116–117
personhood. *See* humans
phenotype, extended, 62
philosophical zombie, 276
physics, 128, 129–130, 135–136
Piaget, Jean, 76
pity, 231
Plato, 41, 197
posthumanism, 150
posttraumatic stress disorder, 83–84
pragmatic linguistics, 244–246, 251, 258
pre-birth nothingness, 209, 210–211
preemptive war, 177
presentism, 137–138, 139
"prisoner's dilemma," 45–47
pronouns, 260–262
proportionality, 183–184

rational, meanings of, 36–37, 44
rational behavior, 269
rational choices, 45–47, 48, 80
rational soul, 28
reason, 32–36
  emotions vs., 35–36, 48–50
  goal attainment and, 40–41, 42–43
  as human capacity, 73–74, 198
  moral development and, 76–77
  moral duty and, 198
reasoning, 73–74, 173, 198. *See also* moral reasoning
Reese, Derek, 86, 88
Reese, Kyle, 9, 18, 37, 127, 133, 149, 177, 183, 185, 210, 221, 254, 255–256, 257
  as John's father, 111, 114–120, 152
  on Judgment Day, 39, 134, 143, 146, 156, 171, 172, 206, 228
  respect for human life and, 206, 213
  on Terminators' characteristics, 15, 35–36, 270
  time travel and, 1, 8, 110–120, 123, 134, 139
  on unfixed future, 138, 145
reference borrowing, 263–264
referential ambiguity, 245–246, 255–256, 258, 259, 261–262, 263
referring descriptions, 255–256
reflex theory, 24, 25
resistance, 122–132, 147, 218–233
responsibility, 166, 201, 224–225
rights, 163, 166–172, 227, 276
Robinson, Will, 51
robot, coining of term, 125. *See also* Terminators
Rousseau, Jean-Jacques, 226, 231
rule utilitarianism, 80n.11
Russell, Bertrand, 3, 161, 162, 173, 254–255, 256, 257, 260, 264

Salceda, Enrique, 10–11
Schwarzenegger, Arnold, 23–24, 52, 55, 74–75, 110, 124, 178, 181, 183, 184, 185, 187, 196, 230, 256
  Austrian accent of, 244
  Terminator violence and, 81n.12
  See also T-101
science fiction, 88–89, 93, 119–120, 150
scientific revolution, 23
Searle, John, 12–13, 14, 38n.14, 271–272
self-awareness, 42–43, 56, 166, 167, 191, 193, 194, 266
self-defense, 163, 164, 166, 170
  just-war theory and, 176–177, 178
self-destruction. *See* suicide
"selfish genes," 41
self-preservation, 35, 36, 40–51, 167, 225–226
self-sacrifice, 196–197, 200–201
semantic meaning, 258, 259–260, 263

sex roles. *See* gender
Shannon, Claude, 241
Shelley, Mary, 49
signs and signifiers, 268–269, 274
Silberman, Dr., 25, 33, 87, 90, 111, 118, 208, 235n.23
simulation, 31, 32, 87–90, 91, 126, 272, 273
Singer, Peter, 165, 235n.22
Skynet, 2, 3, 8, 11–15, 29, 66, 88, 124, 139
  aim of, 40–44, 47–52, 56, 113, 131, 206
  collective responsibility for, 225
  development of, 9, 56, 93–102, 128, 162, 220
  end to history and, 150
  inevitability of, 114, 131
  intelligence of, 55, 56, 94
  interests of, 165–169, 181
  Marxist thought and, 98, 101
  moral status of, 179
  self-awareness of, 197, 206
  self-defense and, 166, 178
  T-101's self-sacrifice and, 190–191, 196–197, 199–200
  technologies of, 62–63
  timelines and, 118, 139, 142
  unleashing of, 227
  war plan of, 176, 178–179, 180, 184, 188, 191
  See also Judgment Day; Terminators
social contract, 47, 51, 226–227, 229, 231
Socrates, 191, 197, 209–210
soul, 22–23, 26, 28, 29–30, 33–34, 35, 37, 208
space-time, 129–130, 137, 138, 142
speaker's meaning, 248–249, 250–251, 258–260
special relativity, theory of, 136
Spinoza, Baruch, 35
stage theory, 70, 76–78
stained warrior, 82–88, 90–92
state of nature, 44, 50, 226, 227
Strawson, P. F., 255, 256, 257
suffering, 165, 223, 229
suicide, 43, 126, 190–192, 194–201, 233
survival of fittest, 181
syntax, 243, 247, 250
  ambiguity and, 245, 254

T-101, 27, 43, 50–53, 63, 87, 131, 151, 152–153, 206, 213, 256, 264
  changes in, 2–3, 124–125, 193
  curiosity of, 168
  death and, 193–197, 205
  free choice and, 195
  gender role reversal and, 74–75
  human aspects of, 9, 10–11, 15, 16, 17, 34, 52–53, 79, 89–90, 102, 124, 163–166, 167, 168, 181, 192, 194, 215–216, 229, 266, 270–272
  humans compared with, 57–58, 60, 267–276
  John's relationship with, 9, 11, 17, 30, 32, 34, 43, 50, 52–53, 61, 75, 79, 88, 89–90, 102, 123, 124, 127, 128, 181–185, 193–195, 202–203, 230, 239–240, 245, 248–249, 250, 266, 272, 275
  Judgment Day and, 1, 154, 178–179, 222
  killing and, 8, 85, 111, 112, 122–123, 142, 184–186, 202, 207, 257
  language use and, 239–240, 242–243, 245, 246, 248–249, 250, 274, 275
  learning ability of, 61, 274–276
  mechanical aspects of, 23–24, 55, 88, 183
  perspective of, 18, 32, 61, 271
  reprogramming of, 102, 127, 194, 274
  reverse engineering and, 30, 31, 33, 88, 153
  self-sacrifice of, 79, 88, 102, 124–125, 126, 167, 190–191, 192, 193, 195–201, 266–267, 276
  thinking and, 9–11, 13–14, 247, 274
  time travel and, 135–138, 140, 142, 172
T-1000, 11, 13, 136, 167, 183, 185, 206, 242, 272–273
  attack on John by, 73, 74, 75, 123, 127, 185
  capacities of, 271
  destruction of, 124, 200, 240
  emotions and, 15–16, 273
  human forms assumed by, 55–56, 88, 186, 272
  language and, 243, 246
technology, 52–66, 89–90, 122, 125–126, 247
  inevitable development of, 131–132
  Marxist philosophy and, 93, 96, 98, 99, 100–104
  See also machines

Terminators, 2–3, 8, 21, 26, 102, 167–168
consciousness of, 15–17, 19
emotional lack of, 34–35, 270
feats of, 61
as human extensions, 62–63
human simulation by, 55–56, 87–90, 88, 186, 272
as killing machines, 181–186, 202–203, 206–207, 270
language capacity of, 239–251
mental life of, 269–274
moral judgments and, 181–184
physical superiority of, 271
purpose of, 94, 97, 113–114, 204
self-preservation and, 45
skills reprogramming of, 33, 59
as soulless, 37
thinking capacity and, 9–11, 13–14, 19, 31–33, 247, 274
time travel by, 184–185
unreasonableness of, 35–36, 37
See also T-101; T-1000; T-X
"the" (use of), 253–265
thesis, definition of, 148–149
thinking being, 3, 9–19, 31–33, 266–276
behavior of, 12–19, 268–269
ethical decisions and, 70, 75–80
intelligence and, 49, 166, 167, 271
moral development and, 70, 75–79
technology as extension of, 63–64, 125–126, 247
Thomas Aquinas, 203, 213
Tillich, Paul, 174n.9
time, 110–120, 133–145, 212, 220
compression of, 112, 113
continuum of, 128–130, 131
death and, 192–193, 210–212
locations in, 135–136
reversal of, 110, 118, 128, 134
time travel, 1, 8, 110, 118, 119, 137–145, 146, 172, 184–185
logical vs. technological possibility of, 134–135
paradox of, 122–123, 128–130, 139–140
space travel vs., 138–139
Tin Man, 34, 92
"tit for tat," 46–47, 48, 49
Todd (John's foster father), 91, 167, 186, 206
transhumanism, 150
Traxler, Lieutenant, 256, 257
Turing, Alan, 38n.14, 40, 125–126, 132, 269
Turing Test, 10, 11, 38n.14, 125–126, 269, 271
T-X, 9–10, 11, 18, 63, 127, 179, 184, 185, 186
capacities of, 16, 34, 271, 273
destruction of, 222

unconscious stereotypes, 48–49, 50
underdetermination, 245, 246, 247
utilitarianism, 70–71, 74, 76, 165–166, 167, 168–172, 199–200, 204–205, 206, 207, 210–211
chairotic decision and, 228–229, 232
definition of, 165, 204, 228
difficulty in implementing, 173

values, 65–66, 72–73, 78
Vick (Terminator), 88

war, 175–189
collective responsibility and, 225
effects of, 83–86, 224
just cause for, 177, 179
just conduct of, 183–184, 185
as last resort, 179–180, 187–188
peace and reconciliation and, 188–189
stain of, 82–88, 90–92
war crimes, 188, 225
weapons technology, 122, 131–132
Weaver, Catherine, 26–27
Weaver, Warren, 241
Wells, H. G., 128
Who-Is-Your-Daddy? Problem, 111, 115–119
Wittgenstein, Ludwig, 230, 268–269, 270, 272, 273, 276
women. *See* gender
word meanings and order, 244, 245
workers, 95–96, 97, 101
World Historical Individuals, 148, 151–155
World War II, 162, 188

Young, Robert, 214

ZieraCorp, 26